Stranded Assets

The topic of 'stranded assets' created by environment-related risk factors has risen up the agenda dramatically, influencing many pressing topics in relation to global environmental change. For example: how best to manage the exposure of investments to environment-related risks so that financial institutions can avoid stranded assets; the financial stability implications of stranded assets and what this means for macroprudential regulation, microprudential regulation, and financial conduct; reducing the negative consequences of stranded assets by finding ways to address unemployment, lost profits, and reduced tax income; internalising the risk of stranded assets in corporate strategy and decision-making, particularly in carbon intensive sectors susceptible to the effects of societal action on climate change; underpinning arguments by civil society campaigns attempting to secure rapid decarbonisation to reduce the scale of anthropogenic climate change; and designing decarbonisation plans developed by governments, as well as companies and investors.

Taken as a whole, this book provides some of the latest thinking on how stranded assets are relevant to investor strategy and decision-making, as well as those seeking to understand and influence financial institutions.

This book was originally published as a special issue of the *Journal of Sustainable Finance & Investment*.

Ben Caldecott is founding Director of the Oxford Sustainable Finance Programme in the Smith School of Enterprise and the Environment at the University of Oxford, UK. He is a leading authority on sustainable finance and investment with a considerable international reputation. He has pioneered key concepts in his field, including the concept of 'stranded assets' and is the leading academic researcher in this area internationally.

Stranded Assets

Developments in Finance and Investment

Edited by
Ben Caldecott

LONDON AND NEW YORK

First published 2018 by Routledge

2 Park Square, Milton Park, Abingdon, Oxon OX14 4RN
605 Third Avenue, New York, NY 10017

Routledge is an imprint of the Taylor & Francis Group, an informa business

First issued in paperback 2021

Publisher's Note

The publisher has gone to great lengths to ensure the quality of this
reprint but points out that some imperfections in the original copies
may be apparent.

British Library Cataloguing in Publication Data
A catalogue record for this book is available from the British Library

ISBN 13: 978-1-138-57423-6 (hbk)
ISBN 13: 978-0-367-52999-4 (pbk)

Typeset in Minion Pro
by RefineCatch Limited, Bungay, Suffolk

Publisher's Note
The publisher accepts responsibility for any inconsistencies that may have
arisen during the conversion of this book from journal articles to book chapters,
namely the possible inclusion of journal terminology.

Disclaimer
Every effort has been made to contact copyright holders for their permission to
reprint material in this book. The publishers would be grateful to hear from any
copyright holder who is not here acknowledged and will undertake to rectify
any errors or omissions in future editions of this book.

Contents

Citation Information

The following chapters were originally published in the *Journal of Sustainable Finance & Investment*, volume 7, issue 1 (January 2017). When citing this material, please use the original page numbering for each article, as follows:

Editorial

Introduction to special issue: stranded assets and the environment
Ben Caldecott
Journal of Sustainable Finance & Investment, volume 7, issue 1 (January 2017), pp. 1–13

Chapter 1

Investment consequences of the Paris climate agreement
Howard Covington
Journal of Sustainable Finance & Investment, volume 7, issue 1 (January 2017), pp. 54–63

Chapter 2

Blindness to risk: why institutional investors ignore the risk of stranded assets
Nicholas Silver
Journal of Sustainable Finance & Investment, volume 7, issue 1 (January 2017), pp. 99–113

Chapter 3

Transition risks and market failure: a theoretical discourse on why financial models and economic agents may misprice risk related to the transition to a low-carbon economy
Jakob Thomä and Hugues Chenet
Journal of Sustainable Finance & Investment, volume 7, issue 1 (January 2017), pp. 82–98

Chapter 4

Social and asocial learning about climate change among institutional investors: lessons for stranded assets
Elizabeth S. Harnett
Journal of Sustainable Finance & Investment, volume 7, issue 1 (January 2017), pp. 114–137

Chapter 5

Assessing the sources of stranded asset risk: a proposed framework
Bob Buhr
Journal of Sustainable Finance & Investment, volume 7, issue 1 (January 2017), pp. 37–53

Chapter 7

Game theory and corporate governance: conditions for effective stewardship of companies exposed to climate change risks
Lucas Kruitwagen, Kaveh Madani, Ben Caldecott and Mark H. W. Workman
Journal of Sustainable Finance & Investment, volume 7, issue 1 (January 2017), pp. 14–36

Chapter 8

A comparative analysis of the anti-Apartheid and fossil fuel divestment campaigns
Chelsie Hunt, Olaf Weber and Truzaar Dordi
Journal of Sustainable Finance & Investment, volume 7, issue 1 (January 2017), pp. 64–81

The following chapter was originally published in the *Journal of Sustainable Finance & Investment*, volume 6, issue 3 (July 2016). When citing this material, please use the original page numbering for the article, as follows:

Chapter 6

Climate change and the fiduciary duties of pension fund trustees – lessons from the Australian law
Sarah Barker, Mark Baker-Jones, Emilie Barton and Emma Fagan
Journal of Sustainable Finance & Investment, volume 6, issue 3 (July 2016), pp. 211–244

For any permission-related enquiries please visit:
http://www.tandfonline.com/page/help/permissions

Introduction: stranded assets and the environment

Since 2011 the topic of 'stranded assets' created by environment-related risk factors, including physical climate change impacts and societal responses to climate change, has risen up the agenda dramatically. The concept has been endorsed by a range of significant international figures, including: UN Secretary-General Ban Ki-moon (McGrath 2014); US President Barack Obama (Friedman 2014); Jim Kim, President of the World Bank (World Bank 2013a; World Bank 2013b); Mark Carney, Governor of the Bank of England and Chair of the G20 Financial Stability Board (Carney 2015); Angel Gurría, Secretary-General of the OECD (Gurría 2013); Christiana Figueres, former Executive Secretary of the UNFCCC (Figueres 2013); Lord Stern of Brentford (London School of Economics 2013); and Ben van Beurden, CEO of Shell plc (Mufson 2014).

The emergence of the topic should be of significant interest to scholars and practitioners alike, as it has influenced many pressing topics facing investors, companies, policy-makers, regulators, and civil society in relation to global environmental change, for example:

- Measuring and managing the exposure of investments to environment-related risks across sectors, geographies, and asset classes so that financial institutions can avoid stranded assets (e.g. see Carbon Tracker Initiative 2011; Caldecott 2011; Caldecott, Howarth, and McSharry 2013; Generation Foundation 2013; Financial Stability Board 2015).
- Financial stability implications of stranded assets and what this means for macroprudential regulation, microprudential regulation, and financial conduct (e.g. see Carbon Tracker Initiative 2011; Caldecott 2011; Bank of England 2015b; Kruitwagen, MacDonald-Korth, and Caldecott 2016).
- Reducing the negative consequences of stranded assets created as societies transition to more environmentally sustainable economic models by finding ways to effectively address unemployment, lost profits, and reduced tax income that are associated with asset stranding (e.g. see Caldecott 2015).
- Internalising the risk of stranded assets in corporate strategy and decision-making, particularly in carbon intensive sectors susceptible to the effects of societal action on climate change (e.g. see Carbon Tracker Initiative 2013; Ansar, Caldecott, and Tibury 2013; Rook and Caldecott 2015).
- Underpinning arguments by civil society campaigns attempting to secure rapid economy-wide decarbonisation in order to reduce the scale of anthropogenic climate change (e.g. see Ansar, Caldecott, and Tibury 2013).
- Keeping track of progress towards emission reduction targets and understanding how 'committed emissions'[1] should influence decarbonisation plans developed by governments, as well as companies and investors (e.g. see Davis, Caldeira, and Matthews 2010; Davis and Socolow 2014; Pfeiffer et al. 2016).

These are some of the most important topics in current policy, investor, industry, and civil society discourses on the environment and look set to remain so for as long as societies continue to transition towards greater environmental sustainability.

What are stranded assets?

There are a number of definitions of stranded assets that have been proposed or are used in different contexts. Accountants have measures to deal with the impairment of assets (e.g. IAS16) which seek to ensure that an entity's assets are not carried at more than their recoverable amount (Deloitte 2016). In this context, stranded assets are assets that have become obsolete or non-performing, but must be recorded on the balance sheet as a loss of profit (Deloitte 2016). The term 'stranded costs' or 'stranded investment' is used by regulators to refer to 'the decline in the value of electricity-generating assets due to restructuring of the industry' (Congressional Budget Office 1998). This was a major topic for utilities regulators as power markets were liberalised in the United States and UK in the 1990s.

In the context of upstream energy production and from an energy economist's perspective the IEA (2013) defines stranded assets as 'those investments which have already been made but which, at some time prior to the end of their economic life (as assumed at the investment decision point), are no longer able to earn an economic return' (IEA 2013, 98). The Carbon Tracker Initiative also use this definition of economic loss, but says they are a 'result of changes in the market and regulatory environment associated with the transition to a low-carbon economy' (Carbon Tracker Initiative n.d.). The Generation Foundation (2013) defines a stranded asset 'as an asset which loses economic value well ahead of its anticipated useful life, whether that is a result of changes in legislation, regulation, market forces, disruptive innovation, societal norms, or environmental shocks' (Generation Foundation 2013, 21).

Different definitions for economists ('economic loss'), accountants ('impairment'), regulators ('stranded costs'), and investors ('financial loss') make it difficult for different disciplines and professions to communicate between each other about very similar and overlapping concepts. Caldecott, Howarth, and McSharry (2013) proposed a 'meta' definition to encompass all of these different definitions, 'stranded assets are assets that have suffered from unanticipated or premature write-downs, devaluations, or conversion to liabilities' (Caldecott, Howarth, and McSharry 2013, 7). This is the definition generally used throughout this Special Issue and the definition most widely used in the literature.

While the environmental discourse appropriated the term in the 2010s and is focused on the environment-related risk factors that can strand assets, asset stranding in fact occurs regularly as part and parcel of economic development. As such it is not a novel phenomenon. Schumpeter (1942) coined the term 'creative destruction' and implicit in his 'essential fact about capitalism' (Schumpeter 1942, 83) is the idea that value is created, as well as destroyed, and that this dynamic process drives forward innovation and economic growth. Schumpeter built on the work of Kondratiev (1926) and the idea of 'long waves' in the economic cycle (Perez 2010).

Neo-Schumpeterians have attempted to understand the dynamics of creative destruction, particularly how and why technological innovation and diffusion results in technological revolutions. This gave rise to the idea of 'techno-economic paradigms' (TEPs), a term coined by Perez (1985), which captures the idea of overlapping technological innovations that are strongly inter-related and interdependent resulting in technological revolutions. Perez (2002) finds five such TEPs: the Industrial Revolution (1771–1829); the Age of Steam and Railways (1829–1875); the Age of Steel, Electricity, and Heavy Engineering (1875–1908); the Age of Oil, the Automobile, and Mass Production (1908–1971); and the Age of Information and Telecommunications (1971–present).

Each TEP was accompanied by the emergence of new sectors and stranded assets in redundant ones. For example, the Industrial Revolution ushered in mechanised cotton production in England that eclipsed India's cottage textile industry (Broadberry and Gupta 2005); the Age of Steam and Railways introduced railway networks that replaced canals and waterways (Bagwell and Lyth 2002); the Age of Steel, Electricity, and Heavy Engineering saw the end of sailing ships and the dominance of steam ships (Grübler and Nakićenović 1991); the Age of Oil, the Automobile, and Mass Production resulted in the rise of the automobile and the decline of railways (Wolf 1996); and our Age of Information and Telecommunications has seen the widespread adoption of digital communication and an information revolution, making analogue communication redundant and technologies from typewriters to telegraphs entirely obsolete. Within each TEP specific companies and brands, physical infrastructure, plant and machinery, and human capital, among other things, have become stranded.

Clearly then, stranded assets can be caused by many factors related to innovation and commercialisation, and these are part of the process of creative destruction articulated in Perez's TEPs and conceived by Schumpeter. Recent research on stranded assets has, however, sought to explore the idea that some of the causes of asset stranding are increasingly environment-related. In other words, that a combination of physical environmental change and societal responses to this environmental change might be qualitatively and quantitatively different from previous drivers of creative destruction we have seen in TEPs. Moreover, such environment-related factors appear to be stranding assets across all sectors, geographies, and asset classes simultaneously and perhaps more quickly than in previous TEPs, and that this trend is accelerating – something that could be unprecedented.

Carbon budgets and stranded assets

From the late 1980s individuals and organisations working on climate and sustainability issues began to acknowledge the possibility that environmental policy and regulation could negatively influence the value or profitability of fossil fuel companies to the point that they could become impaired (Krause, Bach, and Koomey 1989; IPCC 1999; IPCC 2001; IEA 2008). With the concept of a global 'carbon budget' – the amount of cumulative atmospheric CO_2 emissions allowable for certain amounts of anthropogenic climate change – there was a way to determine when impairments ought to begin given a certain climate change target (Allen et al. 2014). When the amount of fossil fuels combusted, plus the amount of carbon accounted for in reserves yet to be burned exceeded the carbon budget, either the climate or the value of fossil fuel reserves would have to give. This concept was dubbed 'unburnable carbon' by the Carbon Tracker Initiative (2011) and was popularised by the US environmentalist McKibben (2011), among others, in the early 2010s.

Unburnable carbon quantified the disconnect between the current value of the listed equity of global fossil fuel producers and their potential commercialisation under a strict carbon budget constraint (Carbon Tracker Initiative 2011; Caldecott 2011). The idea that 'unburnable' fossil fuel reserves could become stranded assets sparked a significant discussion on the risk of investing in fossil fuels (Ansar, Caldecott, and Tibury 2013). It has also helped to spur the development of the fossil fuel divestment campaign (Ansar, Caldecott, and Tibury 2013).

Conjoined with and in parallel, the idea of a 'carbon bubble' also gained traction. This is the hypothesis that unburnable carbon would mean that upstream fossil fuel assets were significantly overvalued, potentially creating a financial bubble with systemic implications for the global economy (Carbon Tracker Initiative 2011; Caldecott 2011). This has inspired divergent responses – from qualified support to outright opposition (e.g. see Caldecott 2012; King 2012; Royal Dutch Shell plc 2014; Exxon Mobil Corporation 2014; Weyzig et al. 2014; EAC 2014).

Unburnable carbon and the carbon bubble were considered to be derived from work conducted and produced in the early 2010s. However, unknown to the proponents of this discourse in the early 2010s, these ideas actually originated much earlier. This only became clear in 2013–2014 and was confirmed by interviews with authors of previously published work.[2]

Krause, Bach, and Koomey (1989) were the first to explicitly make the case for unburnable carbon when they said,

> The mere fact that remaining allowable global carbon emissions are so limited means that any economic infrastructures built up mainly on the basis of fossil fuels risk early obsolescence. In effect, the tight carbon budgets implied by climate stabilization greatly reduce the long-term value of fossil fuels. (Krause, Bach, and Koomey 1989, 164)

Krause, Bach, and Koomey (1989) were also the first to make the explicit link between carbon budgets, fossil fuel obsolescence, and implications for financial markets (i.e. the carbon bubble),

> capital owners in the fossil industries would have to bear an indirect cost i.e. die risks and uncertainties of having to diversify into other business activities. For example, even a well-planned retrenchment [from fossil fuels] could create impacts on the value of stocks in the financial markets. Government financial incentives could be required to make these risks acceptable to capital owners. (Krause, Bach, and Koomey 1989, 172–173)

Krause, Bach, and Koomey (1989) made another significant contribution by highlighting how unburnable carbon is in complete contrast to assumptions used in the energy industry,

> [a carbon budget] means major restrictions on the use of global fossil resources … [our carbon budget] figures clash with the conventional assumption that all conventional oil and gas resources would probably be consumed before a major shift away from fossil fuels would occur. Our analysis suggests that climate stabilization requires keeping significant portions of even the world's conventional fossil resources in the ground. Such a requirement is a stark contradiction to all conventional energy planning and illustrates the magnitude of the greenhouse challenge. (Krause, Bach, and Koomey 1989, 144)

The points are made in exactly the same way in publications more than 20 years later (e.g. see Carbon Tracker Initiative 2011, 2013). Unfortunately, these novel ideas from the late 1980s were largely ignored and then forgotten. One can only speculate as to why this happened and why later work has managed to achieve greater traction, but it must inevitably have something to do with the fact that climate change is an imperative for many contemporary policymakers, businesses, and financial institutions, whereas it simply was not in the late 1980s and early 1990s.

From unburnable carbon towards environment-related risk

One tension within the 2010s discourse of stranded assets is the scope of risks that can cause asset stranding. Early on, some preferred to focus on the idea of scientifically derived carbon budgets being *directly* enforced top-down by governments in a coordinated way (in particular, see Carbon Tracker Initiative 2011). Others have been much more sceptical of coordinated international action and saw carbon budgets being introduced *indirectly* bottom-up through a panoply of different local and national policies, technological change and innovation, and social pressure, among other things (in particular, see Caldecott, Howarth, and McSharry 2013).

The views of individuals and organisations has trended towards the latter view over time (see Hedegaard 2015), including those that originally preferred the 'direct top-down' model over the 'indirect bottom-up' one (e.g. see Carbon Tracker Initiative 2015).

Relatedly, another tension has been the relative status of climate change versus the environment more broadly. Some have been more concerned with stranded assets created by international climate change policy (Carbon Tracker Initiative 2011), others have been more interested in the range of societal responses to physical climate change impacts that extend beyond unburnable carbon (Bank of England 2015b), and others have been concerned with both physical environmental change and societal responses to such environmental change (Bank of England 2015a; Caldecott, Howarth, and McSharry 2013). Again, the views of individuals and organisations has trended towards the latter view, which is more comprehensive and expansive, and has allowed for a wider range of interests to be engaged on the topic, such as those concerned with water risk and stranded water assets (see Lamb 2015) or in sectors that might be affected beyond fossil fuels, such as agriculture (see Caldecott, Howarth, and McSharry 2013; Rautner, Tomlinson, and Hoare 2016; Morel et al. 2016). To underpin a more expansive interpretation Caldecott, Howarth, and McSharry (2013) proposed a typology for different environment-related risks that could cause stranded assets and this is set out below (Figure 1).

Recent developments very clearly illustrate that environment-related risks, and not just those related to unburnable carbon, can have a significant impact on assets today, and these are likely to increase in significance over time (Caldecott et al. 2017). If anything, the available evidence suggests these are much more material, particularly in the short to medium term, than the risk of unburnable carbon or the carbon bubble (Caldecott et al. 2017). For

	Class	Description
PHYSICAL	**Environmental challenges and change**	For example, climate change, water stress, and biodiversity loss.
	Changing resource landscapes	Price and availability of different resources, such as oil, gas, coal and other minerals and metals. For example, Peak oil and the shale gas revolution.
SOCIETAL	**New government regulations**	Introduction of carbon pricing (via taxes and trading schemes), subsidy regimes (e.g. for fossil fuels and renewables), air pollution regulation, disclosure requirements, the 'carbon bubble' and international climate policy.
	Technological change	For example, falling clean technology costs (e.g. solar PV, onshore wind), disruptive technologies, and GMO.
	Evolving social norms and consumer behaviour	For example, fossil fuel divestment campaign, product labelling and certification schemes, consumer preferences.
	Litigation and changing statutory interpretations	For example, court cases, compensation payments, and changes in the way existing laws are applied or interpreted.

Figure 1. Typology of Environment-related Risk. Source: Caldecott, Howarth, and McSharry (2013).

example, air pollution and water scarcity in China threatens coal-fired power generation, which has changed coal demand and affected global coal prices (Caldecott, Tilbury, and Ma 2013); the shale gas revolution in the United States has put downward pressure on coal prices in Europe, stranding new high-efficiency gas plants (Caldecott and McDaniels 2014); and the fossil fuel divestment campaign threatens to erode the social licence of some targeted companies and could increase their cost of capital (Ansar, Caldecott, and Tibury 2013).

1st Global Conference on Stranded Assets and the Environment

Despite its growing prominence as a topic, there remains a great deal of confusion about: what stranded assets are; what assets might be affected; what drives stranding; how financial institutions and companies can manage the risk of stranded assets; what it means for policy-makers and regulators; and how it links to climate change policy. The academic literature on stranded assets also remains relatively limited. Researchers, scholars, and practitioners have generally opted for the publication of working papers, research notes, speeches, government white papers, and reports to disseminate their work as quickly as possible so they can influence a fast-moving discourse.

To critically review and help formulate a better understanding of stranded assets, and to help foster the development of the academic literature on the topic, the Sustainable Finance Programme at the University of Oxford's Smith School of Enterprise and the Environment organised the *1st Global Conference on Stranded Assets and the Environment* on the 24th and 25th September 2015 at The Queen's College, Oxford. The conference brought together over 120 leading scholars and practitioners from a range of disciplines, including economics, finance, geography, management, and public policy. The conference was sponsored by Norges Bank Investment Management and the full agenda and list of speakers at the conference can be found in the appendix at the end of this editorial.

Conference papers were considered for inclusion in this Special Issue of the *Journal of Sustainable Finance & Investment*. The Special Issue contains 8 of the 25 papers presented at the conference and these were selected through a multiple stage short-listing process based on an editorial assessment of quality and novelty, followed by double-blind peer review. Details of the eight papers included are as follows.

The first paper in the Special Issue, *Game theory and corporate governance: conditions for effective stewardship of companies exposed to climate change risks*, examines how investors can successfully convince listed fossil fuel companies to avoid asset stranding through the lens of game theory. The paper tests the effectiveness of owner engagement strategies by studying the conditions for cooperation between investors and their companies. Several parameters are modelled for their impact on the development of sustained cooperative equilibria, including: the benefits and costs of cooperation; the degree of strategic foresight; individual discount factors; and mutual history.

The second paper, *Assessing the sources of stranded asset risk: a proposed framework*, proposes a more efficient framework for assessing where stranded assets might arise, particularly from a bond investor perspective. The author proposes that what are currently called ESG risks are separated into three specific risk categories: (1) Operational or Management Risk; (2) Climate Risk, primarily related to climate mitigation and adaptation; and (3) Natural Capital Risks, a category intended to capture natural capital depletion, subsidy loss risks, and certain geopolitical risks. Stranded assets can arise from all three sources, but those arising from Climate and Natural Capital Risk are more likely to be both significant and irreversible.

The third paper, *Investment consequences of the Paris climate agreement*, develops a model of an energy transition. Projections for growth in renewables and electric vehicles suggest that the oil and gas industry will be disrupted during the 2020s, but that carbon dioxide emissions are unlikely to fall fast enough to keep within a 2° emissions budget. To keep warming to 2°, additional ways of reducing emissions from industry or of accelerating emissions reductions from generation, transport, and buildings will be needed together with an extensive pro-gramme of carbon dioxide removal.

The fourth paper, *A comparative analysis of the anti-Apartheid and fossil fuel divestment campaigns*, attempts a comparison of the similarities and differences between the extant fossil fuel divestment movement and the anti-Apartheid divestment movement. Fossil fuel divestment campaigners and advocates have deployed stranded assets arguments to make the case for divestment and this is the largest and fastest growing divestment movement in history.

The fifth paper, *Transition risks and market failure: a theoretical discourse on why financial models and economic agents may misprice risk related to the transition to a low-carbon economy*, links the traditional market failure literature and the recent research around poten-tial stranded assets risks. The market failure literature provides theoretical evidence of a poten-tial mispricing of stranded asset risks due to the design and interpretation of financial risk models, and the practices and institutions linked to economic agents. Policy intervention will likely be needed to address the design of financial risk models and associated transparency around their results, and the actual institutions governing risk management.

The sixth paper, *Blindness to risk: why institutional investors ignore the risk of stranded assets*, considers if the structure of the investment chain causes investors to be blind to stranded assets. The paper draws on a mixture of academic literature and the author's own experience of industry practice. The paper finds that institutional investors are constrained to measure risk in relation to a benchmark; risk becomes a function of volatility and divergence from peers. The risk of stranded assets is invisible in the decision-making chain. The industry is further constrained by its culture, regulation, and inappropriate incentives.

The seventh paper, *Social and Asocial learning about climate change among institutional investors: lessons for stranded assets*, contributes new empirical data from 58 in-depth inter-views and a global investor survey to explore how climate change is being learnt socially and asocially within the institutional investment industry. This research seeks to identify ways in which the concept of stranded assets can be better disseminated to investment pro-fessionals. This paper should interest both investment professionals keen to learn more about the issue and academic researchers seeking to engage investors on these topics.

The final paper, *Climate change and the fiduciary duties of pension fund trustees – lessons from the Australian law*, examines the obligations of pension (or 'superannuation') fund trustee directors in Australia. The analysis focuses on the obligation to apply due care, skill, and diligence under section 52A of the Superannuation Industry (Supervision) Act 1993 (Cth) (SIS Act). It concludes that a passive or inactive governance of climate change portfolio risks is unlikely to satisfy their duties: whether the inactivity emanates from climate change denial, honest ignorance, or unreflective assumption, strategic paralysis due to impact uncer-tainty, or a default to a base set by regulators or investor peers. Considered decisions to prevail with 'investment as usual' may also fail to satisfy the duty if they are based on outdated meth-odologies and assumptions.

Together these eight papers make a significant contribution to furthering the literature on stranded assets. Perhaps unsurprisingly given the authors' extensive collective experience of finance and investment, there is a strong bias towards research that can directly or indirectly support financial institutions understand and manage the risk of stranded assets. This is welcome, because if stranded assets are effectively priced and integrated into financial decision-making, capital is less likely to flow to assets that are incompatible with environ-mental sustainability and more like to flow to those that are. This is a necessary, albeit insufficient condition, to address climate change and the other environmental challenges facing humanity. The role of finance in this regard, particularly in a world where the politics and policy of dealing with global environmental change appears to be getting harder, has never been more important.

Ben Caldecott

Notes

1. Defined as the future emissions expected from all existing fossil fuel-burning infrastructure worldwide (Davis, Caldeira, and Matthews 2010).
2. These were conducted by the author and took place in March–April 2016 at Stanford University.

References

Allen, M. R., V. R. Barros, J. Broome, W. Cramer, and R. Christ. 2014. "IPCC Fifth Assessment Synthesis Report-Climate Change 2014 Synthesis Report." http://www.citeulike.org/group/15400/article/13416115.

Ansar, A., B. Caldecott, and J. Tibury. 2013. "Stranded Assets and the Fossil Fuel Divestment Campaign: What Does Divestment Mean for the Valuation of Fossil Fuel Assets?" Smith School of Enterprise and the Environment, University of Oxford, (October).

Bagwell, P., and P. Lyth. 2002. "Transport in Britain: From Canal Lock to Gridlock." Accessed August 15, 2016. https://books.google.co.uk/books?hl=en&lr=&id=1JdCtWuaQhcC&oi=fnd&pg=PR7&dq=railway+networks +replaced+canals+and+waterways+england&ots=W-YkMrbBVF&sig=ywv87TQiCFWx1P4D5UqYsqBYe2M.

Bank of England. 2015a. "One Bank Research Agenda." http://www.bankofengland.co.uk/research/Documents/ onebank/discussion.pdf.

Bank of England. 2015b. "The Impact of Climate Change on the UK Insurance Sector A Climate Change Adaptation Report by the Prudential Regulation Authority." http://www.bankofengland.co.uk/pra/Documents/ supervision/activities/pradefra0915.pdf.

Broadberry, S., and B. Gupta. 2005. *Cotton Textiles and the Great Divergence: Lancashire, India and Shifting Competitive Advantage 1600–1850.* pp. 23–25. Accessed August 15, 2016. http://www.iisg.nl/hpw/ factormarkets.php.

Caldecott, B. 2011. Why High Carbon Investment could be the Next Sub-prime Crisis. *The Guardian.*

Caldecott, B. 2012. Review of UK Exposure to High Carbon Investments.

Caldecott, B. 2015. Stranded Assets and Multilateral Development Banks. *Inter-American Development Bank.*

Caldecott, B., G. Dericks, A. Pfeiffer, and P. Astudillo. 2017. "Stranded Assets: The Transiton to a Low Carbon Economy." Lloyd's of London Emerging Risk Report.

Caldecott, B., N. Howarth, and P. McSharry. 2013. "Stranded Assets in Agriculture: Protecting Value from Environment-Related Risks." Smith School of Enterprise and the Environment, University of Oxford. http://www.smithschool.ox.ac.uk/research-programmes/stranded-assets/Stranded Assets Agriculture Report Final.pdf.

Caldecott, B., and J. McDaniels. 2014. "Stranded Generation Assets: Implications for European Capacity Mechanisms, Energy Markets and Climate Policy." Smith School of Enterprise and the Environment, University of Oxford. http://www.smithschool.ox.ac.uk/research-programmes/stranded-assets/Stranded Generation Assets - Working Paper – Final Version.pdf.

Caldecott, B., J. Tilbury, and Y. Ma. 2013. "Stranded Down Under? Environment-related Factors Changing China's Demand for Coal and What this Means for Australian Coal Assets." Smith School of Enterprise and the Environment, University of Oxford. Accessed December 2, 2015. http://www.smithschool.ox.ac. uk/research-programmes/stranded-assets/Stranded Down Under Report.pdf.

Carbon Tracker Initiative. 2011. "Unburnable Carbon – Are the World's Financial Markets Carrying a Carbon Bubble?" http://www.carbontracker.org/wp-content/uploads/2014/09/Unburnable-Carbon-Full-rev2-1.pdf.

Carbon Tracker Initiative. 2015. "Lost in Transition: How the Energy Sector Is Missing Potential Demand Destruction." http://www.carbontracker.org/report/lost_in_transition/.

Carbon Tracker Initiative. n.d. "Carbon Tracker Initiative's Definition of Stranded Assets." Accessed August 23, 2016. http://www.carbontracker.org/resources/.

Carbon Tracker Initiative. 2013. *Unburnable Carbon 2013: Wasted Capital and Stranded Assets.* London: Carbon Tracker Initiative.

Carney, M. 2015. "Breaking the Tragedy of the Horizon – Climate Change and Financial Stability." Speech given at Lloyd's of London by the Governor of … .

Congressional Budget Office. 1998. "Electric Utilities: Deregulation and Stranded Costs." CBO Paper.

Davis, S. J., K. Caldeira, and H. D. Matthews. 2010. "Future CO2 Emissions and Climate Change from Existing Energy Infrastructure." *Science* 329 (5997): 1330–1333. Accessed August 14, 2016. http://www.sciencemag.org/cgi/doi/10.1126/science.1188566.

Davis, S. J., and R. H. Socolow. 2014. "Commitment Accounting of CO2 Emissions." *Environmental Research Letters* 9 (8): 1. http://stacks.iop.org/1748-9326/9/i=8/a=084018?key=crossref.b7c8701dfa5d89a68f45f1956e8793b9.

Deloitte. 2016. "IAS 16 — Property, Plant and Equipment." http://www.iasplus.com/en/standards/ias/ias16.

EAC. 2014. Green Finance E. A. Committee, ed. http://www.publications.parliament.uk/pa/cm201314/cmselect/cmenvaud/191/191.pdf.

Exxon Mobil Corporation. 2014. Letter on to Shareholders and NGOs Carbon Asset Risk. http://cdn.exxonmobil.com/~/media/global/files/other/2014/cover-letter-to-arjuna-capital.pdf.

Figueres, Christiana. 2013. Keynote Address by Christiana Figures, Executive Secretary UNFCCC at the World Coal Association International Coal & Climate Summit. http://www.unep.org/newscentre/Default.aspx?DocumentID=2754&ArticleID=9703.

Financial Stability Board. 2015. FSB to Establish Task Force on Climate-related Financial Disclosures. http://www.fsb.org/wp-content/uploads/Climate-change-task-force-press-release.pdf.

Friedman, T. L. 2014. Obama on Obama on Climate. *The New York Times.* Accessed June 7, 2014. http://www.nytimes.com/2014/06/08/opinion/sunday/friedman-obama-on-obama-on-climate.html?smid=tw-TomFriedman&seid=auto&_r=2.

Generation Foundation. 2013. Stranded Carbon Assets. p.26. http://genfound.org/media/pdf-generation-foundation-stranded-carbon-assets-v1.pdf.

Grübler, A., and N. Nakićenović. 1991. "Long Waves, Technology Diffusion, and Substitution." *Review (Fernand Braudel Center)* 14 (2): 313–343. http://www.jstor.org/stable/40241184.

Gurría, A. 2013. "The Climate Challenge: Achieving Zero Emissions – Lecture by OECD Secretary-General." http://www.oecd.org/about/secretary-general/the-climate-challenge-achieving-zero-emissions.htm.

Hedegaard, C. 2015. "Divestment and Stranded Assets in the Low-carbon Transition – Chair's Summary." OECD's 32nd Roundtable on Sustainable Development, 28th October 2015.

IEA. 2008. *World Energy Outlook 2008.* Paris: International Energy Agency.

IEA. 2013. "Redrawing The Energy Climate Map." World Energy Outlook Special Report, p.134. http://www.worldenergyoutlook.org/media/weowebsite/2013/energyclimatemap/RedrawingEnergyClimateMap.pdf.

IPCC. 1999. Economic Impact of Mitigation Measures: Proceedings of IPCC Expert Meeting on Economic Impact of Mitigation Measures: The Hague, the Netherlands, 27–28 May, 1999, CPB.

IPCC. 2001. *IPCC Third Assessment Report – Climate Change 2001.* Geneva: Intergovernmental Panel on Climate Change.

King, S. M. 2012. Reply to Your Recent Letter on UK Exposure to High Carbon Investments C. C. Capital, ed.

Kondratiev, N. 1926. *The Long Waves in Economic Life.* Eastford, CT, USA: Martino.

Krause, F., W. Bach, and J. Koomey. 1989. *Energy Policy in the Greenhouse.* El Cerrito, CA: Dutch Ministry of the Environment.

Kruitwagen, L., D. MacDonald-Korth, and B. Caldecott. 2016. "Summary of Proceedings: Environment-related Risks and the Future of Prudential Regulation and Financial Conduct – 4th Stranded Assets Forum, Waddesdon Manor, 23rd October 2015." Smith School of Enterprise and the Environment, University of Oxford.

Lamb, C. 2015. "Drying and Drowning Assets – How Worsening Water Security Is Stranding Assets." http://www.strandedassets2015.org/agenda.html; http://www.strandedassets2015.org/uploads/2/6/9/5/26954337/session_v_presenter_ii_catelamb.pdf.

London School of Economics. 2013. "$674 Billion Annual Spend On 'Unburnable' Fossil Fuel Assets Signals Failure to Recognise Huge Financial Risks – Press Release." http://www.lse.ac.uk/GranthamInstitute/news/674-billion-annual-spend-on-unburnable-fossil-fuel-assets-signals-failure-to-recognise-huge-financial-risks-2/.

McGrath, P. 2014. "Ban Ki-moon Urges Pension Funds to Dump Fossil Fuel Investments." ABC.

McKibben, B. 2011. "Global Warming's Terrifying New Math." Rolling Stone.

Morel, A., R. Friedman, D. Tulloch, and B. Caldecott. 2016. "Stranded Assets in Palm Oil Production: A Case Study of Indonesia about the Sustainable Finance Programme." Smith School of Enterprise and the Environment, University of Oxford.

Mufson, S. 2014. "CEO of Royal Dutch Shell: Climate Change Discussion 'has gone into la-la land'." https://www.washingtonpost.com/news/wonk/wp/2014/09/10/ceo-of-royal-dutch-shell-climate-change-discussion-has-gone-into-la-la-land/.

Perez, C. 1985. "Microelectronics, Long Waves and World Structural Change: New Perspectives for Developing Countries." *World Development* 13 (3): 441–463. Accessed August 15, 2016. http://linkinghub.elsevier.com/retrieve/pii/0305750X85901408.

Perez, C. 2002. "Technological Revolutions and Financial Capital." Edward Elgar. https://www.amazon.co.uk/Technological-Revolutions-Financial-Capital-Dynamics/dp/1843763311.

Perez, C. 2010. "Technological Revolutions and Techno-economic Paradigms." *Cambridge Journal of Economics* 34 (1): 185–202. http://cje.oxfordjournals.org/content/34/1/185.abstract.

Pfeiffer, A., R. Millar, C. Hepburn, and E. Beinhocker. 2016. "The '2°C Capital Stock' for Electricity Generation: Committed Cumulative Carbon Emissions from the Electricity Generation Sector and the Transition to a Green Economy." *Applied Energy* 179 (1): 1395–1408.

Rautner, M., S. Tomlinson, and A. Hoare. 2016. "Managing the Risk of Stranded Assets in Agriculture and Forestry." Chatham House Research Paper.

Rook, D., and B. Caldecott. 2015. "Cognitive Biases and Stranded Assets: Detecting Psychological Vulnerabilities Within International Oil Companies." Smith School of Enterprise and the Environment, University of Oxford.

Royal Dutch Shell plc. 2014. "Letter to Shareholders – Stranded Assets." Accessed May 16, 2014. http://s02.static-shell.com/content/dam/shell-new/local/corporate/corporate/downloads/pdf/investor/presentations/2014/sri-web-response-climate-change-may14.pdf.

Schumpeter, J.A. 1942. *Capitalism, Socialism and Democracy*. Routledge. Accessed August 14, 2016. http://aulavirtual.tecnologicocomfenalcovirtual.edu.co/aulavirtual/pluginfile.php/520365/mod_resource/content/1/TEORIAS DEL EMPRENDIMIENTO.pdf.

Weyzig, F., B. Kuepper, J.W. van Gelder, R. van Tilburg, J.W. van Gelder, and R. van Tilbury. 2014. "The Price of Doing Too Little Too Late The Impact of the Carbon Bubble on the EU financial system." In *Green New Deal Series*. Brussels: Green European Foundation.

Wolf, W. 1996. "Car Mania: A Critical History of Transport." Accessed August 15, 2016. https://books.google.co.uk/books?hl=en&lr=&id=DD0samQuijgC&oi=fnd&pg=PR1&dq=rise+of+the+automobile+and+the+end+of+the+steam+railway+&ots=DmO5Le-Z7W&sig=WuYG9kiWjsWptp6C9-toB1shc40.

The World Bank. 2013a. "Toward a Sustainable Energy Future for All: Directions for the World Bank Group's Energy Sector."

The World Bank. 2013b. "World Bank Group Sets Direction for Energy Sector Investments." Accessed July 16, 2013. http://www.worldbank.org/en/news/feature/2013/07/16/world-bank-group-direction-for-energy-sector.

Investment consequences of the Paris climate agreement[*]

Howard Covington

ABSTRACT

This paper develops a simple model of an energy transition. Projections for growth in renewables and electric vehicles suggest that the oil and gas industry will be disrupted during the 2020s, but that, as things stand, carbon dioxide emissions are unlikely to fall fast enough to keep within a 2° emissions budget. To keep warming to 2°, additional ways of reducing emissions from industry or of accelerating emissions reductions from generation, transport and buildings will be needed together with an extensive programme of carbon dioxide removal.

Investor concerns

Investors are becoming aware of the possibility that action to decarbonise the global economy may disrupt business models and change asset values. Some investors have begun to support resolutions put to energy company shareholder meetings to request information about how the energy transition might affect the company's business and value.

Many projections are available of future energy demand and supply. Some of these explore the extensive changes needed if the world is to limit warming to the politically supported 2°C above the level of the late nineteenth century (IRENA 2014). Others seek to justify a view that demand for fossil fuels will be robust in the foreseeable future (BP 2016). The purpose of this study is to formulate an almost trivially simple model of the energy transition that nonetheless contains useful insights about the consequences of pushing ahead with decarbonisation as fast as practicable given the rate at which low-emissions technologies are developing. Its main conclusions are that there is likely to be enough change substantially to undermine the revenues of the petro-economies and the profits of the oil and gas industry during the 2020s and to disrupt business models in high-emissions industries but that holding warming to below 2° will be difficult.

By way of introduction, the next section describes some of the implicit arithmetic consequences for investors of the climate agreement reached in Paris in December 2015. Subsequent sections explore how decarbonisation might be given effect by changes to the world's energy infrastructure.

---

[*]A talk based on an earlier version of this paper was given at the 1st Global Conference on Stranded Assets and the Environment at the Smith School of Enterprise and the Environment at the University of Oxford on 24 September 2015.

Supplemental data for this article can be accessed at 10.1080/20430795.2016.1196556.

Paris arithmetic

In Paris almost all the world's governments agreed to limit global warming to at the most 2°C above the level of the late nineteenth century. Warming is caused by the accumulation in the atmosphere of greenhouse gases from human activities, mainly (but not exclusively) the burning of oil, natural gas and coal to fuel the global economy. Taking likely future emissions of other greenhouse gases into account, and working to a 50% probability, the remaining budget for emissions of the principal greenhouse gas, carbon dioxide, is around 1,000 billion tonnes ($gtCO_2$). Annual emissions of carbon dioxide are currently around 40 $gtCO_2$ (IPCC 2014).

If the global economy's energy infrastructure could be changed so that carbon dioxide emissions were in future to fall at a constant annual rate, then this rate would need to be 4% pa to keep to budget (see Supplementary Information). This would mean that emissions fell by three-quarters by mid-century and by 90% by 2075. These are the kinds of numbers that are sometimes cited as national objectives. Keeping within budget therefore implies a 60-year 'energy transition' during which the global economy is substantially decarbonised. If output grows at 3% pa while emissions are being reduced in this way, then the reduction in emissions per unit of global output would have to be 7% pa. The growth in energy-related emissions ran at 2.7% a year in the first decade of this century, but may now have slowed to almost zero (IEA 2016).

It may not be practicable to cut emissions at 4% a year for 60 years. If, instead, carbon dioxide emissions fell steadily at 2% pa until the end of the century and from then on all further emissions were removed from the atmosphere and stored, the emissions budget would be exceeded by about 650 $gtCO_2$. To keep within budget, these emissions might also be removed and stored – at a rate, say, of 10 $gtCO_2$ pa starting in the mid-2030s.

There are many proposals (ranging from reforestation to liquefaction of carbon dioxide and storage in depleted oil wells) for how industry-scale carbon dioxide removal might be achieved (Caldecott, Lomax, and Workman 2015). The lower end of indicative cost estimates is around $50 per tonne of carbon dioxide. At the current level of emissions, a carbon dioxide price at this level would imply additional costs to emitters of $2 trillion pa and a carbon removal industry of $0.5 trillion pa, about one-third the size of the oil industry when the oil price is $50 per barrel. So that businesses did not relocate to avoid the cost, such a price, and the mechanisms to enforce it, would need international agreement. Many models of the energy transition rely on carbon dioxide removal at this scale to keep within the carbon dioxide emissions budget, although it is far from clear whether it is socially, politically, environmentally, technologically or economically acceptable or possible (Williamson 2016).

Suppose that the global energy infrastructure is progressively changed so that carbon dioxide emissions do indeed decline by between 2% and 4% a year while the economy continues to grow. This implies that demand for fossil fuels will decrease at this rate as energy comes to be used more efficiently and fossil fuels are displaced by the increased use of renewables and nuclear energy. Demand for oil is currently around 95 million barrels a day (mb/d). Around a quarter of this is for feedstock into the petrochemicals industry, so about 70 mb/d is for energy production. A reduction in demand of 2–4% of this amount is equivalent to 1.4–2.8 mb/d. During 2015, surplus supply on this scale caused the oil price to fall by two-thirds from the $90 per barrel or more, where it had been between 2007 and 2014, to touch $30 in early 2016.

It is typical of extractive industries that there is a large sunk cost for preparing a well or a mine and then a much smaller operating cost. Although a high expected product price may be needed to justify investment in a new extraction project, only a relatively low price is necessary to cover operating costs once the initial capital costs have been sunk. A small decrease in demand can therefore trigger a large fall in price as suppliers compete to supply the lower demand and the market price changes from the full unit cost of investing in the next marginally profitable extraction project to the marginal cost of keeping existing projects in production. A steady reduction in demand of a few percent a year for several decades would be likely to send the oil, natural gas and coal prices to historically low levels for several decades while higher cost projects were progressively shut down and supply was gradually cut back to match falling demand. Perhaps anticipating this kind of development, in 2016 Saudi Arabia announced its intention to re-orient its economy so that it can withstand an oil price of $30. During the next few years the price of oil may again rise to $90 per barrel or more as demand and supply come back into balance. If the price were then to fall indefinitely to $30, as the arithmetic of the Paris agreement suggests should be the case, the petro-economies as a whole would lose around $2 trillion of revenues compared to what revenues would have been without decarbonisation.

A price of $50 per tonne on carbon dioxide emissions and a steady fall in demand for oil each imply the potential redirection of $2 trillion, or around 2% of world GDP, each year. Annual transfers of this amount away from carbon dioxide emitters on the one hand and fossil fuel producers on the other would shift the economic balance of some countries and change the business models of several industries. Petro-economies would undergo a period of social and economic adjustment. Some of them might fail as states. The revenues of fossil fuel companies would fall to perhaps a third or so of their level of the recent peak years. The profitability of energy-intensive industries such as electricity generation, steel, chemicals, cement and transport would change. Legacy assets might become uneconomic ('stranded assets') as prices varied and new technologies that helped reduce fossil fuel demand disrupted established industries and resulted in financial distress and bankruptcies. If the world holds to the Paris agreement, these changes will come about during the 2020s, a period that is well within the time-frame of major capital investment projects being considered by company managements and project finance proposals being approved by banks.

The Paris agreement therefore gives investors good reason for concern. Without information on whether and how companies are preparing themselves for the far-reaching changes that it implicitly contemplates, investors cannot properly and responsibly manage their portfolios or approve financing proposals or remuneration plans when asked to do so by the high-emitting companies whose shares they own. We now turn to a simple model to quantify the consequences of an energy transition at the speed contemplated by the Paris agreement.

Method

A model is constructed that summarises the changes that the world's energy infrastructure might undergo. The intention is to make this model as simple as it can be in order to capture the main drivers of carbon dioxide emissions through the energy transition. It is based on the International Energy Agency's 2° energy projections to 2050 (IEA 2014) but modified to incorporate the changes described below. Following the IEA's format, the global economy is divided into four sectors: three energy consuming sectors – transport, industry and buildings (including agriculture and fisheries) – and an electricity-generating sector that supplies electricity to the other three sectors. Following the IEA's judgement about what might be achievable, it is assumed that energy efficiency measures are able to limit the growth in energy demand through the energy transition to 0.4% a year, composed of 0.5% from industry and buildings and 0.1% a year from transport, where it is easier to enact wide-ranging efficiency regulations.

Given this growth, the energy transition is characterised in a simple way by specifying the evolution of the 'shape' of energy supply to the four sectors. This is done by making assumptions for the share of each kind of energy source used within each sector once the energy transition is completed; by specifying a time period to complete the transition in each sector; and by assuming that the growth of each non-fossil fuel source is either at a constant rate or is along a logistic curve. Cumulative carbon dioxide emissions from each sector during the energy transition (and afterwards for the industry sector) are assumed to be proportional to the cumulative amount of fossil fuel consumed by each sector. In this way the uncertainties and complexities of the energy transition are subsumed into a few simple but plausible arithmetic relationships. Process emissions from cement production and emissions from land use changes are treated separately.

The assumptions for the evolution of energy supply are summarised in Table 1. The assumed development of shares of energy supply is based on projections to 2050 described in IEA 2014 but modified by extrapolation through to the end of the energy transition in each sector and also to provide for accelerated electrification of transport through the take-up of electric vehicles and faster growth in wind and solar electricity generation. The main assumptions that underlie Table 1 are as follows.

Table 1.

	Transition	Electricity (%)	Bio (%)	Other (%)	Fossil fuels (%)
Part A: The shape of fuel supply to industry, buildings and transport					
Industry (34% of final energy use)	2015	24	7	4	65
	2075	40	20	5	35
Buildings (37% of final energy use)	2015	29	27	6	39
	2075	50	25	25	0
Transport (29% of final energy use)	2015	0.06	2	0.5	97
	2052	60	30	10	0

	Transition	Wind and solar (%)	Bio (%)	Nuclear and hydro (%)	Fossil fuels (%)
Part B: The shape of fuel supply to electricity generation					
Generation	2015	5	3	28	64
	2065	60	10	30	0

Note: Part A of Table 1 shows the assumed evolution of the shape of energy supply to the three energy consuming sectors and Part B the shape of supply to electricity generation. Electricity supply to transport is for electric vehicles. 'Bio' refers to biomass and waste in industry and generation, biomass in buildings and biofuels in transport. 'Other' refers primarily to the use of waste heat in industry, heat pumps and solar thermal in buildings and hydrogen in transport. Shares of final energy use for the three consuming sectors are estimates for 2015. Shares of supply for 2015 are calculated as the average of supply estimates for 2011 and 2020 in IEA 2014, updated for more recent industry estimates for electric vehicles and wind and solar. Shares of supply at the end of the respective transition periods are discussed in the text. Supply is assumed to grow at constant annual rates other than for electricity in transport and wind and solar in generation, which are assumed to grow along logistic curves, and for fossils fuels which are the difference between demand in each sector and supply from the other sources.

It is assumed that there will be a rapid electrification of industry, buildings and transport so that distributed and/or mobile sources of emissions are replaced by static, localised electricity generation sources from which emissions can be captured. In line with commercial analyses of generation costs (Lazard 2015; Shah 2015) it is assumed that in many geographies from the early 2020s wind and utility-scale solar generation will be cost-competitive with coal generation and that residential and commercial solar generation will reach grid parity. Recognising the political momentum created by the Paris agreement it is assumed that wherever they are economic, these sources of generation will be given preference over competing coal and natural gas generation in order to reduce both air pollution and warming. In addition, it is assumed that some existing coal generation and industrial plants will be adapted to use biomass and waste as a fuel and some will be closed before the end of their useful lives.

In transport, and again reflecting commercial analyses, it is assumed that electric vehicles will be price-competitive with mass-market light petrol vehicles in the early 2020s (Hummel and Houchois 2014), just as technology begins to enable autonomous cars and as ride-hailing apps could change the modes of urban vehicle ownership (Greenblatt and Saxena 2015). Governments are assumed to take the opportunity offered to reduce urban air pollution and constrain warming and so promote the rapid decarbonisation of mass road transport by needed for the widespread adoption of electric vehicles. Transport modes that are not easily susceptible to electrification (road haulage, aviation and shipping) are assumed to be decarbonised by the use of biofuels [IEA 2014].

The assumed evolution of the electricity generation sector recognises that a coal-fired electricity generation plant has a lifetime of around 40 years and such plants are likely to continue to be constructed in developing countries for the next decade. Fossil fuels are accordingly assumed to be eliminated from electricity generation over a period of 50 years, which coincides with the youngest coal plants reaching the end of their lives. Early retirement of coal generation plants may in future be encouraged by an internationally adopted high and rising carbon price and by consumer-owned residential, commercial and industrial rooftop solar PV installations competing with grid-delivered electricity. The rate at which wind and solar penetrate electricity generation may therefore be faster than the natural rate of retirement of the fossil fuel generation fleet. The share of generation finally taken by intermittent renewables depends on progress with developing demand management, interconnection and grid-scale electricity storage. To reflect reasonably rapid deployment, wind and solar are assumed to follow a logistic-shaped penetration curve characteristic of the diffusion of innovations (Rogers 2003; Mayer et al. 2015) that takes their share of generation to 60% in 50 years. It is a matter of conjecture whether grids would be sufficiently flexible to operate by then with this level of intermittent renewables. Grids with 40% solar generation are considered technically possible (Mayer et al. 2015).

The consequence of these assumptions is that electricity generated by wind and solar grows on average at 8.6% a year between 2015 and 2050, compared to IEA's 6.2% a year and industry projections of 4–7% pa for wind and 5–10% pa for solar [GWEC 2014; Mayer et al. 2015]. The effect of assuming that the penetration of wind and solar increases along a logistic curve is that growth is higher in the earlier years and runs at 10.5% a year on average from 2015 until 2040. Hydro, nuclear and biomass are assumed to grow to their assumed final shares at constant annual rates.

Based on the ratio of fleet size to annual new vehicle sales, the light vehicle fleet turns over about every 12 years. To reflect the potential for rapid adoption, it is assumed that electric vehicles increase their penetration of the light vehicle fleet from 0.1% currently to 10% by 2030 along a logistic-shaped penetration curve. It is further assumed that this curve may be extrapolated to 99% penetration, which it reaches in 2052, thus defining a 37-year (or, less precisely, a 35–40 year) transition period for transport. It is assumed that biofuels and hydrogen fuel grow to their final shares at constant rates during this period. Underlying the rapid growth in biofuels is the assumption that second-generation biofuels can be successfully developed. The additional demand for electricity arising from electric vehicles is estimated at a third of the energy content of the oil that would have been used by petrol vehicles that have been displaced

For industry and buildings it is assumed that the change in the shape of energy supply described by Table 1 is completed over the 60 years to 2075, with their use of each non-fossil fuel source of energy supply growing at a constant annual rate in this period. This period reflects the long time required to increase energy efficiency and change the heating plant in the stock of buildings and to re-engineer industrial processes. Fossil fuels are assumed to be eliminated from the buildings sector within this period but not from industry. The problem here is that it may not be possible to eliminate the use of fossil fuels in heavy industrial processes, for example, steel manufacture (Brown et al. 2012). For this reason it is assumed that fossil fuel use by industry continues indefinitely after the transition at its projected 2075 level and that the emissions from this source are captured and stored. (If emissions were assumed to rise after 2075, then the amount of carbon capture would also need to rise from what is projected below.)

The result of these assumptions is an energy transition characterised by three different time periods: 50 years for electricity generation, 35–40 years for transport and 60 years for buildings and industry. During the 50 years in which electricity generation is decarbonised demand for electricity grows on average at 1.7% pa as a result of increased electrification in the other sectors. It is assumed that during these periods, emissions regulations and a high and rising carbon price encourage fossil fuels to be replaced by non-fossil fuels wherever practicable, so that fossil fuel use in each sector becomes the balancing item between overall demand for energy and the available supply from non-fossil fuel sources. Since explicit forms for the growth of each non-fossil fuel source have been assumed, the cumulative use of fossil fuel through the energy transition in each sector may be calculated. Cumulative carbon dioxide emissions from each sector during the energy transition are estimated by assuming that these emissions are proportional to the amount of fossil fuel used. This assumption might be expected to hold if the mix of fossil fuels used in each sector remains roughly constant and holds reasonably well for IEA's 2° projections. The estimated 2015 carbon dioxide emissions from each of the four sectors are shown in the first column of Table 2.

In addition to emissions from the four sectors, carbon dioxide emissions from cement production are significant in their own right. It is assumed that after the enormous growth in cement use that has accompanied the industrialisation of China, cement production increases by 1% pa until mid-century (Brown et al. 2012). Carbon dioxide emissions from this source are assumed to increase at this rate from the starting emissions shown in the first column of Table 2 and then to fall linearly to zero after mid-century, reflecting an assumed gradual substitution of cement by low-emission building materials. This

Table 2. Carbon dioxide emissions in 2015 and projection to 2100.

gtCO$_2$	2015 Emissions	Share of 2015 emissions (%)	Budget to 2100	Projection to 2100
Electricity generation	13.5	34	340	350
Transport	7.4	19	190	180
Industry	9.9	25	250	730
Buildings	3.5	9	90	140
Cement	2.1	5	50	160
Land use	3.5	9	90	90
CO$_2$ removal				−650
Total	40.0	100	1,000	1,000

Note: Table 2 shows carbon dioxide emissions from electricity generation, the three energy consuming sectors, process emissions from cement manufacture and emissions from land use changes. Other than for the land use sector emissions are estimated from average emissions for 2011 and 2020 in IEA 2014. In the case of land use emissions are estimated from IPCC 2014. 'Budget' is the emissions budget to 2100 of 1,000 gtCO$_2$ allocated according to the estimated shares. 'Projection' is estimated emissions to 2100 calculated on the basis described in the text. 'CO$_2$ removal' is what is needed to bring estimated emissions to 2100 back onto budget.

assumption is no more than a convenience with little substance other than an expectation that a high and rising carbon price will encourage the necessary technological developments. Emissions from cement production could turn out to be substantially higher than indicated.

The first column of Table 2 also includes emissions from changes in land use. It is assumed here that political agreements limit emissions from this source in accordance with a notional carbon dioxide emissions budget. For each sector and for cement and land use this budget is constructed by allocating 1000 gtCO$_2$ according to the share of emissions in 2015. The second and third columns of Table 2 show this share and this notional budget allocation that result. Projected emissions are then compared with the notional budget.

The model just described is set out in further detail in the Supplementary information section.

Results

As shown in the last column of Table 2 and illustrated in Figure 1, generation and transport keep approximately to their notional budget. Industry, buildings and cement exceed

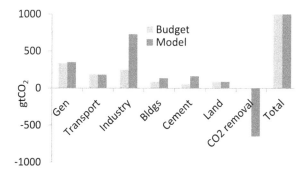

Figure 1. Projected Carbon dioxide emissions to 2100. Note: Figure 1 shows cumulative carbon dioxide emissions from various sources projected between 2015 and 2100 and compares these with a notional budget arrived at by allocating 1,000 gtCO$_2$ among the sources pro rata to estimated emissions in 2015. 'Gen' refers to electricity generation. 'Buildings' includes agriculture and fisheries. 'Land' refers to land use changes. The basis for the projections is explained in the main text.

it, with industry having the largest excess. To restore total net emissions to budget, approximately 650 gtCO₂ of carbon dioxide removal is needed by 2100, an amount consistent with the median estimate of what is needed (Williamson 2016). By this date carbon dioxide emissions have been eliminated from all sectors other than industry, where they continue to run at 7 gtCO₂ pa. Between 2015 and 2075 total emissions accordingly fall at an average annual rate of 2% pa. Provided that it proves feasible to undertake the necessary carbon dioxide removal, Table 1 is therefore a possible representation of a 2° energy transition plan. Without carbon dioxide removal, this plan would result in the 2° objective being exceeded by around 0.3° by 2100, assuming a climate response to cumulative emissions at the mid-point of its expected range (IPCC 2014).

If the transition in electricity generation took 40 years rather than the 50 years assumed, the amount of carbon removal needed to keep to budget would decrease by 85 gtCO₂. If electric vehicle penetration of the light vehicle fleet was 5% by 2030 rather than 10% then the transition in the transport sector would take an additional seven years and the amount of carbon dioxide removal needed would increase by 65 gtCO₂. If energy demand from the industry and buildings sectors were to grow at 1.0% rather than 0.5% pa during the transition in these sectors then the amount of carbon dioxide removal needed to restore the budget would increase by 190 gtCO₂.

The assumed evolution of the electricity generation sector gives wind and solar a 45% share of electricity generated by 2040. Adding in hydro and biomass increases the total share of renewables to approximately two-thirds by then. This is significantly more than expected by some industry observers. Bloomberg New Energy Finance, for example, projects 30% of electricity from variable renewables by 2040 with 46% in total from renewables (BNEF 2015). To meet the growth projected here, installations of wind and solar generation capacity during the 2030s must run at around 500 gW a year, about 5 times the current rate. Roughly 4% of the global fleet of gas and coal generation plants must be retired each year.

The penetration of electric vehicles into the light vehicle fleet is projected to rise from the assumed 10% in 2030 to 70% by 2040, implying annual unit growth of 20% during the 2030s if the light vehicle market remains constant in size at around 1 billion vehicles (and more if this market grows). For comparison, Bloomberg New Energy Finance expects cumulative sales of electric vehicles to increase from 100 million units in 2030 to around 420 million by 2040 (Randall 2016).

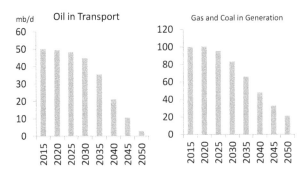

Figure 2. Projected demand for oil in transport and gas and coal in generation. Note: Figure 2 shows how projected demand for oil in transport (million barrels per day) and coal and gas in electricity generation (2015 demand = 100) might be expected to change if fuel supply evolves as depicted in Table 1.

Table 3. Effect of a carbon price on primary energy costs.

Market unit	Oil barrel	Natural gas million BTU	Coal short ton
Indicative current price ($/unit)	40	2.0	45
Primary energy content (gJ/unit)	5.7	1.06	26.6
CO_2 emissions (million tonnes CO_2/eJ)	75	57	84
Indicative current price ($/gJ)	7.0	1.9	1.7
Cost of CO_2 emissions ($/gJ)	3.7	2.9	4.2

Note: The first three rows of Table 3 show approximate market prices (Brent, Henry Hub and Appalachia respectively, April 2016), primary energy content and carbon dioxide emissions for oil, natural gas and coal. The last two rows show current prices per unit of primary energy and compare these with the costs that would result from a price of $50 per tonne being set on carbon dioxide emissions. Primary energy content and carbon dioxide emissions are based on DEFRA 2016. eJ is exa-Joules (10^{18} Joules), gJ is giga-Joules (10^9 Joules).

Figure 2 shows the evolution of the demand for oil in the transport sector and the demand for coal and gas in electricity generation. Demand falls sharply towards the end of the 2020s as electric vehicles and biofuels reduce the demand for oil and wind and solar reduce the demand for natural gas and coal. The fall in demand for oil during the 2020s is about 5mb/d, an amount that might reasonably be expected to lower the oil price to $30 per barrel or less.

A carbon price of the order of $50/tCO_2$ will need to be in place by the early 2030s to stimulate the development of the industrial infrastructure needed for carbon dioxide removal. As illustrated in Table 3, a carbon price at this level adds significantly to the costs of using fossil fuels. This additional cost would be offset, however, by the lower market prices of fossil fuels that would result from the steadily contracting demand for them. A sense of the size of this benefit may be obtained by assuming that if demand for fossil fuels were rising rather than falling, market prices might be around twice the level shown in Table 3, roughly where prices were in 2007–2014. The last two rows of Table 3 imply that the price difference between $40 and $80 per barrel of oil is approximately twice the cost of a carbon price of $50. As part of a package of measures to enable an energy transition, a $50 carbon price would therefore have net benefits for oil consumers. For coal consumers, however, there is a net cost.

Discussion

It is unlikely that the global energy system will evolve along the smooth pathway assumed in this analysis. Progress will more probably be in fits and starts that are the consequence of inherently unpredictable technological, economic and political developments. That said, the simple model developed here gives a sense of what might be the outcome of an optimistic view of the speed of adoption of renewables and electric vehicles.

The conclusion is that changes to the global energy infrastructure will come sufficiently fast to disrupt the markets for oil and natural gas in the 2020s and enable the introduction of a high and rising price on carbon dioxide emissions that will change the economics of many heavy industries. Whether the world can keep within a 2° emissions budget without a much greater effort is doubtful. The model suggests that this will not only require energy efficiency to moderate demand growth, but also the implementation of low-emission energy and transport technologies more rapidly than envisaged here together with carbon dioxide removal on a global scale.

Disclosure statement

No potential conflict of interest was reported by the author.

Notes on contributors

Howard Covington is chair of The Alan Turing Institute, vice-chair of ClientEarth and a senior adviser to Preventable Surprises. He was formerly CEO of New Star Asset Management.

References

BNEF. 2015. *New Energy Outlook 2015*. New York: Bloomberg New Energy Finance.

BP. 2016. "BP Energy Outlook 2035." BP 2016 edition.

Brown, T., A. Gambhir, N. Florin, and P. Fennel. 2012. "Reducing CO_2 Emissions from Heavy Industry." Grantham Institute for Climate Change Briefing Paper No. 7. 2012.

Caldecott, B., G. Lomax, and M. Workman. 2015. "Stranded Carbon Assets and Negative Emissions Technologies." Working Paper. February Smith School of Enterprise and the Environment.

DEFRA. 2016. *Greenhouse Gas Conversion Factor Repository*. London: Department for Environment Food & Rural Affairs. http://www.ukconversionfactorscarbonsmart.co.uk/Filter.aspx?year=38.

Greenblatt, B., and Saxena, S. 2015. "Autonomous Taxis Could Greatly Reduce Greenhouse-gas Emissions of US Light-Duty Vehicles." *Nature Climate Change* 5, 860–863.

GWEC. 2014. *Global Wind Energy Outlook 2014*. Brussels: Author.

Hummel, P., and P. Houchois. 2014. "Will Solar, Batteries and Electric Cars Re-Shape the Electricity System?" UBS.

IEA. 2014. *Energy Technology Perspectives 2014*. Paris: International Energy Agency.

IEA. 2016. *Decoupling of Global Emissions and Economic Growth Confirmed*. Paris: International Energy Agency.

IPCC. 2014. "Climate Change 2013, The Physical Science Basis. Contribution of Working Group 1 to the Fifth Assessment Report of the Intergovernmental Panel on Climate Change". Cambridge University Press. Chapters 6.3.1 (emissions history), 12.4.1 (warming projections) and 12.5.5 (transient climate response to emissions).

IRENA. 2014. *Remap 2030. A Renewable Energy Roadmap*. Abu-Dhabi: International Renewable Energy Agency.

Lazard. 2015. "Lazard's Levelized Cost of Energy Analysis – Version 9.0". New York.

Mayer, J., S. Phillips, N. Hussein, T. Schlegl, and T. Senkpiel. 2015. "Current and Future Cost of Photovoltaics." Fraunhofer-Institute for Solar Energy Systems. Commissioned by Agora Energiewende.

Randall, T. 2016. "Here's How Electric Cars Will Cause the Next Oil Crisis." Bloomberg. http://www.bloomberg.com/features/2016-ev-oil-crisis/?cmpid=yhoo.headline

Rogers, E. 2003. *Diffusion of Innovation*. New York: Free Press.

Shah, V. 2015. "F.I.T.T. for investors – Crossing the Chasm: Solar Grid Parity in a Low Oil Price Era." Deutsche Bank Markets Research.

Williamson, P. 2016. "Emissions Reduction: Scrutinize CO2 Removal Methods." *Nature* 530 (7589): 153–155.

Blindness to risk: why institutional investors ignore the risk of stranded assets[*]

Nicholas Silver

ABSTRACT

There has been an apparent resistance amongst mainstream investors to integrate the risk of stranded assets into investment decisions. This paper considers if the structure of the investment chain causes investors to be blind to risks such as stranded assets. This paper considers how the interaction between financial economic theory, regulation and the practices of the fund management industry gives rise to the way the industry analyses and manages risk. The paper draws on a mixture of academic literature and the author's own experience of industry practice. The paper finds that institutional investors are constrained to measure risk in relation to a benchmark; risk becomes a function of volatility and divergence from peers. The risk of stranded assets is invisible in the decision-making chain. The industry is further constrained by its culture, regulation and inappropriate incentives. The paper concludes that integrating stranded asset risk requires a drastic overhaul of the regulation of, and theory used in, the investment chain. This would better align the investment industry with the long-term capital allocation requirements of society.

1. Introduction

Much of the focus on stranded assets in an environmental context has been on the impact of climate change or, more specifically, the societal response to climate change. If strong action is taken on climate change, to prevent anthropogenic global warming from exceeding safe limits, most of the world's fossil fuel reserves will have to remain left in the ground and there will be 'stranded carbon assets'. There is a risk that fossil fuel companies' stocks will at some point be significantly reduced in value (Caldecott and Rook 2015; Carbon Tracker 2014; Wolf 2014).

Financial assets are to a large extent owned by institutional investors such as pension funds, insurance companies and sovereign wealth funds. If the stranded carbon assets described were to materialise, this would have a significant negative impact on institutional investors' portfolios. The core argument of this paper is that because of the structure and incentives in the financial markets, decision-makers within the investment chain

---

[*]1st Global Conference on Stranded Assets and the Environment 2015.

have little incentive to allow for taking stranded assets into consideration. To understand why this is the case, the paper goes into some detail about how the asset allocation of institutional investors is determined, and what risk means to different actors in the investment chain. It is found that the concept of risk has a different and often contradictory meaning to different actors in the investment chain, which means that the institution is blind to stranded-asset type environmental risks. The paper considers how institutional investors make asset allocation decisions and therefore how they define risk. Risk is defined differently by different actors in the investment chain, making it difficult to integrate stranded assets into the investment decision-making progress. Section 2 describes how institutional investors make asset allocation decisions, focusing, as an example, on defined benefit pension schemes. Section 3 then considers how asset managers are selected and motivated. The construction of a portfolio is to a large extent influenced by financial economics, in particular Modern Portfolio Theory (MPT), which is described and questioned in Section 4. Section 5 then discusses how the different definitions of risks that emerge from the description might influence how institutional investors view stranded assets. Section 6 then discusses the risk of stranded assets and the implications of this paper for investment regulation and practice.

2. How institutional investors make asset allocation decisions

A financial institution is typically a legal entity with a set of financial liabilities and assets. The liabilities are generally contingent on a contracted event happening, for example, an insurance policy pay-out, or a pensioner-member being alive after she has retired. The assets are either held as financial assets (e.g. equity or bonds) or can be a call on a third party, for example, a sponsoring employer in the case of a pension fund.

The problem that a financial institution is trying to solve in deciding on how to invest its assets is how best to allocate the institution's assets between asset classes to minimise the risk of not meeting its liabilities at the lowest cost.

2.1. Selecting a portfolio[1]

There are a range of asset classes in which an institution can invest, often determined by law, the institution's governing constitution, the size of the institution, practical considerations (for example, the cost of investing in an asset class) and professional practice. This stage of the process determines how the assets are allocated between asset classes.

A typical process that the financial institution might take is as follows[2] (Chambers et al. 2005):

(1) Assess the risk appetite and investment beliefs of the financial institution (Koedijk and Slager 2009): The ultimate decision-makers of the financial institution may be a board of trustees (for example, in the case of a pension fund or endowment) or a board of directors (in the case of an insurance company or a bank). In both cases, these boards have a fiduciary duty to act in the best interest of their beneficiaries (in the case of the trustees) or the company's shareholders and other stakeholders (in the case of the directors). The Board therefore needs to define the level of risk that they take to meet their objectives. External considerations also need to be taken into consideration;

for example, if there are any regulations or guidance, in the case of a pension fund the financial strength of the sponsoring employer (the trustees may be less risk averse if the sponsoring employer is a very large, secure entity compared to if it is a small weak company).

(2) Asset Liability Modelling (ALM): The financial institution may undertake an ALM, which is typically a stochastic model of the institution's assets and liabilities under different economic scenarios. This will be described in further detail.

(3) Select range of alternative asset allocation based on different risk/return profiles: as will be described, the ALM will output the cashflows of the institution under different (randomised) economic scenarios for a given asset allocation mix. The distribution of the randomly generated outputs estimates the probability that the institution will not meet its liabilities, which give an estimate of risk. The institution, or its advisers, will determine a range of different asset allocations and analyse the different risks/costs of each asset allocation. The cost might be defined as the contributions that the institution has to receive to meet its liabilities for a given level of risk.

(4) Select most suitable asset allocation: The institution now has a model of the risk and costs of different asset allocations, and needs to determine the one that is the most appropriate given its risk appetite.

(5) Finesse allocation: Once the broad asset allocation has been decided on, the precise asset allocation is determined. This might be done by running the ALM in finer detail around the chosen asset allocation, or specifying tactical asset allocation ranges. Tactical asset allocation is the divergence from the asset allocation decision that will be tolerated given the fund manager's or board's view on current economic circumstances.

(6) Select investment (asset) managers: Once the asset allocation decision has been made, or more usually on an ongoing basis, asset management firms are appointed. For a smaller institution, this might be one company who manages all of the assets, with the specified asset allocation. Larger institutions may manage all or part of the portfolio in-house, and will generally delegate more specific mandates to individual managers, for example, to manage the UK equity portfolio only. The manager could be selected on a number of criteria, for example past performance, their investment style or their specialist expertise in a given mandate.

(7) Monitor and review performance: The manager is usually set a target against a benchmark and reviewed based on their quarterly returns. This is the subject of the next section.

2.2. Example – ALM of a defined benefit pension scheme[3]

To illustrate the process further, I will describe the process of using an ALM. This is illustrated through the example of a defined benefit pension scheme. Other financial institutions will have liabilities with different characteristics, but may also employ ALMs or other stochastic models. An ALM is a stochastic model, in this case of a pension scheme. The ALM randomly generates a large number of scenarios. Each scenario projects the cashflow payments the scheme has to make and the income it receives from a given asset allocation. The model is run a large number of times, typically with 10,000 scenarios.

In any given scenario, the scheme will either be able to meet its obligations or not. So, the large number of scenarios gives an estimate of the probability that the assets meet the liabilities of the scheme for the given asset allocation, for a given income from the scheme (for example, contributions from members and employer in the case of a pension scheme).

The model also gives a distribution of the cashflows. A simplified output is given in Figure 1.

Figure 1 shows the funding level of the scheme going forward through time for the range of scenarios run under the ALM. The 'cone' increases as the possible range of outcomes widens through time. In the case of Figure 1, rather than the cashflows being projected, a discounted value of future cashflows is the output in the future. The funding level is the market value of assets divided by the discounted value of liabilities, so 100% is fully funded, and less than a 100% means the scheme is in deficit and hence more contributions will have to be made to the scheme to meet its liabilities.

Many financial institutions face explicit and/or implicit solvency regulations. Even if the institution is able to meet its future cashflow, it has to demonstrate that it is currently solvent, that its funding level is above some level. This form of ALMs illustrated by Figure 1 gives the risk of not meeting this objective.

The ALM model is re-run for different asset allocations; each asset allocation will give a different spread of results and hence a different probability that the scheme will be able to meet its obligations.

In the ALM, the liabilities are the payments that the scheme is obliged to make to its pensioners or other beneficiaries. Under a defined benefit scheme, the level of pension is determined by a formula, related to the scheme members' salary. Hence the payments are related to the formula, to the salary increases between now and retirement, to inflation and to the life expectancy of members.

On the asset side of the balance sheet, the ALM assumes that each asset class has a volatility and return characteristic based on a mixture of historic performance and economic theory. In the model, these are related to underlying economic variables which are generated by an economic scenario generator (ESG) for each scenario. The economic variables

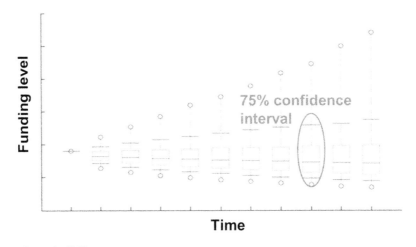

Figure 1. Example ALM.

are also used to determine some of the factors affecting the liabilities such as inflation and salary growth.

In this sketch of an ALM, there are a number of different ways of looking at risk.

Firstly, *Risk* is the probability that the scheme does not meet its liabilities. In the model described in Figure 1, the risk is slightly different. The scheme is assumed to be ongoing, and Figure 1 shows the funding level reducing. *Risk* in this case is that the funding level will fall below 100% or some other solvency level that the scheme has to meet. If this is the case, then the sponsor or members will have to make extra contributions. In such an ongoing arrangement, there will be an annual contribution from the sponsoring employer and/or members. Under certain asset allocations, the output of the ALM may suggest that this contribution could be lower but give rise to a greater volatility of outcomes than under a different asset allocation. This is where the risk and cost inherent in different asset allocations need to be balanced off each other.

In the actual mechanism of the model, *Risk* is related to volatility of different asset classes, as these will give rise to extra variability. If we refer back to potentially stranded environmental assets, this measure of risk will not see the risk; a potentially stranded asset will not necessarily have a higher historical volatility. Also, the decision is at the asset class level, and the potential stranded assets will be within or across asset classes.

3. How stock-pickers are selected and motivated[4]

Once the stages described in Section 2 have been undertaken, some or all of the investment decisions are delegated to one or more asset management firms, depending on the size and strategy of the financial institution. There can be a variety of criteria on which the fund manager is chosen or retained, for example fund management style, past performance, fee level and service, or they might be specialised in a particular asset class in which the fund would like to invest.

3.1. Asset allocation[5]

Based on the ALM and other discussions, the institution would have decided on a distribution of assets between different asset classes. In each asset class, an index is usually chosen against which investment performance is measured. The index chosen might depend on the granularity of the analysis and size of the asset allocation. So, for example, a UK pension fund might have allocation in UK equity, which might be invested against the UK FTSE index. However, for the non-UK allocation, this might be invested against a global UK equity index, rather than regional or country level specification. However, if an asset manager was appointed to manage the non-UK equity, they might in turn delegate investment of parts of this to more specialised internal or external managers, who would be measured against a regional or country level index.

Maybe the most basic choice in style is between a fund that is passively managed and one that is actively managed. A fund that is passively managed, also known as an index tracker, is essentially invested by a computer programme to track a specified index. An active manager employs humans to make investment decisions on which stocks to select.

The decision between active and passive is less dramatic than it might seem; because the active manager is investing against an index, they take relatively small positions away from the index. There are some managers who specialise in taking large positions on a small number of stocks, but these managers are rarely given the bulk of the portfolio to invest in, and are usually seen as a diversification play. This means that active managers are effectively index managers with a bit of discretion. Passive managers try to sell themselves based on lower cost, active managers on the argument that they can foresee trends and are talented stock-pickers.

Active managers try to differentiate themselves from each other through different styles. For example, some managers describe themselves as 'value' investors; that is, they look to buy stocks that may be undervalued, for example, because they are unfashionable or overlooked. In contrast, 'growth' investors look for stocks with a good future prospect, for example, high-tech stocks. These are the two most common traditional styles, but a host of others have developed recently, or a blend of styles is commonly employed (Kemp, Richardson, and Wilson 2000).

However, even though managers may have different criteria for different stocks, they are essentially investing in all the stocks in an index, and if they like or dislike a stock, all this means is that they are buying slightly more or less of it than everyone else. A typical refrain I have heard frequently from fund managers is 'we aim to be in the second quartile'. Fund managers' performance is judged against their peers, so this statement means that the fund manager aims to be between the 25th and 50th percentage of fund managers. They do not aim to be in the top quartile, because this might imply that they are taking undue risk. The *risk* here defined would be divergence from an index.

3.2. Stock-picker motivation

The asset manager is typically compensated with a percentage of funds under management. So a fund manager might charge, say, 1% of all funds under management. Typically, a financial institution will employ an investment consultant, who will advise on investment issues. In the case of a pension fund, the trustees do not necessarily have investment expertise, and therefore will rely heavily on the advice of the investment consultant.[6] One of the roles of the investment consultant is to monitor the performance of the fund manager. The fund manager will produce returns on a regular basis, typically every quarter. The returns are compared with the fund manager's peers, that is, other fund managers. The assets are valued on a mark-to-market basis.

Whilst the asset manager will not necessarily be sacked because of a poor quarter performance, because this is the metric that everyone is looking at, performance against peers on a relatively short-term basis becomes the most important characteristic of a fund manager's output. As the fund manager is compensated with a proportion of funds under management, his main incentive is to attract as high level of funds as possible, whilst the main *risk* is losing funds under management (Kay 2012). Again, it is hard to see criteria of risk can 'see' the risk of stranded assets, provided that these stranded assets are part of the index, managers diverging from this index by reducing holdings of stranded assets are apparently taking on more risk.

4. MPT and its discontents

Why are assets invested against an index if it gives rise to all of the aforementioned problems? First, there is an element of pragmatism. A trustee or other decision-maker in a financial institution does not know what the future will bring or which industry sectors or stocks will win out. However, they might be confident that the economy will grow, and moreover there will be some relationship between the growth of the economy and the institution's liabilities; for example, in the case of a pension scheme, the liabilities are salary-linked, and salaries can only increase if the economy grows. So, a practical approach to buying into the growth of the economy would be to buy an index of all of the major stocks and bonds in that economy. Broadly speaking, and in the long term this should follow the growth of the economy. The second reason that funds are invested in this way is because of MPT.

4.1. The dominant paradigm

MPT is a theory from the academic discipline of financial economics, which is widely used in the financial services industry. Part of its attraction is it lends itself very well to accurate mathematical modelling and its practical usefulness (Turner 2012). I do not intend to regurgitate MPT in great detail in this paper, but refer the reader to a standard financial economics textbook, such as that of Fabozzi et al. (2010).

However, I will give a brief sketch of this theory and explain how it justifies investing against an index. MPT was developed between the 1950s and 1970s following Markowitz (1952). Since then it has come in for a great deal of criticism, and many practitioners and regulators have adjusted their models to take into account some of the criticism. However, even so it still forms the central backbone of the model on which investment practice and regulation are based, and defines the language which shapes the discourse and practice of finance.

MPT is based on a number of simplifying assumptions about the real world, notably that markets are efficient, that the price of an asset incorporates all relevant information and that investors are rational, that is they act in a way to maximise their utility taking into account all relevant information, and there are zero transaction costs.

As markets are efficient, when new information arises, the markets immediately react to the news to reach a new equilibrium price. As this information is random, the price follows a random walk, which was developed as a mathematical description of how gas molecules move when bombarded by other particles.

As the markets are efficient, following this random walk, investors cannot beat the market. What they can do though is construct portfolios which are efficient, that is, having the lowest amount of risk for a given level of return (or the maximum return for a given amount of risk). *Risk* here is defined as sensitivity to market movements (this is often referred to as Beta) based on historical price movements. Expected return can be increased by purchasing stocks with higher Beta and hence taking more risk.

Beta of different stocks are correlated to a different extent; hence risk can be reduced by developing an optimal portfolio with the maximum diversity, that is holding a range of assets which are uncorrelated. As markets are efficient and agents are rational, the index portfolio can be used as a proxy for an efficient portfolio and hence risk is the divergence from the index.

As above, risk measured in this way will not view stranded assets as a risk; a potentially stranded asset will not necessarily have been more volatile historically.

4.2. An alternative paradigm – agent-based modelling

In this section, I will describe an alternative model to MPT which attempts to describe how markets work, based on a technique called agent-based modelling. Agent-based modelling has been used in a number of fields, and is now being widely applied to economics. Agent-based modelling is used to describe Complex Adaptive Systems (CASs); the premise behind the technique is that the system being modelled displays characteristics which emerge from the interaction of agents. Examples of CASs include the brain, life, ant colonies and the economy.

I have chosen a very simple and early agent-based model of a market, which, because of its simplicity, is easy to understand, and highlight the differences with MPT (Farmer 2001).

For simplification, Farmer (2001) hypothesises two kinds of traders, a seasonal trader and a technical trader. There is no movement in the underlying 'value' of the commodity in the market. The seasonal traders buy and sell in a predictable pattern – they could represent, for example, farmers who have to sell when their crops are harvested. The technical traders are purely in it for the money and are allowed to develop a variety of trading strategies; the more successful a strategy is, the more capital the trader gets and the more they influence the market. The model is run over a large number of time periods, with the price of the asset output in each time period. The result is shown in Figure 2.

What happens is that the market becomes 'efficient' after about 5000 iterations when the technical traders make money off the seasonal traders and 'iron' out the predictable seasonal fluctuations. But after that, as you see, the model suddenly goes mad. This is because the technical traders, who have now acquired practically all the capital (as shown in graph B), start trading against each other, devising ever more sophisticated trading strategies which work for a while until another trader develops a better strategy. This phase, after the 5000th iteration, appears to be random, but is not – all of the inputs to the model are non-random. The high volatility is generated purely by the agents trading against each other and continually developing competing strategies.

This is obviously a very simple model and even the author admits that it cannot be used for practical investment applications. There are a number of issues with the model that make it unrealistic; for example, the swings in the market prices are of the wrong order of magnitude compared to a real market. It also makes unrealistic assumptions; indeed some of which are the same as underlying MPT such as rational agents. Does an agent based model (ABM) of this sort really challenge MPT, which has been developed over 60 years now, has had countless number of papers and research carried out on it and is the basis behind much of academic financial economics, regulation and financial practice?

MPT has been criticised for a number of years for not being realistic, firstly in terms of its unrealistic assumptions and also that it cannot explain a number of basic facts about the market, for example, in a real market returns are 'fat tailed'; that is, there are more extreme returns than predicted by MPT, there are periods of high volatility generated by the market itself and there is a correlation between this volatility and trading volume. For good summaries of critiques of MPT, see Keen (2011) and Beinhocker (2007).

Probably a main flaw of MPT is that it assumes away the finance sector, if markets are efficient, there would be no need for fund managers as they could not possibly beat an efficient market. In contrast, Farmer (2001) gives a convincing explanation of why there are

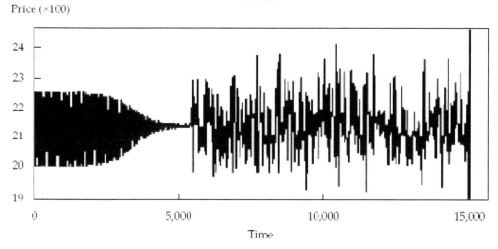

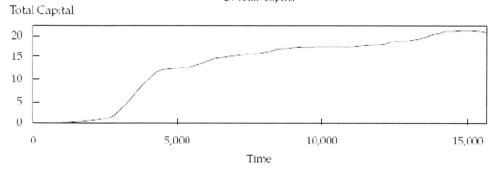

Figure 2. Agent-based model (Farmer 2001).

fund managers; they are competing against each other and the most successful strategies lead to a large accumulation of capital which drives the market price: exactly as anyone who has had anything to do with finance would observe.

Just like MPT, Farmer (2001) is also based on similar unrealistic assumptions. However, there is one crucial difference with MPT, and that is that there are more than one heterogeneous agents (under MPT all agents are homogeneous economic rational agents). By changing this assumption, Farmer (2001) explains fat tails, high volatility and the correlation between volatility and trading volume. Crucially, it also explains the existence of a large dynamic financial services industry, all competing against each other. Farmer admits his model is just a start, and it seems that the other unrealistic assumptions which are crucial to MPT, such as rational agents and no transaction costs, are not crucial when developing more realistic ABM of the market. One of the points of Farmer (2001) is that by introducing heterogeneous agents you get a model which resembles a real market; you can refine this model by making it more realistic, as opposed to MPT which *relies* on the unrealistic assumption of homogenous agents. Moreover, the ABM model supports insights from previous generations of economists such as Keynes (1936) and Minsky (1992).

The insight from Farmer (2001) and other ABMs is that the market price is driven by the interaction of the agents in the market. The implications from this insight are extremely awkward for academic economists, current regulation and for much current risk management practice:

- The economy is a dynamic CAS. This is not really a conclusion from Farmer (2001), but is an observation of what the economy actually is, and why agent-based modelling is an appropriate tool to use to model markets. A CAS is a physical system which demonstrates certain features; such as emergence (that is, the behaviour of the system arises from the interaction of the agents that make up the system), complexity (the system contains many parts which interact in a variety of ways), self-similarity (parts of the system resemble each other) and self-organisation (order arises from the interaction of parts of the system) which the economy and markets have been shown to demonstrate (Mandelbrot 2008).
- Market does not tend to equilibrium: A CAS, as demonstrated by the ABM, does not tend to equilibrium, but is in a constant state of dynamism.
- 'Efficiency' is a meaningless concept: Economics places much emphasis on efficiency, for example, that markets are efficient when the price reflects all of the information. The price is actually determined by the interaction of the agents, not by external information.
- Price is not the same as value and can diverge from value in the short term. The short term can last many years; in the words of Keynes 'in the long-run we are all dead'.

All of the above have profound implications for the regulation of financial markets, which are regulated on the assumption that the economy is a general equilibrium system. For example, if price diverges from value, there is no justification for using a market price. Worse, the normative justification for using markets to allocate capital is undermined – in the Arrow–Debreu formulation (Arrow and Debreu 1954), markets are Pareto efficient, and any divergence from the market makes someone else worse off. However, if the price is driven by participants rather than information, this is clearly not the case.

The implications of an ABM/complex system approach for stranded assets is that fund managers are basing investment decisions on trying to out-compete each other, and this to a large extent drives the price of underlying assets. This can cause divergence from 'fundamental' values for many years. Again, there is no reason why if investments are made under this approach, then the risk of stranded assets would figure in any shape or form.

4.3. Culture of financial markets

Another interesting insight comes from the field of anthropology. Cultural theory of risk was developed by Douglas (1994). Individuals associate societal harms with conduct that transgress social norms; hence their perception of risk is informed by these social norms.

Cultural life and outlooks are characterised by different solidarities, which Thompson (2008) defines as hierarchical, individualism, fatalism and egalitarianism. These solidarities are a certain set of values by which groups define themselves, and therefore any information that undermines these values will not be processed by the group because it would undermine the core set of beliefs which define the group. Hence the solidarity will define acceptable risks, but will be blind to some risks which are generated by the group itself.

Anthropologists have undertaken many ethnographic studies of the finance industry. They have found that 'financial professionals operate in a bureaucratic world, where they are expected to embody the figure of the investor by following stringent and often contradictory rules' (Hart and Ortiz 2014). Employees working in the finance industry pursue a number of strategies of competition and collaboration with their peers, and often use valuation methodologies which are quasi-theological in nature. Tsanakas et al. (2014) argue that models are normally inconclusive; how data and outputs from models are interpreted and what financial decisions are made based on the outputs are highly dependent on the culture of the organisation.

There is also a linkage between academic financial economic and the industry which mutually promotes a certain view of the way markets work, how risk is defined and hence what regulation and government policy should be pursued (Hart and Ortiz 2014).

Douglas (1994) also identifies a political dimension to the analysis of risk; risk is identified in a way that strengthens the political and financial power of those that are promoting the risk. This view is corroborated by research showing that the financial system generates risk which it then gains from by selling products which manage this risk generated by the system itself (Turner 2012; Vayanos and Woolley 2008).

The conclusion of this discussion is that *risk* is defined by the financial community which supports the community's culture and intellectual framework under which it operates. This framework and culture support the finance sector's power and wealth. Risks which undermine or are opposed to this framework will be resisted as they undermine the belief system under which finance is practised, and would also undermine the political and financial power of the sector.

So, investment managers will view stranded assets as a risk, depending on whether or not it fits into the culture under which they operate.

5. Stranded assets

Much of the focus on stranded assets in an environmental context has been on the impact of climate change or, more specifically, the societal response to climate change.

It has generally been agreed between governments and scientists that to avoid dangerous climate change, global greenhouse gas emissions have to be kept to such a level as to limit anthropogenic global warming to below 2°C. The implication is that most of the world's fossil fuel reserves – a third of oil reserves, half of gas reserves and over 80% of current coal reserves – will have to remain left in the ground if we are to achieve 2°C or less and therefore at some point will become stranded assets (McGlade and Ekins 2015). The value of fossil fuel companies' stocks, such as oil and gas companies and mining companies, to a large extent, depends on the value for these reserves, meaning there is a risk that these stocks will at some point be significantly reduced in value (Caldecott and Rook 2015; Carbon Tracker 2014; Wolf 2014). If such a stranded asset scenario were to manifest, it would not just be companies' stock (equity) prices that would be affected; for example, corporate bonds could be negatively impacted if they were secured against or reliant on income generated from fossil fuel assets. There would also be secondary impacts; for example, banks with large exposure to fossil fuel companies might be affected, and even some government bonds, if that country's economy were particularly fossil fuel dependent.

Carbon Tracker (2014) estimates that the combined value of the top 100 oil and gas companies along with the top 100 coal companies was $7.42 trillion as of February 2011. If most of these assets were to become un-burnable, a large proportion of this value will be lost with the severe economic damage that this would entail.

More formally a stranded asset is an asset where there is the risk of negative shock at time t: for all $t > t_s$.

The value of a financial asset is the sum of the discount value of future cashflows. So, for a stock with future dividends $d(i)$, its value is:

$$\sum_{n=0}^{\infty} \frac{d(n)}{(1+i)\hat{n}}. \tag{1}$$

However, if an event occurs at time t, which reduces the ability of the company to produce dividends, to $r(i)$, where $r(i)$ is much less than $d(i)$, the value of the stranded asset should be:

$$\sum_{n=0}^{t-1} \frac{d(n)}{(1+i)\hat{n}} + \sum_{n=t}^{\infty} \frac{r(n)}{(1+i)\hat{n}}. \tag{2}$$

The value of Equation (2) will be considerably less than Equation (1). More specifically $r(n)$ will be $f(n)^{*}d(n)$ where $f(n)$ is less than 1. However, $f(n)$ is subject to uncertainty, as is what the value of t is; that is, when the stranded asset impact will occur.

If we take an event such as the manifestation of stranded carbon assets, then this will not just affect a single company, but all companies that have fossil fuel assets. For an institution which is invested in the index, as described in Section 2, this will be a large negative shock, although there may be positive shocks to other sectors, such as to the renewable energy sector.

If we assume that all markets are efficient, then stranded carbon assets should not be a risk at all. The market price reflects all known information. The stranded carbon assets have become a well-known phenomenon, the annual Conference of Parties meetings as part of the United Nations climate negotiations (UNFCCC) process is widely covered in the media, and hardly a day goes by when there is not some article in the mainstream media about climate change. So according to the efficient market hypothesis, the risk of stranded carbon assets is already reflected in the market price and it is therefore not a risk, or it is a risk that is being managed by the market and a market participant will be able to hedge the risk.

There are two possible conclusions, which are not necessarily mutually exclusive:

(1) The market has examined the UNFCCC process, and looked through government rhetoric and has decided that there is very little risk that fossil fuel assets will not be burned.
(2) Markets are not efficient. Risk perception is defined by the culture of the financial system itself and stock prices are driven by the interaction of the participants of agents. Incorporating a view on stranded assets would undermine this culture. The price of an asset can diverge from its value as described by Equations (1) and

(2) for many years. There is no obvious reason that agents should incorporate stranded assets into their decision-making process, when they make money by competing against other agents. Finally, stock-pickers make investment decisions against an index and their peers. This is inherently backward looking, and again there is little motivation for them to incorporate the risk of stranded carbon assets into their investment making decision as it will not cause them to win new investment mandates.

6. Conclusion

There is a risk that world governments will take strong action to limit greenhouse gas emissions. This will mean that much of current fossil fuel reserves will have to be left in the ground and will remain unburnt. This in turn means that there is a risk that a large proportion of the assets of companies engaged in the fossil fuel industry will lose much or most of their value. This will have a large negative impact on the assets of financial institutions and hence the solvency of insurance companies, pensions and savings.

Financial institutions are blind to this risk because their asset allocation decisions are based on a historical view of risk which does not factor in future events. Stock-picking is delegated to asset managers who are motivated to invest in an index, based on an incorrect view of markets that they are efficient. Neither the institution or the asset manager is able to integrate the risk of stranded assets into their model; their view of risk is culturally defined to exclude such risk and they are not motivated to do so.

Alternatively, the market is aware of the very low probability that governments will successfully ban fossil fuels and therefore create stranded carbon assets, and has already factored it in to prices to the extent investors consider appropriate. Or as we transition to a low-carbon economy, investors will switch to firms which service these economies. There is evidence that the market is actually over-keen to switch to new technologies, as was witnessed during the dot-com bubble (Shiller 2000) and it has been argued that this is happening now with low-carbon technologies such as the electric car (Broughton 2015). A pragmatic solution may be based on the premise that whether or not this risk of stranded carbon assets will manifest is unknowable and subject to uncertainty, and that markets are highly volatile in the short term anyway. In the long run, over which institutions such as pension funds invest, asset returns should be approximately in line with economic growth, with old technology stocks being replaced by new technology stocks.

Another perspective is that price is driven by the interactions of agents in a market. The interaction of agents or 'irrational exuberance' (Shiller 2000) creates bubbles and crashes. For example, between 1994 and 2000, the NASDAQ index increased five-fold only to fall back almost to its 1994 level by 2003. In 2015, the Chinese stock market more than doubled in less than a year, before falling back to below its level at the start of the year. The gains and losses involved in these movements were internally generated by the market themselves rather than from an external risk.

Financial institutions' investment allocation is a collaborative effort made by a combination of different actors to whom different responsibilities are delegated. These actors have differing perceptions of risk, and their risk perception is guided by the incentives under which they operate and the culture of the organisations in which they work. In practice, investment practice is guided by measurement of short-term performance against peers, where risk is defined in relation to historic short-term volatility and divergence from a benchmark index. A forward-looking external risk, such as stranded assets, which does not have an obvious relationship with these factors does not therefore fit into an institution's risk perception and the institution is therefore effectively blind to this risk.

Notes

1. In addition to the paper referenced, this section also draws on the author's own experience and interviews that the author has undertaken with other professionals.
2. In this section, I have taken the process that a pension fund would go through. Other institutions, such as insurance companies, would go through an equivalent process (see, e.g. Ahlgrim, D'Arcy, and Gorvett 2004).
3. In addition to Booth et al. (1999), this section also draws on the author's own experience and interviews that the author has undertaken with other professionals.
4. In addition to the references cited, this section also draws on the author's own experience and interviews that the author has undertaken with other professionals.
5. Chambers et al. (2005).
6. There are other models of governance, such as fiduciary management, but the outcome is often the same as described here.

Disclosure statement

No potential conflict of interest was reported by the author.

Notes on contributor

Nicholas Silver is an actuary and economist whose specialities include risk management, social insurance and environmental finance. Nick is a director of Callund Consulting, a specialist consultancy which advises governments on developing social insurance, pensions and capital markets, in which capacity he has worked in over 30 countries. Nick is on Council (the governing body) of the Institute and Faculty of Actuaries, and recently won The President's Award for outstanding contribution to the Profession. Nick is a founder and director of the Climate Bonds Initiative (CBI), an NGO focused on mobilising the bond market to fund climate change solutions. Nick is a visiting fellow at the London School of Economics, Anglia Ruskin University and Cass Business School and lectures at Trinity College, Dublin as well as these institutions. He has also written a number of papers and articles on economics, government debt, and climate change. Nick has been widely quoted in the media and two separate papers he authored have been cited in parliamentary debates. Nick has an MSc in Public Financial Policy from the London School of Economics.

References

Ahlgrim, K., S. D'Arcy, and R. Gorvett. 2004. *Asset-liability Modelling for Insurers: Incorporating a Regime-Switching Process for Equity Returns into a Dynamic Financial Analysis Model.* http://www.actuaries.org/ASTIN/Colloquia/Bergen/Ahlgrim_DArcy_Gorvett.pdf.

Arrow, K. J., and G. Debreu. 1954. "Existence of an Equilibrium for a Competitive Economy." *Econometrica* 22 (3): 265–290.

Beinhocker, E. 2007. *The Origin of Wealth.* London: Random House (ISBN: 9780712676618).

Booth, P. J., R. Chadburn, D. Cooper, S. Haberman, and D. James. 1999. *Modern Actuarial Theory and Practice*. Chapman & Hall/CRC.

Broughton, P. 2015. "To be rational about Tesla is to miss the point." *Financial Times*, August 26.

Caldecott, B., and D. Rook. 2015. *Summary of Proceedings 3rd Stranded Asset Forum*. Smith School of Enterprise and the Environment.

Carbon Tracker. 2014. Unburnable Carbon. http://www.carbontracker.org/wp-content/uploads/2014/09/Unburnable-Carbon-Full-rev2-1.pdf

Chambers, A., A. Barnes, M. Barnes, L. Beukes, D. Dyer, P. Fulcher, M. Kemp, A. Lawrence, A. Tatham, and N. Winter. 2005. *Liability Driven Benchmarks for UK Defined Benefit Pension Schemes*. London, UK: Institute and Faculty of Actuaries.

Douglas, M. 1994. *Risk and Blame: Essays in Cultural Theory*. London: Routledge.

Fabozzi, F. J., F. Modigliani, F. J. Jones, and M. G. Ferri. 2010. *Foundations of Financial Markets and Institutions*. 4th ed. Upper Saddle River, NJ: Prentice Hall.

Farmer, D. 2001. "Towards Agent Based Modelling for Investment." *The Association for Investment Management and Research* 61–70.

Hart, K., and H. Ortiz. 2014. "The Anthropology of Money and Finance." *Annual Review of Anthropology* 43: 465–482.

Kay, J. 2012. *The Kay Review of UK Equity Markets*. UK Government.

Keen. 2011. *Debunking Economics – Revised and Expanded Edition: The Naked Emperor Dethroned?* London: Zed Books.

Kemp, M., M. Richardson, and C. Wilson. 2000. *Investment Management Style Analysis*. Institute and Faculty Actuaries.

Keynes, J. 1936. *The General Theory of Employment, Interest and Money*. London: Palgrave McMillan.

Koedijk, K., and A. Slager. 2009. "Do Institutional Investors have Sensible Investment Beliefs." *Rotman International Journal of Pension Management* 2 (1): 12–20.

Mandelbrot. 2008. *The (Mis)behaviour of Markets: A Fractal View of Risk, Ruin and Reward*. London: Profile Books.

Markowitz, H. 1952. "Portfolio Selection." *The Journal of Finance* 7 (1): 77–91.

McGlade, C., and P. Ekins. 2015. "The Geographical Distribution of Fossil Fuels Unused When Limiting Global Warming to 2°C." *Nature* 517: 187–190.

Minsky, H. 1992. *The Financial Instability Hypothesis*. Working Paper No. 74: 6–8.

Shiller, R. 2000. *Irrational Exuberance*. Princeton, NJ: Princeton University Press.

Thompson, M. 2008. *Organising and Disorganising*. Axminster: Triarchy Press.

Tsanakas, A., M. B. Beck, T. Ford, M. Thompson, and I. Ye. 2014. "Model Risk and Culture." *Actuary Magazine*, December 2014.

Turner, A. 2012. *Economics After the Crisis*. Cambridge, MA: The MIT Press.

Vayanos, D., and P. Woolley. 2008. *An Institutional Theory of Momentum and Reversal*. The Paul Woolley Centre for the Study of Capital Market Dysfunctionality, Working Paper Series No. 1.

Wolf, M. 2014. "A Climate Fix Would Ruin Investors." *Financial Times*.

Transition risks and market failure: a theoretical discourse on why financial models and economic agents may misprice risk related to the transition to a low-carbon economy

Jakob Thomä and Hugues Chenet

ABSTRACT

This paper provides a theoretical discourse linking traditional market failure literature and the recent research around potential stranded assets risks associated with the transition to a low-carbon economy (defined here as 'transition risks'). While it does not seek to prove a mispricing in practical terms, it demonstrates the extent to which the market failure literature provides theoretical evidence of a potential mispricing of these risks, as a result of the design and interpretation of financial risk models, and the practices and institutions linked to economic agents. The evidence supports a growing body of practical literature highlighting transition risks in financial markets. It suggests that there may be a case for policy intervention to address the market failures and associated potential mispricing of risk. It also suggests however that this intervention will likely need to address both the design of financial risk models and associated transparency around their results, and the actual institutions governing risk management. A key challenge in this regard involves resolving the principal–agent problem in financial markets and the associated 'tragedy of the horizons'.

1. Introduction

The past few years have seen a growing narrative around potential financial risks associated with the transition to a low-carbon economy, largely focused on the future of fossil fuels and the power sector (Meinshausen et al. 2009; Robins, Chan, and Knight 2012; Leaton 2013; Caldecott, derricks, and Mitchell 2015).[1] This body of research argues that the transition to a low-carbon economy leads to value creation and destruction that can potentially impact the financial viability of assets on corporate and government balance sheets, a situation that can in turn impact the credit-worthiness and valuation of financial assets (e.g. equities and bonds). These risks are usually labelled 'transition risks', a short form this paper will use to describe this family of risks.

A key underlying assumption, either explicit or implicit, of this literature is that financial markets currently misprice the risks associated with the transition to a low-carbon economy. A consequence of this could be the creation of a bubble in valuation of assets and companies dependent on fossil-fuel energy. This is the concept of 'transition risk', which could – in theory – have system-wide impact and affect financial stability. 'Transition risks' and the 'carbon bubble' thesis are referenced across publications on the topic. The Financial Stability Board, on the initiative of Mark Carney – Governor of the Bank of England – and the French Treasury, has started assessing the issue. The French Parliament has passed a law mandating climate-related risk disclosure. The Swiss and German governments have both launched research inquiries on the potential financial stability risks arising from the transition to a low-carbon economy.

To date, the research around these risks has primarily focused on examining the potential materiality of these types of risks to financial market assets and actors. Notable examples include research on transition risk to physical assets (Fulton et al. 2015; McGlade and Ekins 2015; Caldecott et al. 2016), financial assets (Robins, Chan, and Knight 2012) and financial portfolios (Mercer 2015). Less explored in this debate is the question of whether financial market actors are already correctly pricing these risks, challenging the 'bubble' assumption. For example, research from organizations highlight risks to physical assets and capital expenditure plans, noting for example potential $2 trillion worth of capital expenditure that may not be profitable under a 2°C transition (Fulton et al. 2015). Robins, Chan, and Knight (2012) suggest impact on share prices of fossil-fuel companies of 30–50%. Mercer (2015) in turn shows little cross-asset impact, but some significant impacts within asset classes.

While there is growing consensus that these risks may materialize, it is unclear whether they are already priced into current asset prices. This is particularly the case for fossil-fuel companies that have lost in some cases upwards of 50% of their market capitalization in the past 2 years or even coal mining companies that have seen growing bankruptcies in the United States. Similarly, high-carbon European utilities have also suffered. While there is academic evidence of a sudden tipping point in climate policies that can create sudden, unexpected transition risks (Aghion et al. 2014), such literally does not directly question how actors may or may not already be pricing probabilities of such 'surprises'.

The question of asset mispricing is key for two objectives. First, it is important from a financial stability perspective, as asset mispricing can lead to asset bubbles that may have systemic effects or at the very least create financial risks for some actors and asset classes. Second, and linked to the first, asset mispricing is also relevant from a policy and social perspective. Asset mispricing can lead to inefficient capital allocation, which in turn may inhibit growth as capital does not go to its best use. In this particular case, this may be even more problematic insofar as such inefficient capital misallocation may exacerbate economic inefficiencies that relate to the mispricing of the social cost of carbon. Thus, mispricing not only inhibits growth, but also has an additional negative impact on public welfare more generally, through negative health impacts (Lancet 2015) and other social and political costs.

The objective of this paper is to link the theoretical literature around market failure associated with correctly pricing risk with the literature on transition risk in order to test the premise that financial market actors currently misprice potential risks associated with the transition to a low-carbon economy. The paper will thus not contribute to the question of whether the transition to a low-carbon economy *will* be material for financial market actors. Rather, it seeks to build the theoretical basis as to why, *should these risks be material*, financial market actors may misprice these risks. In this sense, the paper provides the complementary analysis to the existing risk literature on this topic.

The paper reviews the existing literature on market failures and seeks to link it to the risk characteristics commonly associated with transition risks. Crucially, the paper only focuses on transition risks and does not address mispricing related to other climate-related risks (e.g. physical risks, litigation risks). The analysis demonstrates that transition risks exhibit a number of characteristics that, according to the market failure literature, are likely to lead to mispricing. This can be linked to the theoretical evidence on market failure as it applies to financial market models and economic agents. Developing transition risk models and associated evidence of the presence of these risks, according to the results of this paper, thus only addresses one side of the equation and needs to be complemented by activities related to tackling the broader market infrastructure and the actions of economic agents within.

The paper thus provides concrete input as to the potential for the existing body of research to improve the efficient pricing of these risks in financial markets. In addition, it suggests that there is at least theoretical evidence that these types of transition risks may be mispriced, suggesting the potential for the presence of capital misallocation related to investments associated with the transition to a low-carbon economy, both in high-carbon and low-carbon assets. This may be material for policymakers and regulators exploring the question of efficient capital allocation. It may also be material for the broader debate about achieving global climate goals. It also points the way for needed future research avenues.

The paper is organized as follows. Section 2 briefly introduces the efficient market hypothesis (EMH). Section 3 connects the market failure literature to financial market models and transition risks. Section 4 focuses on the market failure literature as it informs the assessment of economic agents. Here too the discussion is then linked to transition risks. Section 5 provides some concluding remarks.

2. A short history of the EMH

The starting point for any analysis on market failure is the EMH. Fama (1970) and Samuelson (1965) developed the EMH more or less in parallel.[2] The EMH is based on the notion that 'a market in which prices always "fully reflect" available information is called efficient' (Fama 1970, 383). In such a scenario, information is fully available to all market participants equally and integrated into price formation instantly (Fama 1970).[3] According to Jensen (1978, 95), 'there is no other proposition in economics which has more empirical support than the EMH'.

Whether a financial market is informationally efficient or not matters in two ways: 'First, investors care about whether various trading strategies can earn excess returns (i.e. "beat the market"). Second, if stock prices accurately reflect all information, new investment capital goes to its highest-valued use' (Jones and Netter 2014). In order for the EMH to exist, two conditions are crucial. Firstly, as highlighted above, prices need to fully (and equitably) reflect available information, allowing market participants to distinguish between different investments. Second, market participants need to operate as rational, utility-maximizing agents, an assumption also known as the 'rational choice theory'.

The idea of the self-interested, utility-maximizing individual entered the economic discourse with the early Classical economists, notable among them being Smith (1776, 105), who coined the famous adage that 'it is not from the benevolence of the butcher, the brewer, or the baker that we expect our dinner, but from their regard to their own interest'. In the nineteenth century, Mill (1844, 48) then linked this self-interest to utility and rationality, arguing that political economy 'concerned with [man] solely as a being who desires to possess wealth, and who is capable of judging the comparative efficacy of means for obtaining that end'.[4] The concept of rational, utility-maximizing entered today's discourse, on the shoulders of Walras, Pareto, Jevons and others, in the form of the Rational Choice Theory, pioneered by Robbins (1938) at the London School of Economics. At the heart of the rational choice theory is the 'homo oeconomicus', the economic man.[5]

Today, the EMH forms a core tenet of finance, both as it is taught at universities (Krugman 2009) and increasingly thought of in practice. The growth of passive investing (PWC 2014) is arguably a function of the growing consensus that market actors cannot beat the market, given its 'random walk' characteristics. Modern portfolio theory, as developed by Markowitz (1952), Tobin (1958), Sharpe (1964) and others relies on the assumption that optimal investing strategies involve adopting market assumptions around prices and diversifying portfolios accordingly.

At the same time, a growing literature is starting to challenge the EMH, suggesting the presence of a number of 'market failures' that market actors can exploit and that may lead to the mispricing of financial risk. Market failures can be defined as:

> the failure of a more or less idealized system of price-market institutions to sustain 'desirable' activities or to stop 'undesirable' activities. The desirability of an activity, in turn, is evaluated relative to the solution values of some explicit or implied maximum-welfare problem. (Bator 1958, 351)

It should be noted that the purpose of this review is not to *a priori* evaluate the theoretical literature on this topic as a whole. It does not seek to contribute to this debate. The analytical exercise proposed here is neither evidence of proof nor a criticism of either the EMH or its critics. Instead, the review is designed to provide a better theoretical understanding of how the EMH can *in theory* break down if certain conditions are not satisfied and how this can explain the potential mispricing of transition risks.

3. Transition risks and the design of risk models

This section will review elements of the market failure literature that can inform on the design and interpretation of financial market risk models. It will emphasize in particular the treatment of 'tail risks' in these models, the distribution assumed therein, and the extent to which financial market models can capture complexity, in particular as it relates to risk and uncertainty.

One of the strongest theoretical criticisms of the utility-maximization model comes from Simon (1957), who coined the term 'bounded rationality'. Simon (1957, 198) argues, and it is worth quoting him at length, that:

> the capacity of the human mind for formulating and solving complex problems is very small compared with the size of the problems whose solution is required for objectively rational

behaviour in the real world [...] The first consequence of the principle of bounded rationality is that the intended rationality of an actor requires him to construct a simplified model of the real situation in order to deal with it. He behaves rationally with respect to this model, and such behaviour is not even approximately optimal with respect to the real world.

As a result, people use heuristics as opposed to optimization. Agents do not optimize, but 'satisfice'.[6]

From an agent's perspective, this may be 'optimal'. Equally, from an investment perspective, this means that agents may not realize (or even attempt to realize) maximum returns. In this case, price formation does not reflect all information, given that agents have not attempted to optimize.[7] As a result, prices may become skewed, leading *potentially* to capital misallocation.[8]

The issue of model is core to the question of transition risks. Transition risks are unlikely to be captured by traditional risk models – models which are equated to be representatives of real-world risks. There are a number of reasons for this, most notably perhaps the breakdown of the normal distribution principle associated with these risks and the lack of historical data (Simon 1957). As suggested in Figure 1, the distribution of transition scenarios is not normal insofar as it exhibits a weight in one direction – there seems to be a visual weight that drags the bottom part of the curve downward. The chart thus suggests a skewed distribution in one direction – in this case in the direction of the probability related to a 2°C decarbonization pathway. Naturally, this distribution is somewhat 'artificial', perhaps more of a 'social distribution' than a quantified one – the number of 2° C scenario is not necessarily testament to its probability. But nevertheless, as a proxy for distribution, it shows a skew.

While the normal distribution assumption is no longer as core to finance as it used to be,[9] it still forms the basis of all core models, including the models introduced by Markowitz (1952) in the context of modern portfolio theory, Arrow-Debreu models (1954), Black-Scholes Options Pricing Model (1973) and more recent models of credit risk (Vasicek).[10] It is also used by the International Monetary Fund stress-testing models for example (Ong 2014).

One core reason of using the normal distribution is the additional complexity a nonnormal distribution introduces in the models – a complexity potentially avoided at least

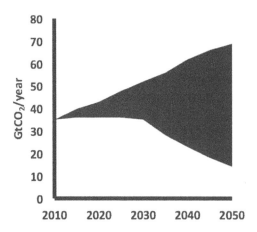

Figure 1. Range of IPCC scenarios. Source: Modified from IPCC 2014.

in part as a result of the bounded rationality principle. Agents satisfice by using simplified assumptions to reduce complexity. This may make sense for an agent that does not seek to optimize. It may however create systematic biases in models that lead to sub-optimal pricing of risks.

The bounded rationality thesis related to the nature of models would thus potentially apply to transition risks, as evidence suggests these risks are unlikely to be distributed in a normal manner – if the mean is a transition pathway of for example 5°C the probability of under-shooting that pathway (i.e. achieving less than 5°C warming) is significantly higher than over-shooting that pathway – based on the 'social distribution' logic defined above where 2°C is the official goal. Normal distribution assumptions may systematically bias against the skewed risks related to the transition to a low-carbon economy.

There are other ways agents may not optimize, notably in terms of dealing with tail risks. The idea that investors do not deal with risks equitably finds its roots in the Prospect Theory, developed by Kahnemann and Tsversky (1979) and Tsversky and Fox (1995). Tsversky argues that investors appear risk-averse for small losses, but indifferent to, or at the very least less impacted by large losses. In other words, the level of risk aversion is at least partly a function of the size of the loss, where investors are willing to take larger bets with a higher risk of loss. More recently this literature has been popularized in its application to models by Taleb (2007) and his work on tail risks, which he describes as 'black swans' or 'fat tails'. Taleb (2007) highlights the extent to which financial market models under-weight probabilities at the tail end of the distribution.

As outlined above, the skewed nature of climate roadmaps suggests risks associated with this transition are not normally distributed. Another way the risks are not normally distributed is potentially their characteristic as involving 'fat tails'. While 2°C is seen as unlikely,[11] it remains the global policy commitment. The extreme end of the tail may thus be more likely than in a normal distribution – where the probability of an event

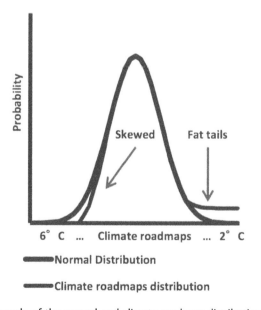

Figure 2. Illustrative example of the normal and climate roadmap distribution. Source: Authors.

outside two standard deviations is about 5%. While possible and perhaps probable, it is not clear whether transition risks will indeed have fat tails. Figure 2 visualizes the joint impact of a skew and fat tail on a distribution function.

At the same time, what does appear apparent is that the 2°C event can be seen as extreme. It is on the lower end of the spectrum of climate roadmaps and far removed from the current business as usual – defined for example by the International Energy Agency as the 'Current Policy Scenario' associated with roughly 6°C global warming. What is thus possible is that financial markets collectively are willing to take risks associated with the 2°C transition in the vein of Prospect Theory. In other words, even if the probability of the tail event is not over-stated, its ramifications in models are under-stated as a result of the cognitive bias of market actors vis-à-vis these tail risks.

The discussion here in a way pre-empts the subsequent discussion in the next section on cognitive biases related to market actors' *actions*, beyond models. It also has a place here however, insofar as financial market models may reflect this bias in two ways. First, inputs chosen in the analysis, for example, the scenarios around cash flows and so on tend to congregate around the mean or median assumption, in particular when it comes to climate transition questions.[12] Second, the emphasis on single indicator outputs for example in discounted cash flow models highlights mean results without creating transparency around potential tail risks.

Appropriate at this stage then is the reference to a strand of literature that, while having its origin in the traditional classical and neoclassical economics, has been picked up by the market failure literature as well. This relates to the distinction between risk and uncertainty, a distinction first introduced in the economic debate by Frank Knight in 1921 and then further developed by Keynes in the General Theory (1936).[13] According to Knight (1921, 19–20),

> risk means in some cases a quantity susceptible of measurement, while at other times it is something distinctly not of this character […] It will appear that a measurable uncertainty, or 'risk' proper, as we shall use the term, is so far different from an *unmeasurable* (sic!) one that it is not in effect an uncertainty at all. We shall accordingly restrict the term 'uncertainty' to cases of the non-quantitative type.

This definition is largely uncontested to the knowledge of the authors.

The idea of risk and uncertainty was particularly made relevant in the context of the financial sector by Minsky (1992), who argued that the inability to quantify all future risk scenarios was one of the factors that led to financial crises. Simon (1957) argued that uncertainty, unlike risk, implies that contingencies cannot be assigned probability distributions and hence cannot be fully insured against. This is particularly the case in future-oriented decisions such as investment. Thus economic agents might fall back on rules-of-thumbs. The key idea then is that, in the presence of both risk and uncertainty, investors may not be able to make optimal decisions.

Transition risk is likely to be particularly subject to this constraint. As outlined above, climate change models and associated roadmaps are highly complex and subject to a wide range of assumptions. Data to input models is not necessarily available or available at affordable costs to investors. Already quantifying the possibilities associated with each degree of warming is a particular challenge, which is also why the 'fat tail' assumption cannot be validated at this stage. In addition, even if these probabilities could be quantified, each degree of warming is associated with a range of different technological roadmaps, some emphasizing one technology over another. There are over a 100 different roadmaps (Caldecott, Tilbury, and Carey 2014). For example, given the potential deployment of carbon capture and storage, a range of different fossil-fuel production volumes can be linked to a specific climate outcome. All of these of course pre-supposes capacity to assess and quantify these challenges, which the bounded rationality literature suggests is lacking. There is no reason to believe climate literacy is particularly high among financial sector actors – given that climate change related risks do not involve a historical precedent at a sufficient scale – and thus relevant historical data – that would have formed part of the education of individuals working in financial markets and their ability to integrate these challenges into models.

4. Transition risks and economic agents

There are two key characteristics of the market failure literature on economic agents relevant from a transition risk perspective that fall outside the scope of models, namely the role of time-inconsistent preferences and the role of institutions. Each of these aspects will be discussed in turn and linked to the analysis of the expected characteristics of transition risks.

One of the main tenets of the rational choice theory in terms of utility-maximization is the time-consistency of preferences by economic agents – in other words a 'no regret' position at point $t + 1$ relative to their choices at point t.[14] If this was not the case, utility would not be maximized inter-temporally. Mathematically, this can be described as individuals having an exponential discount function, implying that we discount the future at a steady rate.[15] Most economic modelling and analysis has been founded on the premise that 'we do not suppose time to be allowed for any alteration in the character or tastes of the man himself' (Marshall 1967). 'What is assumed is that consumers are fairly consistent in their tastes and actions – that they do not flail around in unpredictable ways, making themselves miserable by persistent errors of judgement or arithmetic' (Samuelson 1937).

As crucial as this condition for the theory of utility-maximizing agents, as weak is its theoretical and empirical foundation. In practice, economic agents discounting usually resembles hyperbolic discount function (Thaler 1981; Laibson 1997).[16] The hyperbolic discount function suggests economic agents have 'present-biased preferences', where the immediate future is discounted highly, but the long-term future progressively at a lower rate.

In terms of finance, this is important because it suggests that investors may not optimize inter-temporal returns.[17] In the case of transition risks, inter-temporal inconsistency is particularly important because transition risks are likely to be long-term and thus heavily discounted over the short-term. Transition risks may thus be mispriced in the context of hyperbolic discount functions not because investors do not *believe* the risks will materialize, but that their financial impact is discounted. In the same vein, from a broader capital allocation perspective, this may also suggest more long-term pay offs from 'climate-friendly' investments may similarly be discounted. Discounting is obviously visible in financial risk models as well, although here the issue is probably the practice of extrapolating current trends rather than the discounting. Beyond models however, hyperbolic discount functions lead economic agents to ignore long-term trends. Thus even where models can integrate long-term risks, these are not considered by the economic agent because the cash flows associated with these events are discounted by the actors themselves. By extension, there is no incentive to engage in an exercise beyond extrapolation given that potential hits to long-term cash flows are not material to the economic agent.

There may be another reason long-term risks are not integrated and this relates to externalities and principal–agent problems. The discussion on market failures has thus far focused on whether agents are rational and maximize their utility. It is important to also address the other part of the equation highlighted in the beginning, namely the extent to which financial markets are informationally efficient, independent of the rational nature of actors. This other side of the literature focuses on questions of market design creating inefficiencies, notably through transaction costs, agency costs in the context of the principal–agent problem and asymmetric information, and externalities.[18]

Principal–agent problems describe a situation where both the incentives and the information of a principal (for example an owner of assets or a voter) and the agent (the asset manager or politician, respectively) are not aligned.[19] Whereas the differences in incentives and interests for the two parties are likely to be a frequent (if not omnipresent) characteristic of these types of transactions, they become problematic in the context of asymmetric information, allowing the agent to capitalize on superior information to the principal.[20] The associated costs of this information asymmetry are called 'agency costs' (Jensen and Meckling 1976).

Externalities in turn are 'the cost or benefit that affects a party who did not choose to incur that cost or benefit' (Buchanan and Craig Stubblebine 1962, 200). The presence of externalities will lead to prices that are sub-optimal as they do not integrate the full range of cost and benefits associated with an asset (Greenwald and Stiglitz 1986).

The externalities associated with climate and the environment are usually referred to as the 'tragedy of the commons', after a seminal essay of the same name published by Garret Hardin in 1968. Interestingly, the analysis of externalities usually does not distinguish between inter-temporal externalities, where the affected party is somebody in the future and geographic externalities, where the affected party is in the same geography (analytically speaking). In terms of climate change, the question of externality has usually focused on the extent to which the costs of climate change are externalized by those who are responsible for it (Stern 2006).

Costs associated with climate change are socialized across the economy and will likely in some way impact all economic actors negatively, more or less.[21] Costs associated with the transition to a low-carbon economy will be more focused however. These types of costs are likely to impact only a few sectors, industries or even just a select number of companies within industries. Similar to physical risks, these costs can also be externalized.

In financial markets, this may be the case in the presence of principal–agent problems. In such a scenario, short-term asset managers externalize long-term costs associated with their investments to asset owners. They are able to do this given the challenges around measuring long-term performance and risk of asset managers (WEF 2012). Asset managers may thus, even if financial models reveal long-term risks, ignore this risk as it is externalized to asset owners over the long-run – at some potential assumed short-term benefit. Part of this externalization happens in the models and use of data and thus can be linked to the first part of the discussion above. Even when these models are adjusted however, it does not respond to the principal–agent, externality, and time-inconsistency problem; this is the reason the discussion here focuses on the economic agent rather than the model itself. To reiterate, short-termism may be a problem in particular when discussing transition risks given the long-term nature of these risks (Figure 3).

Beyond time horizons, institutions can also play a role for transition risk assessment in financial markets. The role of institutions is marginalized in the individual's rational, utility-maximizing behaviour.[22] The most obvious evidence for this lies in the fact that the actual preferences determining utility are treated as exogenous variables in neoclassical models (Savage 1950). According to North (1993, 360), 'history demonstrates that ideas, ideologies, myths, dogmas, and prejudices matter. [...] [Institutions] are made up of formal constraints (e.g. rules, laws, constitutions), and informal constraints (e.g. norms of behaviour, conventions, self-imposed codes of conduct), and their enforcement characteristics)'. Hence, the idea of an embedded economy: the economy functions in a specific social-historical context.

To the extent that rational choice theory acknowledges this, it is argued that rational individuals in the context of competitive market ensures the formation of efficient institution (i.e. minimizing transaction cost etc.), including incidentally cultural institutions.[23] This ignores a number of behavioural elements however, notably path-dependency, where existing economic institutions are the contingent result of particular historical developments and therefore have no a priori claim to optimality or efficiency. Perhaps the most famous example in this regard is the QWERTY-keyboard, which is said to have

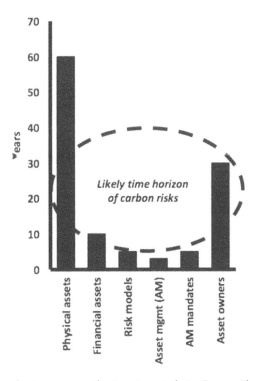

Figure 3. Illustrative time horizons across the investment chain. Source: Thomä, Dupré, and Chenet (2014).

been established for optimal typewriter typing (to avoid bunching of keys), but no longer being optimal for computers (David 1985).[24] This has also been described as 'evolutionary economics' (Nelson and Winter 1982).

One important aspect to highlight in this regard is that institutions can create decision-making parameters that are 'rational' for the individual, but where the rationality is specific to the institutional context. For example, it is rational for asset managers to maximize short-term value given the institution of short-term remuneration to which that asset manager is subject to. It would naturally be irrational from a profit-maximization perspective to do the same if their remuneration was tied to more long-term performance and value.

The 'atomism' of the rational choice theory falls short in other respects as well, beyond a discussion of institutions. The key here is that individuals in a group will be confronted with a different utility function (and a different desire to satisfy that utility function) relative to being in isolation. Bikhchandani and Sharma (2001) for example argues that herding behaviour partly explains booms and busts, where market participants exhibit 'irrational exuberance' and move as a crowd into a sector, overvalue their prices and ultimately move out, leading to a crash.[25] It is better to be wrong in a group (Brennan and Li 2008).[26]

While it is difficult to find evidence on herding behaviour related to climate change, there is evidence that the transition to a low-carbon economy, despite success in recent years, is not fully on the radar screen of investors. The NGO Asset Owner Disclosure Project (AODP) finds that about half of all surveyed asset owners have a 'no score' on climate change issues and another 35% score a D.[27] At the same time, other surveys (Mercer 2013; Novethic 2015) do identify action on climate change. Evidence is thus not unequivocal.

5. Conclusion

The previous section emphasized two ways the market failure literature influences risk management practices in financial markets. Section 3 focused on the insights financial market failure literature provides in terms of the assessment of the design of financial risk and valuation models. It then sought to show how these design features could create barriers to transition risk assessment, notably in their treatment of skewed, tail risks, and challenges around turning uncertainty into quantifiable risk. Section 4 then emphasized issues around the conduct of economic agents, notably the presence of time-inconsistent preferences, principal–agent problems and externalities. While these three features naturally also inform the design of models, they were identified as primarily as challenges in the market failure literature that related to the interpretation and use of models.

This study admits freely that the distinction between these two categories (i.e. models and economic agents) can be challenged, given the overlap and interplay between the two factors. At the same time, the key take-away from the review of the theoretical literature relates to the fact that transition risk assessment challenges may not be confined to the models. In other words, there is a case to be made that there is a mis-assessment of transition risks in financial markets and that this mis-assessment relates at least in part to the institutions around risk assessment. This suggests that solving this challenge requires not just better, smarter risk models, but in equal measure addressing key features of market design – notably the principal–agent problem and externalities – and potential 'irrationality' of market actors – notably their time-inconsistent preferences.

To date, the narrative and literature on transition risks has primarily focused on the issue of models. A review by Chenet, Thomä, and Janci (2015) identifies over 30 different reports integrating transition risk into traditional financial market models and risk assessment. Many of these models address the key challenges defined in Section 3, notably the use of tail-end scenario assumptions and addressing issues around uncertainty. While they do not necessarily challenge the models themselves, they show that these models can capture transition risks. These models also at least in part tackle questions explored in Section 4, notably in the form of looking at more long-term time horizons or bringing events forward to today, visible in the work of Mercer and Profundo for the Green European Foundation (Chenet, Thomä, and Janci 2015).

This work however is only starting to address the structural challenges. Notable examples in this regard are research by Caldecott, derricks, and Mitchell (2015) on investment consultants and a new research initiative by the 2° Investing Initiative on the 'Tragedy of the horizons'. There are other examples in this space, for example the UK initiative 'Preventable Suprises'. Key open questions remain, namely whether the way forward is an 'integration' approach, where these risks are integrated into traditional models to improve pricing, or a 'stress-test' approach where financial market actors use traditional risk tools for 'business-as-usual' assumptions, but are shown potential downside risks and resilience implications under extreme scenarios through models utilizing long-term scenario analysis. The way forward here will require further research. To date, the discussion on what approach works best has been limited.

The discussion here involved a theoretical discourse designed to inform research work on the question of the potential mispricing of transition risks. It is worth reiterating that the authors do not provide evidence as to the scale or materiality of these risks in and of themselves. Rather, the vantage point of the paper is on how, if these risks do exist, one could assume for them to be properly priced, based on the large theoretical literature on asset mispricing. It thus equally does not contend that transition risks deserve more or less attention than other risks, from a pure financial perspective. Rather, it suggests that mispricing of these risks, if they occur, are particularly damaging versus other types of risks because of the dual negative impact highlighted in the introduction, that is both the inefficient allocation of capital from a financial perspective and the associated potential increased costs of the transition to a low-carbon economy, which implies capital misallocation from a social perspective.

While the methodological design in terms of focusing on a theoretical analysis versus quantitative tools limits the explanatory power, the analysis does point to a few key conclusions.

First, the particular characteristic of transition risks suggest that they are susceptible to market failure. This relates to the likelihood that these risks are likely to be long-term, non-normally distributed, tail-end risks. There is thus reason to believe that an intervention may be needed from long-term asset owners and/ or regulators likely exposed to the potential capital misallocation associated with this market failure. Naturally, taking a more societal view, this call for action also appears justified given the global objective of limiting global warming to 2°C and the role investments play in realizing this objective.

It should be noted that, perhaps obviously, the toolbox of financial analysis may in itself provide some of the solutions to the problems described in this paper. This relates notably to the Real Options analysis or valuation, which allows investors to price options related to actual physical investment decisions and potential adverse impacts under various socio-economic scenarios.

At the same time, their long-term nature also suggests that there are institutional barriers linked to economic agents. Responses thus should not be limited to a focus on design of models and potential linked activities around risk transparency, for example in the form of expanded disclosure, but also address the broader institutional barriers – in effect, in the words of Carney (2015), responding to the 'tragedy of time horizons' that grips climate change more generally.

Notes

1. These types of risks should be distinguished from physical risks associated with climate change itself (e.g. droughts, floods, storms etc.). This paper also does not cover legal risks. It thus only focuses on one of the three risks first identified in the taxonomy developed by Dupre and Chenet (2013) and since then picked up by the Financial Stability Board (2015).
2. Although Fama and Samuelson introduced the term to today's economic discourse, modern economics now traces the origins of the efficient market hypothesis to the Ph.D. of Louis Bachelier and the idea of a 'random walk' of financial markets (1900).
3. Fama in fact differentiated between weak, semi-strong and strong efficiency, a distinction, while relevant in general, is not relevant for the review in this study.
4. Interestingly, contrary to popular belief, not all of the Classical economists relied on this assumption, Ricardo being a notable exception.
5. Despite the apparent worship of the economic man, this man is treated with some ambivalence, like Frankenstein, who rejected his own monster. The political economist Fukuyama (1992, 314) thus concluded that 'the life of rational consumption is […] in the end, boring.'
6. Related to this concept is the idea of 'selective rationality', articulated by Leibenstein (1966) in the context of his work on 'x-efficiency'.
7. This is not to be confused with agents not integrating all information as a result of costs. Here, allocative efficiency according to the rational actor still exists because the costs associated with the acquisition of information are seen to be higher than the associated benefits. In the scenario presented here however, actors do not integrate all information, even if this is profitable because they do not seek maximum profits. The distinction will be revisited later.
8. A scenario could be envisioned where agent satisficing has an equal effect on all financial assets and thus not lead to a skewing of prices. While possible, the 'zero error' hypothesis seems unlikely given that there is no good reason why an unconstrained decision-making process should have a distribution with a mean of zero. Such a scenario, while worthy of further research, will not be explored in further detail in this paper.
9. See for example a review by Alloway (2012) in the Financial Times, although this review simply caveats that normal distribution is *not always* the norm.
10. Haldane and Nelson (2012) provides a review of the history of normal distribution in financial market models, from which this paper borrows heavily.
11. See for example Pidcock (2012) and Iacurci (2014).
12. These assumptions may be more diverse in the case of economic stress-tests now part of the standard toolbox of regulators.
13. Knight arguably holds the economists crown for under-statement, in particular in hindsight, by beginning the book with the line: 'There is little that is fundamentally new in this book' (Knight 1921, vii).

14. Of course, rational choice theory does not assume we do not regret our decisions given 20/20 hindsight. Rather, it assumes that we do not disagree with our 'former' self's decision, given the information set available at the time the decision was made.

15. While the discussion here focuses on the market failure associated with time-inconsistency in terms of allocative efficiency, the same problem obviously persists for policy, where it is more frequently labelled the dynamic-inconsistency problem (Kydland and Prescott 1977; Barro 1983).

16. While the hyperbolic discount function has achieved popularity with the rise of behavioural economics, the notion of time-inconsistent preferences is obviously not new and can be, at least in the field of economics, traced back to Smith and Hume (Palacios-Huerta 2003).

17. Hyperbolic discount functions may be rational from an individual's perspective. If long-term paybacks are more uncertain, for example due to trust issues or external uncertainties, it may be rational to prefer a short-term payoff. Uncertainty may also exist about the ability to capture that payoff, particularly in finance. Equally, uncertainty is only one factor in explaining the hyperbolic discount function. Moreover, uncertainty is not an exogenous variable, but will be a function of a range of endogenous factors.

18. A range of other factors have been purposefully excluded in this debate, notably the presence of incomplete markets (Magill and Quinzii 1996), the literature on transaction costs (Coase 1937; Dahlman 1979) and the role of power in determining prices (Bowles 1985). While other factors may also play a role, the discussion is limited to these factors that seem immediately material for the questions around transition risk. Other factors which may prove to be equally material over time, were excluded however at this point, given the lack of immediately obvious link.

19. The term 'Principal' and 'Agent' have their origin in law, where it refers to two parties of a contractual agreement.

20. The concept of information asymmetry has been developed most prominently by Akerlof (1970), who won the 2001 Nobel Prize in Economics for his work in this field.

21. That is not to say all economic actors will face the same costs, nor that all geographies will be affected the same. Rather, that some economy-wide costs at global scale and across most countries will affect most actors in some way.

22. Institutions in this study are understood in the political economy tradition (North 1993).

23. The origin of this analysis is with Coase (1960), who applied this logic to law, where modern common law is frequently said to be driven by economic 'efficiency' considerations, as opposed to 'natural rights' considerations. See also Medema (2010).

24. It is an open question as to whether other keyboards would be more optimal in terms of typing on a computer. In any event, however, the legacy of the QWERTY-keyboard, having established its pre-dominance largely independent of efficiency considerations, cannot be denied.

25. Keynes (1936) famously called the financial markets 'a beauty contest'.

26. Much of the literature here is inspired by Mackay (1841)

27. The AODP ranks based on credit ratings from AAA to D and an 'X' for when no evidence/ response was identified.

Acknowledgements

The authors would like to acknowledge the inputs of Didier Janci and Catherine Karyotis to this paper.

Disclosure statement

No potential conflict of interest was reported by the authors.

Funding

This work was supported by European Commission H2020 [grant number 696004].

References

Aghion, P., C. Hepburn, A. Teytelboym, and D. Zenghelis. 2014. "Path-dependency, Innovation and the Economics of Climate Change." New Climate Economy Report: The Global Commission on the Economy and Climate.

Akerlof, George A. 1970. "The Market for 'Lemons': Quality Uncertainty and the Market Mechanism." *Quarterly Journal of Economics* 84 (3): 488–500. http://socsci2.ucsd.edu/~aronatas/project/academic/Akerlof%20on%20Lemons.pdf.

Alloway, Tracy. 2012. "Modelling: Normal Distribution Is Not Always the Norm." *Financial Times Online*, April 13.

Bachelier, Louis. 1900. "La Théorie de la Speculation." *Annales scientifiques de l'E'cole Normale Superieure* 3 (17): 21–86.

Bator, Francis M. 1958. "The Anatomy of Market Failure." *The Quarterly Journal of Economics* 72 (3): 351–379.

Bikhchandani, Sushil, and Sunil Sharma. 2001. "Herd Behavior in Financial Markets." *IMF Staff Papers* 47 (3): 279–310.

Bowles, S. 1985. "The Production Process in a Competitive Economy: Walrasian, Neo-Hobbesian, and Marxian Models." *American Economic Review* 75: 16–36.

Brennan, Michael J., and Feifei Li. 2008. "Agency and Asset Pricing." UCLA Finance Working Papers.

Buchanan, James, and W. M. Craig Stubblebine. 1962. "Externality." *Economica* 29 (116): 371–384.

Caldecott, Ben, Gerard derricks, and James Mitchell. 2015. "Stranded Assets and Subcritical Coal: The Risk to Companies and Investors." Oxford University Smith School of Enterprise and the Environment Stranded Assets Programme Working Paper.

Caldecott, Ben, Lucas Kruitwagen, Gerard Dericks, Daniel Tulloch, Irem Kok, and James Mitchell. 2016. "Stranded Assets and Thermal Coal: An Analysis of Environment-related Risk Exposure." Oxford University Smith School of Enterprise and the Environment Stranded Assets Programme Report.

Caldecott, Ben, James Tilbury, and Christian Carey. 2014. "Stranded Assets and Scenarios." Oxford University Smith School of Enterprise and the Environment Stranded Assets Programme Discussion Paper.

Carney, Mark. 2015. "Breaking the Tragedy of the Horizon – Climate Change and Financial Stability." Speech given at Lloyd's of London, September 29.

Chenet, Hugues, Jakob Thomä, and Didier Janci. 2015. "Financial Risk and the Transition to a Low-Carbon Economy: Towards a Carbon Stress-testing Framework." 2° Investing Initiative / UNEP Inquiry Working Paper.

Coase, Ronald. 1937. "The Nature of the Firm." *Economica* 4 (16): 386–405.

Coase, R. H. 1960. "The Problem of Social Cost." *The Journal of Law and Economics* III: 1–44.

Dahlman, Carl J. 1979. "The Problem of Externality." *Journal of Law and Economics* 22 (1): 141–162.

David, Paul. 1985. "Clio and the Economics of QWERTY." *American Economic Review* 75 (2): 332–337.

Dupre, Stanislas, and Hugues Chenet. 2013. "Landscaping Carbon Risk for Financial Intermediaries" 2° Investing Initiative Working Paper. Accessed July 9, 2016. http://2degrees-investing.org/IMG/pdf/landscaping_carbon_risk_website.pdf.

Fama, Eugene. 1970. "Efficient Capital Markets: A Review of Theory and Empirical Work." *Journal of Finance* 25 (2): 383–417.

Financial Stability Board. 2015. "Task Force on Climate-Related Financial Disclosures."

Fukuyama. 1992. *End of History and the Last Man*. New York: First Free Press.

Fulton, Mark, James Leaton, Paul Spedding, Andrew Grant, Reid Capalino, Luke Sussams, and Margherita Gagliardi. 2015. "The $2 Trillion Stranded Assets Danger Zone: How Fossil Fuel Firms Risk Destroying Investor Returns."

Greenwald, Bruce, and Joseph E. Stiglitz. 1986. Externalities in Economies with Imperfect Information and Incomplete Markets. *Quarterly Journal of Economics* 101 (2): 229–264. http://qje.oxfordjournals.org/content/101/2/229.short.

Haldane, Andrew, and Benjamin Nelson. 2012. "Tails of the Unexpected." Speech given at "The Credit Crisis Five Years On: Unpacking the Crisis." conference held at the University of Edinburgh Business School, June 8–9.

Hardin, Garett. 1968. "The Tragedy of the Commons." *Sciences* 162 (3859): 1243–1248.

Iacurci, Jenna. 2014. "Global Warming Goal of 2 Degrees Dwindling." *Nature World News*, September 22. Accessed November 11, 2015. http://www.natureworldnews.com/articles/9139/20140922/global-warming-goal-of-2-degrees-dwindling.htm.

Jensen, Michael C. 1978. "Some Anomalous Evidence Regarding Market Efficiency." *Journal of Financial Economics* 6 (2): 95–101.

Jensen, Michael C., and William H. Meckling. 1976. "Theory of the Firm: Managerial Behavior, Agency Costs and Ownership Structure." *Journal of Financial Economics* 3 (4): 305–360.

Jones, Steven, and Jeffrey M. Netter. 2014. "Efficient Capital Markets." Library of Economics and Liberty.

Kahnemman, Daniel, and Amos Tsversky. 1979. "Prospect Theory: An Analysis of Decision Under Risk." *Econometrica* 47 (2): 263–292.

Keynes, John Maynard. 1936. *The General Theory of Employment, Interest and Money*. Cambridge: Macmillan University Press.

Knight, Frank. 1921. *Risk, Uncertainty, and Profit*. Boston, MA: Hart, Schaffner and Marx.

Krugman, Paul. 2009. "How Did Economists Get It so Wrong?" *NY Times*, September 6.

Kydland, F. E., and E. C. Prescott. 1977. "Rules Rather than Discretion: The Inconsistency of Optimal Plans." *Journal of Political Economy* 85 (3): 473–491.

Laibson, David. 1997. "Golden Eggs and Hyperbolic Discounting." *Quarterly Journal of Economics* 112 (2): 443–478.

Lancet. 2015. "Health and Climate Change: Policy Responses to Protect Public Health." 2015 Lancet Commission on Health and Climate Change.

Leaton, James. 2013. "Unburnable Carbon 2013: Wasted Capital and Stranded Assets." Carbon Tracker Initiative report.

Leibenstein, Harvey. 1966. "Allocative Efficiency vs. 'X-Efficiency'." *The American Economic Review* 56 (3): 392–415.

Mackay, Charles. 1841. *Memoirs of Extraordinary Popular Delusions and the Madness of Crowds*. London: Richard Bentley. https://vantagepointtrading.com/wp-content/uploads/2010/05/Charles_Mackay-Extraordinary_Popular_Delusions_and_the_Madness_of_Crowds.pdf.

Magill, Michael J. P., and Martine Quinzii. 1996. *Theory of Incomplete Markets*. Vol. I. Cambridge: MIT Press.

Markowitz, H. M. 1952. "Portfolio Selection." *Journal of Finance* 7 (1): 77–91.

Marshall, Alfred. 1967. *Principles of Economics*. London: Macmillan for the Royal Economic Society.

McGlade, Christophe, and Paul Ekins. 2015. "The Geographical Distribution of Fossil Fuels Unused When Limiting Global Warming to 2°C." *Nature* 517: 187–190.

Medema, Steven. 2010. *The Hesitant Hand: Taming Self-interest in the History of Economic Ideas*. Princeton, NJ: Princeton University Press.

Meinshausen, M., N. Meinshausen, W. Hare, S. C. B. Raper, K. Frieler, R. Knutti, D. J. Frame, and M. R. Allen. 2009. "Greenhouse-gas Emission Targets for Limiting Global Warming to 2°C." *Nature* 458: 1158–1162.

Mercer. 2013. "Global Investor Survey on Climate Change." 3rd Annual Report on Actions and Progress – Commissioned by the networks of the global investor coalition on climate change.

Mercer. 2015. "Investing in a Time of Climate Change." Mercer report.

Mill, Jon Stuart. 1844. *Essays on Some Unsettled Questions of Political Economy*. London: Longmans, Green, Reader and Dyer.

Minsky, Hyman. 1992. "The Financial Instability Hypothesis." Levy Economics Institute of Bard College Working Paper No. 74.

Nelson, Richard, and Sidney G. Winter. 1982. *An Evolutionary Theory of Economic Change*. Harvard: Harvard University Press.

North, Douglass. 1993. "Economic Performance through Time." Nobel Prize Lecture 1993.

Novethic. 2015. "Responsible Investors Acting on Climate Change." Novethic report.

Ong, Li. 2014. *A Guide to IMF Stress Testing: Methods and Models*. Washington, DC: International Monetary Fund.

Palacios-Huerta, Ignacio. 2003. "Time-inconsistent Preferences in Adam Smith and David Hume." *History of Political Economy* 35 (2): 241–268.

Pidcock, Roz. 2012. "Can We Still Limit Warming to Two Degrees?" Carbon Brief, December 12.

PWC. 2014. "Asset Management in 2020: A Brave New World." PWC report.

Robbins, Lionel. 1938. "Interpersonal Comparison of Utility: A Comment." *The Economic Journal* 48 (192): 635–641.

Robins, Nick, Wai-Shin Chan, and Zoe Knight. 2012. "Coal and Carbon." HSCB investor report.

Samuelson, Paul. 1937. "A Note on Measurement of Utility." *Review of Economic Studies* 4: 155–161.

Samuelson, Paul. 1965. "Proof that Properly Anticipated Prices Fluctuate Randomly." *Industrial Management Review* 6 (2): 41–49.

Savage, L. J. 1950. *The Foundations of Statistics*. New York: Wiley Press.

Sharpe, William F. 1964. "Capital Asset Prices: A Theory of Market Equilibrium under the Conditions of Risk." *The Journal of Finance* 19 (3): 425–442.

Simon, Herbert. 1957. *Models of Man: Social and Rational*. New York: John Wiley and Sons.

Smith, Adam. 1776. *An Inquiry into the Nature and Causes of the Wealth of Nations*. London: Methuen.

Stern, Nicholas. 2006. "What is the Economics of Climate Change?" *World Economics* 7 (2): 1–10.

Taleb, Nassim. 2007. *Black Swans: The Impact of the Highly Improbable*. New York: Random House Publishing Group.

Thaler, R. H. 1981. "Some Empirical Evidence on Dynamic Inconsistency." *Economic Letters* 8 (3): 201–207.

Thomä, Jakob, Stan Dupré, and Hugues Chenet. 2014. "The Turtle becomes the Hare: Short-termism in Financial Markets." 2° Investing Initiative Working Paper.

Tobin, J. 1958. "Liquidity Preferences as Behavior Towards Risk." *Review of Economic Studies* 25 (2): 65–86.

Tsversky, Amos, and Craig R. Fox. 1995. "Ambiguity Aversion and Comparative Ignorance." *The Quarterly Journal of Economics* 110 (3): 585–603.

WEF (World Economic Forum). 2012. "Measurement, Governance and Long-Term Investing." World Economic Forum report.

Social and asocial learning about climate change among institutional investors: lessons for stranded assets

Elizabeth S. Harnett

ABSTRACT

Institutional investment portfolios are currently, and will increasingly be, affected by the risks and opportunities resulting from climate change. This paper contributes new empirical data from 58 in-depth interviews and a global investor survey to explore how climate change is being learnt socially and asocially within the institutional investment industry. This research seeks to identify ways in which the relatively novel concept of 'stranded assets' can be better disseminated to investment professionals. Importantly, both social and asocial learning can affect investment decisions, with some actors usefully providing information via both channels. Better learning, language and leadership within the institutional investment system could facilitate the dissemination of climate and stranded asset discourses among investors, but an imperative to communicate effectively rather than simply communicating more is noted. This paper should interest both investment professionals keen to learn more about the issue and academic researchers seeking to engage investors on these topics.

1. Introduction

Institutional investors will be key actors in combating climate change. They are exposed to the risks and opportunities of climate change, and represent a large pool of capital that could help finance the $53trillion needed to develop a low-carbon economy (IEA 2014). Recognition of these issues within investment institutions appears to be increasing: with membership to groups such as the Principles of Responsible Investment (PRI) and the Montreal Carbon Pledge growing rapidly (UNEP FI 2014; IIGCC 2015). A growing literature highlights how environmental change makes investments across a range of sectors and asset classes at risk from being stranded (Caldecott, Howarth, and McSherry 2013; Harnett, Harnett, and Edstrom 2014). However, the understanding that environmental factors could strand assets and will have a financial impact on investment portfolios is far from universal (EUROSIF 2014; Sievänen 2014).

This paper explores how investors are learning about Responsible Investment (henceforth, RI) topics, seeking to outline which information sources investors use to learn about climate change. It illuminates investors' dependence on both social and asocial learning strategies, and highlights the useful role of some industry actors in providing opportunities for both. This paper uses this exploration of learning to frame recommendations for better communication between academics, researchers and investors on the subject of environmentally driven stranded assets.

This paper analyses findings from 58 semi-structured interviews with a range of investment industry professionals to explore the current state of social and asocial learning about climate change and 'stranded assets' within the UK and Australia. These countries were chosen because of the high level of potential stranded asset exposure in their asset markets, and their differing institutional investment structures and climate policies. The Assets Under Management (AUM) of organizations interviewed in Australia equalled A $778bn, almost 30% of total A$2.6tr AUM (Reserve Bank of Australia 2015). Interviewed organizations in the UK represented £6.5tr, 24% of the combined Western Europe and the Middle East[1] market (BCG 2015). A global survey of 154 investors provides additional insight.

In defining institutional investors, this study focuses on both asset managers and asset owners, with particular focus on Pension Funds (PF) and Superannuation Funds (SF). Insurance companies are excluded from this study, despite the importance of climate risks to the sector (London Assembly 2015). Incorporating them would represent an important extension of this research. Throughout this paper the terms 'investor' and 'institutional investor' are used interchangeably.

Sections 2 and 3 explore existing literatures exploring RI and stranded asset debates, and communication and learning theories, respectively. Section 4 outlines the methodologies used. Section 5 examines the diversity of information sources used by investors to learn about climate change, before Sections 6, 7 and 8 delve into more detailed analysis of the asocial, social and dual learning strategies of investors, respectively. Section 9 explores the need for greater translation of climate science into investable hypotheses. Section 10 offers a discussion and recommendations for the diffusion of stranded asset discourses. Section 11 concludes and highlights useful future research.

2. Climate change, stranded assets and RI

Climate change will increasingly impact investment portfolios (OECD 2012; Wolf 2014). Institutional investors are likely to be particularly at risk through their role as Universal Owners. Such investors typically have large diversified portfolios, whereby performance is partly reliant on the performance of the economy as a whole and therefore likely to be negatively affected by the range and scale of climate change impacts (Hawley and Williams 2007). It is predicted that without significant mitigation and adaptation action from governments, businesses, investors and consumers in the coming years, global warming is unlikely to stay below the 2°C target of 'acceptable' warming (IPCC 2014). Beyond this point, feedback loops are likely to accelerate and exacerbate the negative consequences of climate change through a series of 'rolling collapses' within the economy, environment and society (Towers Watson 2012; World Bank 2012).

In 2011, the Carbon Tracker Initiative highlighted a potential 'carbon bubble' (Carbon Tracker 2011), building on Krause, Bach, and Koomey (1989) who suggested that fossil fuel companies could be overvalued due to future climate regulation. Research suggests that 60–80% of publicly listed fossil fuel reserves are 'unburnable' if the world is to avoid disastrous climate changes (Carbon Tracker 2013; Kepler 2014). This would likely be reflected in stranded assets and lower share prices, creating large economic losses among investors, corporations and governments. Stranded assets can occur when 'environmentally unsustainable assets suffer from unanticipated or premature write-offs, downward revaluations or are converted to liabilities' (Caldecott, Howarth, and McSherry 2013). The impact of asset stranding on investors may be even higher if excess reserves are burnt: subsequent climate changes could irrevocably alter the environment, affecting economic production and investment risk and returns (IPCC 2014). Asset stranding is already occurring: for example, European gas-fired power stations premature closures cost nearly €6bn in 2013 (Caldecott and McDaniels 2014). Carbon Tracker (2016) thus suggests that oil majors could be worth $100bn more if they plan for and invest in a 2°C world.

Investments which depend on the natural environment, particularly those exposed to the 'stress-nexus' of water–energy–food, are increasingly at risk from such significant premature write-downs as regulation tightens, natural capital is impaired, clean technologies develop and socio-political pressures increase (Harnett, Harnett, and Edstrom 2014). Beneficiaries and NGOs are therefore calling for investors to calculate their exposure to 'stranded assets' risks, catalysing greater corporate engagement and shareholder resolutions against fossil fuel companies (Dupré et al. 2015; Srinivas 2015). Campaigns for decarbonization and divestment from dirty fossil fuels have also gained momentum (Flood 2015), with the Divest–Invest movement attracting 500 signatories with $3.4 trillion AUM pledging to move capital out of fossil fuels and into environmentally beneficial investments in 2015.[2]

RI refers to considering environmental, social and governance (ESG) factors in investment decision-making (EUROSIF 2012). However, to integrate RI asset owners and asset managers must first learn about their exposure to ESG risks and the investment opportunities available to manage and mitigate these risks. Information asymmetries, a lack of standardized corporate ESG disclosures, and inherent uncertainty and complexity in climate change scenarios all contribute to a lack of information and learning opportunities surrounding RI and hinder its integration into investment decisions (Eccles and Serafeim 2013; Sievänen 2014).

This paper compares institutional investor learning about climate change and stranded assets in the UK and Australia. Both investment markets have significant carbon exposure, strong and growing institutional investment systems, and an activism surrounding RI (EY 2015; World Bank Database 2015). Given the size of institutional investment assets in these two countries, (pension assets are equivalent to the entire annual economic output in both countries [OECD 2014]), more responsible management of these assets could, potentially, provide significant impetus in shifting capital towards lower carbon economies.

3. Theories of learning and communication

Learning occurs in both social and asocial environments. Haas and Haas (1995) suggest that capacity to learn is based on the 'willingness to make use of available knowledge' that can be acquired through study, experience, or being taught. Communication, however, is defined in this paper as the imparting or exchanging of information by speaking, writing or using some other medium. Communication is therefore fundamental to facilitating learning, but is not sufficient: learning depends on the recipient accepting (or rejecting) the information being shared.

3.1. Asocial learning

Asocial learning in this paper will refer to new information that is learned by an individual through the private consumption of information (Pidgeon and Fischhoff 2011; Rendell et al. 2011). Asocial learning is common in investment decisions, as asset managers often used detailed analysis of raw data on individual companies, sectors and markets (Voss 2015). The channel of delivery is shown to have a tangible impact on the take-up of information by investors. Easily accessible information within mainstream media has greater stock market impact than the same data released in scientific journals (Huberman and Regev 2001). Market-wide climate announcements and media coverage are thus more likely to affect investment decisions. A 2012 report found a growing consensus among investors that increased corporate transparency and disclosure could facilitate greater RI, with 80% saying that ESG data are relevant to investment decision-making (A4S/GRI 2012). This report also highlighted the diversity of sources used to gather data, with the majority of respondents using multiple channels: direct engagement with companies and formal reporting channels were seen as the most important. This paper expands on and challenges these findings to explore key sources of information and the learning strategies used by investment actors.

3.2. Social learning

Social learning appears to facilitate the rapid dissemination of new ideas, especially when learnt from peers (Hara 2009) and if practices are expected to have positive outcomes (Rotter 1954). This suggests attention to climate change information is more likely if espoused by investors' co-workers or peers, and also if low-carbon or climate-aware strategies offer good returns (financial and/or reputational). Social learning is perhaps particularly useful for investors who have limited time and attention capacities due to the nature of their jobs (Peng 2005; Peng and Xiong 2006).

This section comments on the utility of different social learning theories (summarized in Table 1) in underpinning the empirics of this paper.

Both formal and informal 'communities of practice' facilitate peer-learning and the dissemination of group norms and practices. Such groups can be formed between colleagues within organizations or external groups promoting cross-collaboration and knowledge-sharing (Smith and Mackie 2007). In the case of climate change-related investor groups, these communities of practice also promote learning within and between different groups, with some members belonging to multiple groups, so knowledges, identities and norms learned can be transferred between members of different groups (Guyatt 2007). Social learning can also help to overcome confirmation bias, whereby individuals are prone to selecting information that confirms existing beliefs. This can limit the likelihood of asocial information changing beliefs, compared to exposure to others' opinions and information via social learning (Nickerson 1998; Jonas et al. 2001).

Table 1. Summary of social learning theories.

Theory	Key literature	Literature linked to climate and/or investment	Explanation
Social Learning	Bandura (1963) Reed et al. (2010)	Bursztyn et al. (2014) Nilsson and Swartling (2009) Hall (1993)	Learning as a cognitive process that occurs in social environments rather than taught environments or through individual work.
Peer-learning	Hara (2009) Pelling et al. (2008)	Bursztyn et al. (2014) Cambridge Network (2015)	Collaborative learning amongst peers is shown to expedite the learning process.
Group norms	Abrams and Hogg (1988) Hornsey (2008)	Masson and Fritsche (2014) Whitmarsh, Lorenzoni, and O'Neill (2012) Dunlap and McCright (2008) Fielding et al. (2012)	Social and professional groups provide guidelines for appropriate behaviour through the internalization of accepted behaviours, and the transfer of accepted knowledges.
Communities of practice	Wenger (2011) Smith and McKeen (2003)	A4S (2015) Bursztyn et al. (2014) Guyatt (2007)	Groups of people who share a concern or a passion for something, and meet together to discuss and learn how to improve the situation through regular cooperation.

Source: Author.

Rendell et al. (2011) explore the role of peer copying in processing new information. While imitation is an important cognitive process through which we adopt new behaviours, it is also potentially dangerous as the lines of social learning can become entangled in false information. While highly educated investors are perhaps less likely to fall into this trap, 'groupthink' and 'herding' are common market traits (Kahneman 2011). Investors adapt their own decisions based on others' investments due to 'social learning' and 'social utility' (Bursztyn et al. 2014), and this can cause herding and market speculation (Devenow and Welch 1996; Kahneman 2011). As such, the reasoning and motivations behind any copied behaviour must be considered (Fielding, Hornsey, and Swim 2014), and asocial learning is required to ensure that up-to-date and accurate information is consumed, particularly when new information is regularly published as is the case in RI and investment markets (Rendell et al. 2011).

3.3. Communicating climate change

The communication of climate research is important, as the decisions of policy-makers, investors and the public will affect future planetary conditions (Painter 2013). The IPCC has been instrumental in summarizing and publishing the latest climate science (Hulme and Mahony 2010). However, their ability to communicate these risks effectively remains questionable, with a persistent gap between the climate science, policy action and the public understanding of the risks (Sterman 2011; Capstick et al. 2014).

A growing literature explores the psychological, social, institutional and political barriers to accepting climate science. To formulate the most effective communication strategy the audience and framing strategies need to be considered (Pelling et al. 2008; CRED 2009). Moser (2010) suggests that audiences need to 'receive ample, clear, sufficiently strong, and consistent signals that support the necessary changes'. Weigold (2001) and Bostrom, Böhm, and O'Connor (2013) suggest targeting specific audiences; such efforts are beginning to be established in financial communities, with Cambridge University releasing concise, sector-specific, summaries of the IPCC (CISL 2015). However, significant gaps in disseminating the importance of climate change to investors remains, with Eccles and Serafeim (2013) noting the continued lack of ESG information in quarterly earnings reports which are central to investor's asocial learning. Importantly, simply increasing the amount of information available may not facilitate more efficient learning, and could lead to 'information overload' (Agnew and Szykman 2010; Gleick 2011).

This paper thus explores the actors facilitating both social and asocial learning, having identified a significant paucity of academic research exploring different actors' roles in facilitating investor learning on RI topics. This could then usefully inform strategies for academics and industry actors communicating these topics, including stranded assets.

4. Methodology

The primary research for this article took place between November 2014 and August 2015. The results are based on a comparative study of 58 in-depth interviews undertaken in the UK and Australia, and a broader global survey of investors.

4.1. Interviews

Fifty-eight interviews were conducted, 29 each in the UK and Australia. Table 2 provides a tabulated breakdown of the 60 interview participants (one interview in each country was attended by two individuals). As is common in more qualitative business studies, this research utilized convenience sampling instead of more systematic techniques (Eriksson and Kovalainen 2008). These respondents are thus not presumed to be representative of the wider market, but as gaining access to business-people, or 'elites', especially in the financial world, is often particularly difficult (Thomas 1993; McDowell 1998; Harvey 2010), it was decided that the methods and sampling adopted would yield the most interesting and insightful results. Furthermore, snowballing techniques reduced subjectivity, as participants were often willing to suggest additional individuals to interview (Atkinson and Flint 2001).

Existing contacts within the Oxford University Smith School and the economic consultancy Absolute Strategy Research acted as 'gatekeepers'.[3] Emails were sent out to clients of both institutions explaining the research topic and requesting participants; while this provided a range of interviewees, there is some self-selection bias as those most interested in the topic are more likely to respond. Key organizations in RI, including leading NGOs and

Table 2. Breakdown of interview participants by role and organization type.

	Director or Executive	RI analyst	Investment manager	Head of RI	Researcher	Policy director	Total
Asset manager	4	4	7	3	3	–	21
Pension fund	5	8	2	2	1	–	18
Climate/RI NGO	5	1	–	–	–	3	9
Consultant	1	2	–	1	–	–	4
Data/Research provider	2	–	–	1	–	–	3
PF body	2	–	–	–	–	1	3
Other	1	1	–	–	–	–	2
Total	20	16	9	7	4	4	60

investment organizations were approached directly following desk-based analysis. These two sampling strategies were used to ensure a diversity of jobs and sectors were represented, and (where possible) the most senior investment or RI individual was targeted. In addition to NGOs, consultants, brokers and data providers, interviewees represented a range of investment sectors, including mainstream asset managers, corporate and public PF, ethical funds, infrastructure funds and a sovereign wealth fund.

Interviews were semi-structured, and varied depending on the individuals' profession (mainstream investor, RI professional or intermediary), their interests and experience. Prompt questions were designed in light of existing literature, historical investor surveys and the key research questions. As is often the case in qualitative research, the interview process was an iterative one (Pope, Ziebland, and Mays 2000): issues raised in early interviews, including an initial pilot interview, provided additional prompts and questions for subsequent interviews (Ziebland and McPherson 2006). Due to the sensitivity of the information discussed, particularly regarding investment practices, quotations have been anonymized, with references based on their location and the order in which the interviews were conducted (i.e. UK01 and Aus01 for the first interview in each country).

4.2. Survey

A structured, web-based, invitation-only survey was a secondary research method employed to provide broader insights to a consistent set of questions regarding investment learning. A pilot study of nine individuals, with varying knowledge of climate change and/or investment experience, contributed to the non-linear process of survey creation following the interview process and literature search. The final survey included 29 questions. This survey reduced response bias by randomizing the order in which answer options appeared, and emphasized that results would be shared with participants to increase likelihood of 'true' responses. Both positive and negative phrasing of questions was used and answers were triangulated to ensure that respondents were answering consistently.

The survey was disseminated through the Oxford World Financial Digest (OXWFD), an online news outlet aimed at international investment professionals. This survey accumulated a rich data set of 154 responses: 38.7% of survey respondents were Executives and a further 27.8% were Investment Managers. Only 4.7% were ESG/RI specialists, but 88.3% of survey respondents said that they were 'somewhat' or 'very' familiar with sustainability investment topics. 40.6% worked in Asset Management organizations. However, a key limitation of the survey design was that the disclosure of location was not mandated, so almost half of responses are not attributable to a specific country; survey results are thus used to support the interview comparisons of Australia and the UK by providing a broader insight into the global investment market.

4.3. Data analysis

Survey and interview data were analysed using a number of different techniques, including statistical analysis on quantitative data, and textual analysis on qualitative data. The interview data, where appropriate, has been quantified through tallying responses to structured questions to facilitate comparison to survey data. Coding software 'NVivo' facilitated collective analysis of the data. This software platform helped to organize and analyse data through coding, search, query and visualization tools. Codes were cross-examined and combined to 'understand the patterns, the recurrences' of responses by framing the ways in which data illuminated, questioned and clarified key themes and answered research questions (Miles and Huberman 1994; Saldana 2009; Guest 2012).

The results are specific to the time and place of the research, and my own interpretation and understanding of participants' responses (Schoenberger 1991). However, every effort has been made to accurately represent the views and data generated, and address biases where possible. The methodologies are clearly outlined in Harnett (2015), and repeatable in different settings.

5. Investment communication channels

Only 3 survey respondents (out of 112 responses to this question) and none of the 60 interviewees said that they had 'never' read an article about climate change risks or opportunities. Forty-two per cent of survey participants had read an article in the last week. This figure is likely to be higher than normal due to a speech by President Barack Obama announcing America's first national standards to limit carbon dioxide in the week of the survey.[4] Regardless of such unintentional event bias, the findings of both methodologies suggest that a market for climate-related information does exist.

We live in the 'Information Age' (Hara 2009): an era defined by the Internet and online/mobile communication. This has made dissemination of ideas and content much easier, and made data more accessible, with many interviewees using 'Internet searching' (Aus07) to source climate information. However, many interviewees noted that 'anyone can write anything at any time, its unfiltered, and its not peer reviewed' (Aus11), so additional discernment is often required to determine reliability before the views and ideas can be accepted and learnt from the internet. Investors thus rely on a wide range of sources to triangulate ideas and ensure that they are getting the best information (Voss 2015).

Table 3 outlines the range of information sources used by investors to gather and internalize information about climate change, based on interview and survey responses. Information sources that facilitate both social and asocial learning are represented. This demonstrates investors' dependence on both learning types, but also the fact that these strategies are not necessarily mutually exclusive.

Of these sources, interviewees relied on brokers and mainstream data providers most frequently (Figure 1). Both UK and Australia interviewees rely heavily on traditional providers of financial information to source their climate-related information. Further

Table 3. List of information sources.

Asocial	Both asocial and social	Social
Academic publications	Brokers	Experts
Company reports	Climate/RI groups	Face to face meetings in work
Data providers (ESG)	Consultants	Social discussions outside work
Data providers (General)	Internal research	Social media
Industry and national bodies	Law firms	
Investment journals	NGOs	
IPCC reports	Regulators	
Lobby group reports		
Mainstream news		
RI news		

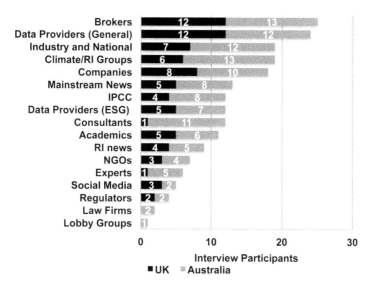

Figure 1. Information sources on climate change. Source: Research interviews.

emphasis of the materiality of climate and stranded asset risks within these channels could be key to reaching a broad investment audience. However, more dedicated climate research from climate groups (19 mentions), the IPCC reports and ESG data providers (12 mentions each) are also prominent, particularly in Australia where these sources gained 28 mentions. Australian interviewees typically used a wider range and higher number of information sources.

The following sections will outline investors' reliance on social, asocial and dual (social *and* asocial) learning strategies, analysing the scope and scale of the dissemination of climate information and stranded assets discourses undertaken by different actors.

6. Asocial learning sources

Asocial learning is seen as key to the diffusion of knowledge about climate change and investment, with access to data, peer-reviewed science and the latest trends in climate and investment all important. The wide range of actors aiding in the asocial dissemination of this information allows investors to access the information they need rather than being at the mercy of their peers' and colleagues' opinions, interests and subjectivities (Table 4). Appendix 1 and 2 illustrate survey results for information sources used in accessing climate information and sources that inform investment decisions.

Market data providers are the most relied-upon information by survey participants when making investment decisions (74% use data regularly or always), but are also key sources of climate information, with 24 interviewees and 54.1% of global survey participants listing them as an important data source on climate change. This supports the findings of A4S/GRI (2012), which found that formal reporting channels were important sources of ESG information. Sixteen interviewees mentioned Bloomberg and 12 mentioned the MSCI database as providing good climate and ESG data. Ensuring that climate information is readily available on these platforms is vital to its integration in investment decisions in both the UK and Australia, but awareness of available information

Table 4. Asocial learning sources.

Academic publications
Company reports
Data providers (ESG)
Data providers (General)
Industry and national bodies
Investment journals
IPCC reports
Lobby group reports
Mainstream news
RI news

varied. There was an expressed frustration that 'there is a lot of good research done but it is not taken up' (UK17). Greater discussion within the industry of the data available on these platforms, and efforts to increase the coverage of topics such as stranded assets, could therefore be beneficial.

Corporate reports were also ranked highly in the A4S/GRI (2012) survey findings. However, only 18 interviewees commented on their use (the fifth most common source), and just 27.9% of survey respondents used corporate reports for climate information, challenging the A4S/GRI finding. Seventy-six per cent of survey respondents, however, said they use corporate reports to guide their investment decisions; integrating climate information (and its materiality to financial performance) into annual reports could be key to greater climate awareness within investment decisions.

Mainstream news was the most relied-upon information source about climate change among survey participants, with 81.1% of international survey participants using mainstream news. However, only 13 (22%) interviewees used mainstream news to gather climate information. The wording of the question could have caused this discrepancy: in the survey, 'mainstream media' was referred to as 'newspapers, online content, television, etc.', whereas this definition was not clarified in the interviews. Concurrently, the level of climate expertise was greater among interviewees; 50% of interviewees had a job related to RI compared to only 4.7% of survey participants. Thus the lower proportion of media usage by interviewees could be due to their greater access to, and confidence in using, specific climate-related data, and greater scepticism around the legitimacy of media reporting: an Asset Management Executive said of climate change 'there is a lot talked about it in the media, but a lot of it is fairly alarmist and maybe not very insightful' (Aus14), and another interviewee lamented the 'dearth of rigour' in the press (Aus21). However, these results highlight the importance of imbuing mainstream news channels with timely, accurate and relevant climate information for investors, especially as this can help mainstream investors with little alternative information. One interviewee noted that:

> People like Carbon Tracker are trying to make the academic stuff more digestible … It puts it into the more colloquial language and is more impactful … I think using mainstream media and social media is much more effective. I think there is progress being made by the academics and I would support them doing more. (UK25)

Although there has been a proliferation of RI news outlets, websites and blogs, interviewees suggested that these websites have limited outreach to mainstream investors and mostly aid the learning of those already informed and interested in RI issues, with interviewees demanding greater coverage in mainstream channels.

Nineteen interview participants noted the importance of national, international and industry organization reports in highlighting important climate-related issues, citing the IEA, the OECD and the World Bank as useful sources. These were mentioned more in Australia (12 mentions) than the UK (7 mentions), perhaps due to their focus on broader global and regional scale issues, which were considered more frequently by Australian interviewees. While providing insight into past and future trends, some participants commented that report findings are often difficult to convert into actionable information.

Investment journals were used to gather climate change information by 48.6% of survey respondents, and in informing investment decisions by 80.7%. Furthermore, 75 survey respondents (69.4%) used academic reports to help inform their investment decisions at least sometimes, and 12 interviewees discussed the use of the IPCC reports and 11 mentioned using academic articles for learning about climate change. However, many interviewees agreed that academic reports provide general knowledge rather than investment-relevant information: IPCC reports were described as 'not necessarily helpful … it provides some evidence but it doesn't necessarily translate that into something that is helpful in terms of making investment decisions' (Aus17). As such, more work needs to be done in translating the findings of key reports into investment hypotheses, with Section 9 exploring this in more detail. Regardless, it is clear that asocial learning retains an important role in the learning processes of investors, and that those communicating the importance of stranded assets need to ensure that rigorous research is available through a range of asocial channels.

7. Social learning sources

Social learning opportunities were noted as important in disseminating climate change information through the investment markets, and particularly vital for changing perceptions and beliefs about the materiality of climate change and stranded assets to investment decisions (Table 5).

Learning from those of similar experiences, backgrounds and profession is a key knowledge-sharing process (Hara 2009; Reed et al. 2010), with early-adopters of RI helping to 'socialize that message and let it be heard amongst the broader investment and business communities' (Aus16). Groups of peers appear to help normalize discourses and beliefs around the materiality of climate change: 'The vast benefit of it is how quickly you can get things done because the existing trust is already there' (Aus28). Although apparent in both the UK and Australia, greater emphasis on informal 'communities of practice' was noted among Australian interviewees, perhaps due to the geographical remoteness, the smaller nature of the industry and the greater reliance on external interaction and cooperation: 'Australia is a small place. There are only two cities where anything happens (around RI) and we all know each other' (Aus28).

Table 5. Social learning sources.

Experts
Face to face meetings in work
Social discussions outside work
Social media

Perhaps the most useful social learning technique described by different interviewees was the concept of 'peer-learning':

> I talk to my peers about how they are looking at certain issues; you don't necessarily tell them everything but over time you develop a group that you trust ... I think it is hugely important in our field and that information is very useful for us to take internally to use as leverage. (UK24)

Those engaging with such groups saw informal social learning as vital, particularly for RI professionals, with only 9 of the 60 interviewees saying that they favour 'formal' learning over 'informal' learning. Interviewees emphasized the systemic nature of the climate problem, arguing that collaboration was needed to affect the necessary policy and corporate changes: 'We felt like we were fighting the same battle so we almost ended up sharing approaches: what worked and what didn't work so that has built a nice platform' (UK17). A novel finding was that social media, including Twitter and LinkedIn, is playing an increasingly important role in disseminating key reports and RI updates, and facilitating peer discussions and the filtering of research.

Top-down leadership is arguably necessary for firm-wide integration of climate considerations (Juravle and Lewis 2009; Mercer 2015), and consequently peer-learning among senior managers could stimulate widespread systemic and institutional change. Such networks are perhaps less common due to acute concerns around Chinese Walls, confidentiality and conflicts of interest. However, these groups are beneficial because 'everyone struggles to bring case studies to life when it isn't through face-to-face interaction' (UK18). Examples of such high-level 'communities of practice' include the 'Cambridge Leaders Academy CEO Group'[5] and The Prince's Accounting for Sustainability 'CFO Leadership Network'.[6] The important part of such peer-learning groups is

> finding that core group of insiders who can be your advocates. They are respected and seen as credible and are 'one of the club'. Therefore they can say what everyone else may have been saying, but it will be heard. (UK18)

Such advocacy among peers from trusted individuals/organizations could be key to overcoming confirmation bias among those sceptical of climate changes' materiality. This suggests that forming smaller groups of Executives supportive of action on climate change and stranded assets could be particularly effective in encouraging RI.

However, the extent of peer-learning internationally was challenged to a certain extent by the survey results: only 26% used face-to-face meetings to gather information about climate change. This is perhaps suprising given the recent rise of NGO and investor-led groups focusing on this issue, including the PRI, Global Sustainable Investment Alliance and the Global Investor Coalition on Climate Change, which were all noted by interviewees as facilitating useful peer-learning. However, lower participation rates in these groups and the lower proportion of RI specialists meant that survey participants were less likely to undertake specific learning activities on climate change. Furthermore, discussion of climate change was limited within investment institutions surveyed: 83.3% never have climate change as a standing agenda point in Investment Committee Meetings, and only 12.5% discussed climate risk 'regularly' or 'always' with clients. While 'ad hoc' and 'reactionary' discussions about climate change were occurring in investment organizations, evidenced by the 70.5% of survey participants who discuss it at least sometimes, the lack of formality and frequency identifies the current limit of opportunities for social learning as a barrier to the integration of RI into investment decisions.

Social learning also needs to be moderated by asocial learning to avoid the pitfalls of social 'copying' and 'groupthink' (Rendell et al. 2011) and ensure that participants can stay abreast of scientific and policy developments (Pidgeon and Fischhoff 2011). One interviewee commented of the informal RI networks 'there is insufficient cross-pollination of ideas. It's no different to the boys club … It's probably more porous and progressive minded, but you do wonder if there is enough different thinking coming through' (Aus28).

As such, social learning opportunities were acknowledged by interviewees as an especially important learning process around climate change, particularly when encouraged by senior leadership and facilitated by intermediaries and experts. However, it faces challenges from those concerned about competitive advantage, a continued perception that climate change is not material enough to investment decisions, and the relative lack of social learning opportunities for mainstream investors. Greater outreach by RI groups to non-members, and the facilitation of social learning opportunities on stranded assets at mainstream investment events could be key to increasing the dissemination of ideas.

8. Dual social and asocial learning sources

Given the above benefits and limitations to both social and asocial learning, this paper argues that those organizations and communication channels that combine both social and asocial learning opportunities are likely to be most effective (Table 6).

As well as writing their own reports on a range of RI subjects, such actors draw attention to other research reports and facilitate networking and social learning opportunities during client meetings and presentations on key topics, including stranded assets. Several interviewees, particularly in Australia, suggested that such discussions had been key to persuading them that climate change was relevant and could be integrated on a practical level into investment decisions.

External research providers, including brokers and consultants, ranked highly amongst survey and interview participants as key to facilitating learning. More research needs to be done on this topic, as little literature exists on the climate research capacity of these groups (c.f. Caldecott and Rook 2015). 59.5% of survey participants use external research for climate information, and brokers were the most-discussed source of climate information by interviewees in both UK and Australia (25 out of 60 interviewees). One SF RI manager commented 'I find that the work done by the brokers is really useful in distilling information into an investment context' (Aus05).

However, not all interviewees were so impressed: an Executive in a sustainability-focused asset management firm commented, 'We have found that traditional "broking"

Table 6. Dual learning sources.

Brokers
Climate/RI groups
Consultants
Internal research
Law firms
NGOs
Regulators

research is not as long-term oriented or covering these issues as well as we would like' (UK28). Although some brokers are providing useful social and asocial learning on climate issues, coverage varies between brokerage houses and perhaps depends on which stocks and sectors they are broking as to the extent they view climate change and stranded assets as relevant. This supports Dlugolecki and Mansley (2005) who found that brokers tend to be sector-oriented, and focused on emission regulations, with many viewing climate change as too long-term.

Although 12 interview participants mentioned the role of investment consultants in sourcing climate information, 11 of these were Australians, and Mercer was the only investment consultant praised by name for their climate work. The level of coverage of RI issues, and the extent to which climate reports are made public, varies dramatically between organizations, affecting the learning opportunities available to investors. A sustainability NGO director commented: 'I have heard of one investment consultant who explicitly didn't cover ESG unless you paid extra for it, even if it was material' (UK05). While almost 50% of survey participants use consultants in their investment decisions, only four 'always' use them – the least of any option given. As such, consultants communicating on climate change and stranded assets should perhaps focus on a strategic rather than asset investment level. Interestingly, no participants mentioned management consultants such as McKinsey, who have large environmental research capabilities and products.

NGOs and investor-led groups focusing on climate change provide opportunities for both social and asocial learning. Literature, such as Guyatt (2013), increasingly notes their important role in facilitating RI. Nineteen interviewees noted their role in primary research, collaborative engagement and networking. Thirteen of these were Australian interviewees, compared to just six in the UK. This difference could perhaps be due to the apparent cohesion within Australia's RI networks centred around the Investor Group on Climate Change (IGCC), which was mentioned as positively impacting the climate policy and investment spheres and facilitating networking. However, whilst climate groups were useful for members, their scope was often seen as simply 'preaching to the converted' (UK08). This perhaps reduces their contribution to convincing mainstream investors of the materiality of climate and stranded assets, but once an investor was looking for information these groups were seen as key sources of learning. Interview participants supported greater outreach by these groups.

While most asset management institutions have research teams, there is a growing trend towards establishing in-house RI/ESG research capacity (Bourghelle, Jemel, and Louche 2009). Thirty of the 58 organizations interviewed had internal climate-related research analysts, but only 24.2% of survey respondents knew of such capacity. 29.7% of survey respondents used internal research to learn about climate change and 79% use it in investment decisions, suggesting that there is still a gap between mainstream investment research and climate issues. Although some mainstream researchers cover climate change, an ESG team is perhaps more likely to facilitate social and asocial learning within an organization due to their greater capacity and expertise on these issues. This was clear during the interview process, with ESG researchers more likely than mainstream equivalents to discuss the topic with colleagues and encourage access to reports and data analytics. Such research can play an important teaching role for mainstream investors and can cement decisions about RI at the individual, executive and institutional level.

Bos (2014), however, cautions that 'to accomplish true ESG integration, one should make ESG an integral part of the investment analysis performed by the mainstream analysts'. The success of an ESG team could perhaps be seen in its own demise if it successfully trains mainstream analysts to integrate ESG factors (Arjalies 2010). However, interviewees argued that 'we shouldn't expect our general managers to be experts in everything' (Aus25), and that until ESG integration is further developed, the presence of ESG teams in-house can enable bespoke and practical guidance, in the form of written research, participation in meetings and personal relationships with colleagues which could spark further interest and understanding around climate change and stranded assets exposure.

Regulators and law firms can also provide such social and asocial information, but only a few research participants acknowledged their role explicitly. However, they potentially could play a key role in change industry norms within the investment system towards greater acceptance of RI.[7]

The dual role of these actors communicating both socially and asocially is implicitly accepted throughout the investment industry, but has gained little attention within the academic literature. Greater explicit attention could facilitate better communication and learning. The organizations explored above could be key to disseminating stranded asset research through their capacity to cater to both social and asocial learning needs of investors, but current focus on climate change by these actors was criticized as concentrated in only a few industry leaders.

9. Translating the science

In addition to understanding the learning mechanisms of investors, and the use of different information sources, it is important to understand what is being communicated, and whether the information is being presented in a relevant manner and language for investors.

> First and foremost, we want to deliver superior performance for our clients. Anything that we have access to that will help us do that, we will look at. The challenge is then to prove that is material. A lot of progress has been done in terms of the ESG quality of the analysis but we still have quite a way to go (UK24)

Survey data found that many financial actors still feel that there is not enough information available, with only 20% of 110 survey respondents saying that there is adequate information to properly analyse corporate exposure to climate change. In contrast, 70% of interviewees (25 interviewees out of 36 interviewees that commented on this issue) said that there is sufficient information available on climate change: comments included 'This is not an information problem' (UK19) and 'I don't think getting hold of information is a problem' (UK04). Furthermore, five Australian and six UK participants said that there was 'too much information', with seven interviewees mentioning that they suffered from 'information overload' (three in Australia, four in the UK). This variation in views between the survey and interview participants was pronounced, and again can be linked to the greater proportion of interviewees having an RI capacity in their job and involvement in RI groups, perhaps leading to confirmation bias whereby those convinced by the climate science seek out more information than those still sceptical of its relevance to investment decisions. Even though climate-related research and corporate disclosures are being released through a range of platforms, it is not fully integrated into decision-making. This is perhaps where more RI teams, consultants and brokers could become important conduits for research and the education of investors around the availability and use of existing climate information.

Translating academic knowledge into an actionable investment thesis is key to its integration into investment decision-making (UNEP FI 2009). This translation is currently inadequate: only 30% of survey participants said that the language used in climate change communications was appropriate for the investment community. Climate communications were seen as 'politicized', 'full of jargon or difficult to follow' and 'alarmist arguments'. The lack of funding for climate-related investment research could be one reason for the deficit of investor-appropriate language and research, with only 4.7% of survey respondents knowing of climate research budgets within their organization. Alongside technical and non-relevant language, interviewees in both countries also commented that most climate reports were too long: 'when a big report comes through on climate that is relatively technical that might be 50 or 100 pages, I find it very hard to read' (Aus13). Another said: 'Time is a major factor for me and for investment teams. So generally good, concise exec summaries are the things I like to look at' (Aus15). This corroborates Peng (2005), which posits that investors have limited time and attention for learning and processing information. This should act as a warning for those communicating stranded assets to investors: simply providing more information is not sufficient to increase consideration of ESG factors and stranded assets, the information needs to be relevant to investment decisions, and of a suitable language and length.

However, a desire for more and different information does exist. Figure 2 explores the additional information desired by survey respondents, finding that 58.7% wanted better data on how climate change is affecting portfolio/economy returns, and 46.8% wanted better company data on exposure to climate change. Such efforts are already underway in academia and industry, such as Caldecott et al. (2016) which explores asset-level exposure to climate change among thermal coal assets, but these are still limited in their scope and impact.

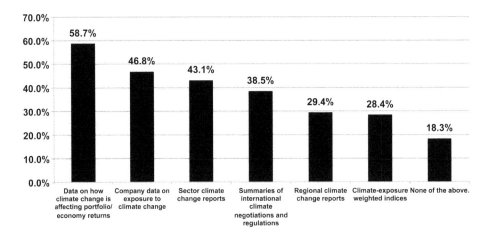

Figure 2. What additional information would be helpful to better account for climate change in investment decisions? Source: Research survey.

Furthermore, the timelines and immediate relevance of climate risks were also noted as important by interviewees. One interviewee commented that translating the science into investment actions was difficult: 'given the nature of climate change it is very difficult to pin down when certain things are going to occur, so that has made it quite challenging' (Aus15). 38.5% of survey respondents said that summaries of policies and regulation could enhance understanding of likely impacts and the time-frames for investment exposure. Time-frames around stranded assets was highlighted as being potentially useful, with one asset manager saying 'if you had some models where you could point to stranding potential then that would be more helpful' (UK09). Another said 'unless you can put a value and a timeline on the stranding then it isn't that helpful for investors' (UK10).

Both UK and Australian interviewees suggested the need for more high-profile case studies and mainstream coverage of the materiality of climate, the need for more investment products that offered opportunities to benefit from the low-carbon transition, and praised work that shifted discourses from moral campaigns towards material financial risks, such as being done by those interested in stranded assets:

> I think that the recent work … by groups like Carbon Tracker around stranded assets, backed up by the IPCC findings around the carbon budget, has helped to present to investors a much simpler thesis. (Aus16)

As such, greater focus on examples and timelines of stranded assets could help emphasizing the materiality of climate change to current and future investment decisions, but this needs to be communicated clearly through both social and asocial learning opportunities.

10. Discussion

Existing academic literature has given only limited attention to the issue of how mainstream investors are most efficiently and effectively informed about climate change exposure, and how these ideas inform investment decision-making. This analysis should help frame future research and communication aimed at translating climate science and stranded assets risks for the investor audience. Importantly, this paper has identified the on-going demand for this information and the need to communicate through a range of social and asocial learning opportunities. Specifically, better understanding, funding and outreach among those actors offering dual learning methods could be particularly advantageous.

Australian interviewees, who tended to use a wider range of information sources, mentioned information provided by consultants and climate groups more frequently suggesting that there is greater knowledge-sharing between firms in Australia. UK interviewees relied more heavily on internal research teams, perhaps due to the greater scale and capacity of these teams due to the differing nature of the investment industry. The failure of investment firms to explicitly budget for purchasing third-party climate change-related investment research could be limiting the amount of information of a suitable length, language and detail available to help investors integrate climate into everyday decisions. Further emphasis on the materiality of climate change for financial risk and return facilitate greater efforts towards RI, with stranded asset discourses praised as helping in this process. Such information and discourses could lead to greater consideration of these risks at the Investment Committee Meetings and C-suite level, which might increase demand for, and integration of, such information. A novel finding was the increasing role of social media in providing a filter and sharing platform within the RI profession, providing a channel for reaching wider audiences and reducing the risk of information overload.

Investors in both the UK and Australia engage in social and asocial learning about climate change and stranded assets. This research suggests scope for further development of informal 'communities of practice' within the investment system for learning about stranded assets, with such groups facilitating social peer-learning and asocial knowledge development through sharing of climate research. Such networking opportunities could be particularly important among Executives, where the greatest leverage exists for firm- and industry-wide change. Executive networking opportunities already exist to a limited extent in the UK, but could be scaled up in both the UK and Australia in line with existing formal and informal networks of RI professionals. Networks of individuals and the role of social learning appeared stronger in Australian than in the UK, possibly a result of the geographic remoteness and small scale of the investment industry, causing a greater reliance on collaboration and knowledge sharing. However, the multiple climate groups in both countries need to be more aware of reaching out beyond their own networks to ensure that the benefits of peer-learning and research reports extend beyond RI professionals to mainstream investors and that members continue to learn about new discourses such as stranded assets.

As such, this paper recommends that those wishing to disseminate stranded asset discourses use a co-ordinated communication strategy. This should tap into the diversity of information sources and learning strategies used by investors. Simply producing more detailed research or organizing conferences about the likelihood and impacts of stranded assets, although needed, will not be sufficient to convince investors of the merits of the concept or facilitate its integration into investment decisions. Targeting information specifically for investors, and encouraging internal mainstream and RI researchers to write their own research, synthesize key reports and hold regular meetings with peers and colleagues to discuss these topics could aid the translation of academic science of stranded assets and climate change into investment hypotheses. A key recommendation resulting from these findings is the need for researchers to focus their engagement with organizations that regularly engage investors through *both* social and asocial learning opportunities, notably climate groups, consultants, internal research teams and brokers. This could be key to catalysing greater learning about stranded assets, building on investors' dual learning and informational needs. However, mainstream media and data platforms remain particularly important for those investors not already aware of climate and stranded asset concepts, so concise, rigorous and easily accessible information on these platforms will also be key to catalysing a shift towards a lower carbon economy and more RI.

11. Conclusions and future research

This paper has explored the learning surrounding climate change and stranded asset risks within institutional investment organizations in the UK and Australia. These countries were chosen because of the high level of climate change exposure in their asset markets, and their differing institutional investment structures. As an extension to this research, American, European and Asian institutional investors could be studied using the same methodologies to expand comparisons and understandings of learning and RI within the international institutional investment system. Similarly, a study of how the insurance industry is learning about these long-term climate risks could be interesting future research.

Changing investment behaviour to take greater account of climate-related issues and stranded asset risks is possible, and already occurring, but this research suggests that there remains scope for this to be scaled up and intensified. Increased collaborations, communication and peer-learning are needed, and greater recognition of the benefits of offering both social and asocial learning opportunities could further facilitate the dissemination of the stranded assets concept. Better learning, language and leadership within the institutional investment system could stimulate greater integration of climate change thinking and accounting for stranded asset exposure, but could also, perhaps, help push private capital towards funding the estimated \$53trn of investment required to deliver a more sustainable, lower carbon global economy.

Notes

1. Western Europe and Middle East used in calculation due to the geographic scope of interviewed organizations' AUM despite their investment office location in the UK.
2. http://divestinvest.org.
3. Rice (2010) suggests adopting a business-like or 'inside' approach, using 'gatekeepers' to gain access to initial interviewees.
4. For example, this announcement was widely covered in the Economist, the BBC, the Guardian, CNN, the *New York Times* and the *Wall Street Journal* in the week beginning 3rd August 2015. The President said 'I am convinced that no challenge poses a greater threat to our future, to future generations, than a changing climate', (The Economist 2015).
5. https://www.cambridgenetwork.co.uk/learning/peer-learning/.
6. http://www.accountingforsustainability.org/cfos/network-of-chief-financial-officers.
7. For example, law firms Minter Ellison and Client Earth are producing novel research and litigation emphasizing investors' institutional and individual liability to climate risks, and the Bank of England has been pioneering in its capacity as a regulator calling for greater accounting for stranded asset and climate exposure in investment portfolios. Both types of organization provide written research as well as attending client meetings and running workshops.

Acknowledgements

I would like to begin by expressing my gratitude to Ben Caldecott and Gordon Clark, my supervisors within the Oxford Smith School, whose guidance and support was invaluable in preparing and writing this paper. My heartfelt thanks also go out to my reviewers, friends and family who read and commented on early drafts. Thanks must also go to all those who have participated in my research, generously sharing their time and experience. Without you this would be a very different project, your perspectives and experiences added invaluable depth and insight to this research. I would also like to thank Absolute Strategy Research and the Oxford University Smith School of Enterprise and the Environment for their kind sharing of contacts, which made this research possible. My particular thanks must go to Luke MacRedmond, for his readiness to share contacts and desk-space in Australia.

Disclosure statement

No potential conflict of interest was reported by the author.

Funding

The fieldwork required for the writing of this paper would not have been possible without the generous provision of scholarships and financial assistance from Jesus College, Oxford and the Oxford University Department of Geography and the Environment.

References

A4S. 2015. "The A4S CFO Leadership Network." The Prince's Account for Sustainability. Accessed June. http://www.accountingforsustainability.org/cfos/network-of-chief-financial-officers.

A4S/GRI. 2012. *What Investors and Analysts Said – The Value of Extra-Financial Disclosure.* London: The Prince's Accounting for Sustainability Project and the Global Reporting Initiative.

Abrams, D., and M. A. Hogg. 1988. "Comments on the Motivational Status of Self Esteem in Social Identity and Intergroup Discrimination." *European Journal of Social Psychology* 18 (4): 317–334.

Agnew, J. R., and L. Szykman. 2010. "Annuities, Financial Literacy and Information Overload." *Pension Research Council WP* 33: 1–41.

Arjalies, D. 2010. "A Social Movement Perspective on Finance: How Socially Responsible Investment Mattered." *Journal of Business Ethics* 92: 57–78.

Atkinson, R., and J. Flint. 2001. "Accessing Hidden and Hard-To-Reach Populations: Snowball Research Strategies." *Social Research Update* 33 (1): 1–4.

Bandura, A. 1963. "The Role of Imitation in Personality Development." *Dimensions of Psychology*: 1–16.

BCG. 2015. *Global Wealth 2015: Winning the Growth Game.* Boston Consulting Group. Accessed September 2015. https://www.bcgperspectives.com/content/articles/financial-institutions-growth-global-wealth-2015-winning-the-growth-game/?chapter=2.

Bos, J. 2014. "Integrating ESG Factors in the Investment Process." *CFA Institute Magazine*, January.

Bostrom, A., G. Böhm, and R. E. O'Connor. 2013. "Targeting and Tailoring Climate Change Communications." *Wiley Interdisciplinary Reviews: Climate Change* 4 (5): 447–455.

Bourghelle, D., H. Jemel, and C. Louche. 2009. "The Integration of ESG Information into Investment Processes: Toward an Emerging Collective Belief?" *Vlerick Leuven Gent Working Paper Series* 26: 1–39.

Bursztyn, L., F. Ederer, B. Ferman, and N. Yuchtman. 2014. "Understanding Mechanisms Underlying Peer Effects: Evidence from a Field Experiment on Financial Decisions." *Econometrica* 82 (4): 1273–1301.

Caldecott, B., N. Howarth, and P. McSherry. 2013. *Stranded Assets in Agriculture: Protecting Value from Environment-Related Risks.* Oxford: Smith School of Enterprise and the Environment.

Caldecott, B., K. Kruitwagen, G. Dericks, D. J. Tulloch, I. Kok, and J. Mitchell. 2016. *Stranded Assets and Thermal Coal: An Analysis of Environment-Related Risk Exposure.* Oxford: Smith School of Enterprise and the Environment.

Caldecott, B., and J. McDaniels. 2014. "Stranded Generation Assets: Implications for European Capacity Mechanisms, Energy Markets and Climate Policy." [Online]. Working Paper, Smith School of Enterprise and the Environment. Accessed August. http://www.smithschool.ox.ac.uk/research-programmes/stranded-assets/Stranded%20Generation%20Assets%20-%20Working%20Paper%20-%20Final%20Version.pdf.

Caldecott, B., and D. Rook. 2015. *Summary of Proceedings: Investment Consultants and Green Investment.* 3rd Stranded Assets Forum, March. Waddesdon Manor, Oxfordshire.

Cambridge Network. 2015. *Peer Learning.* Cambridge Network. [Online]. Accessed June. https://www.cambridgenetwork.co.uk/learning/peer-learning/.

Capstick, S., L. Whitmarsh, W. Poortinga, N. Pidgeon, and P. Upham. 2014. "International Trends in Public Perceptions of Climate Change Over the Past Quarter Century." *Wiley Interdisciplinary Reviews: Climate Change* 6 (1): 35–61.

Carbon Tracker. 2011. *Unburnable Carbon: Are the World's Financial Markets Carrying a Carbon Bubble?* London: Carbon Tracker Initiative.

Carbon Tracker. 2013. *Unburnable Carbon 2013: Wasted Capital and Stranded Assets*. London: Carbon Tracker Initiative.

Carbon Tracker. 2016. *Oil Majors Worth More Adopting 2̊C Pathway, Independent Stress Test Finds*. London: Carbon Tracker Initiative.

CISL. 2015. *IPCC Climate Science Business Briefings*. Cambridge Institute for Sustainability Leadership. [Online]. Accessed June. http://www.cisl.cam.ac.uk/business-action/low-carbon-transformation/ipcc-briefings.

CRED. 2009. *The Psychology of Climate Change Communication: A Guide for Scientists, Journalists, Educators, Political Aides, and the Interested Public*. New York: Center for Research on Environmental Decisions.

Devenow, A., and I. Welch. 1996. "Rational Herding In Financial Economics." *European Economic Review* 40 (3): 603–615.

Dlugolecki, A., and M. Mansley. 2005. *Asset Management and Climate Change*. London: Tyndall Centre for Climate Change Research.

Dunlap, R. E., and A. M. McCright. 2008. "A Widening Gap: Republican and Democratic Views on Climate Change." *Environment: Science and Policy for Sustainable Development* 50 (5): 26–35.

Dupré, S., J. Thomä, S. Dejonckheere, R. Fischer, C. Weber, C. Cummis, and A. Srivastava. 2015. *Climate Strategies and Metrics: Exploring Options for Institutional Investors*. [Online] UNEP FI, 2 Degrees Investing and GHG Protocol. Accessed August, 2015. http://www.unepfi.org/fileadmin/documents/climate_strategies_metrics.pdf.

Eccles, R., and G. Serafeim. 2013. "A Tale of Two Stories: Sustainability and the Quarterly Earnings Call." *Journal of Applied Corporate Finance* 25 (3): 66–77.

Eriksson, P., and A. Kovalainen. 2008. *Qualitative Methods in Business Research. Introducing Qualitative Methods Series*. London: SAGE.

EUROSIF. 2012. *SRI Study 2012*. EUROSIF.

EUROSIF. 2014. *SRI Study 2014*. EUROSIF.

EY. 2015. *Tomorrow's Investment Rules 2.0*. London: Ernst & Young LLP.

Fielding, K. S., B. W. Head, W. Laffan, M. Western, and O. Hoegh-Guldberg. 2012. "Australian Politicians' Beliefs about Climate Change: Political Partisanship and Political Ideology." *Environmental Politics* 21 (5): 712–733.

Fielding, K. S., M. J. Hornsey, and J. K. Swim. 2014. "Developing a Social Psychology of Climate Change." *European Journal of Social Psychology* 44 (5): 413–420.

Flood, C. 2015. *Fossil Fuel Divestment Gathers Momentum*. 3rd ed. London: Financial Times.

Gleick, J. 2011. "Information Overload." *New Scientist* 210 (2806): 30–31.

Guest, G. 2012. *Applied Thematic Analysis*. Thousand Oaks, CA: Sage.

Guyatt, D. J. 2007. "Mobilising Collaborative Opportunities between Pension Funds." Available at SSRN 2033516.

Guyatt, D. J. 2013. "Effective Investor Collaboration: Enlarging the Shadow of the Future." *Rotman International Journal of Pension Management* 6 (2): 56–64.

Haas, P. M., and E. B. Haas. 1995. "Learning To Learn: Improving International Governance." *Global Governance* 1 (3): 255–284.

Hall, P. A. 1993. "Policy Paradigms, Social Learning, and the State: The Case of Economic Policymaking in Britain." *Comparative politics* 25 (3): 275–296.

Hara, N. 2009. *Communities of Practice: Fostering Peer-to-Peer Learning and Informal Knowledge Sharing in the Work Place*. 1st ed. Berlin Heidelberg: Springer-Verlag.

Harnett, E. S. 2015. *Communicating Climate Change: How Learning, Language and Leadership Can Impact Institutional Investment Decisions in Australia and the United Kingdom*. Published master's thesis, University of Oxford, Oxford. Available at http://www.fir-pri-awards.org/wp-content/uploads/Master_Harnett.pdf.

Harnett, I., E. Harnett, and E. Edstrom. 2014. *Stranded Assets: A New Concept but A Critical Risk. Absolute Thematics Paper*. London: Absolute Strategy Research.

Harvey, W. S. 2010. "Methodological Approaches for Interviewing Elites." *Geography Compass* 4 (3): 193–205.

Hawley, J., and A. Williams. 2007. "Universal Owners: Challenges and Opportunities." *Corporate Governance: An International Review* 15 (3): 415–420.

Hornsey, M. J. 2008. "Social Identity Theory and Self Categorization Theory: A Historical Review." *Social and Personality Psychology Compass* 2 (1): 204–222.

Huberman, G., and T. Regev. 2001. "Contagious Speculation and a Cure for Cancer: A Nonevent That Made Stock Prices Soar." *The Journal of Finance* 56: 387–396.

Hulme, M., and M. Mahony. 2010. "Climate Change: What Do We Know about the IPCC?" *Progress in Physical Geography* 34 (5): 705–718.

IEA. 2014. *Special Report: World Energy Investment Outlook*. France: International Energy Agency/ OECD.

IIGCC. 2015. *Climate Change Investment Solutions: A Guide for Asset Owners*. London: Institutional Investor Group on Climate Change.

IPCC. 2014. "Summary for Policymakers." In *Climate Change 2014: Impacts, Adaptation, and Vulnerability. Part A: Global and Sectoral Aspects. Contribution of Working Group II to the Fifth Assessment Report of the Intergovernmental Panel on Climate Change*, edited by V. R. Barros, and C. B. Field, 1–32. Cambridge: Cambridge University Press.

Jonas, E., S. Schulz-Hardt, D. Frey, and N. Thelen. 2001. "Confirmation Bias in Sequential Information Search after Preliminary Decisions: An Expansion of Dissonance Theoretical Research on Selective Exposure to Information." *Journal of Personality and Social Psychology* 80 (4): 557–571.

Juravle, C., and A. Lewis. 2009. "The Role of Championship in the Mainstreaming of Sustainable Investment (SI): What Can We Learn From SI Pioneers in the United Kingdom?" *Organization & Environment* 22 (1): 75–98.

Kahneman, D. 2011. *Thinking, Fast and Slow*. New York: Farrar, Straus and Giroux.

Kepler Cheuvreux. 2014. *Stranded Assets, Fossilised Revenues*. Energy Transition and Climate Change. ESG Sustainability Research, Kepler Cheuvreux.

Krause, F., W. Bach, and J. Koomey. 1989. Energy Policy in the Greenhouse. London: Earthscan Books.

London Assembly. 2015. *Weathering the Storm: The Impact of Climate Change on London's Economy*. London: London Assembly Economic Committee.

Masson, T., and I. Fritsche. 2014. "Adherence to Climate Change-Related Ingroup Norms: Do Dimensions of Group Identification Matter?" *Eur. J. Soc. Psychol.* 44: 455–465.

McDowell, L. 1998. "Elites in the City of London: Some Methodological Considerations." *Environment and Planning A,* 30 (12): 2133–2146.

Mercer. 2015. *Investing in a Time of Climate Change*. Mercer. Accessed December 2015. http:// www.mercer.com/our-thinking/investing-in-a-time-of-climate-change.html.

Miles, M. B. and A. M. Huberman. 1994. *Qualitative Data Analysis: An Expanded Sourcebook*. Thousand Oaks, CA: Sage.

Moser, S. C. 2010. "Communicating Climate Change: History, Challenges, Process and Future Directions." *Wiley Interdisciplinary Reviews: Climate Change* 1 (1): 31–53.

Nickerson, R. 1998. "Confirmation Bias: A Ubiquitous Phenomenon in Many Guises." *Review of General Psychology* 2 (2): 175–220.

Nilsson, A. E., and Å. G. Swartling. 2009. "Social Learning about Climate Adaptation: Global and Local Perspectives." Stockholm Environment Institute, Working Paper.

OECD. 2012. "The Role of Institutional Investors in Financing Clean Energy." OECD Working Papers on Finance, Insurance and Private Pensions.

OECD. 2014. *Pension Markets in Focus 2014*. OECD. Accessed August 2015. https://www.oecd.org/ daf/fin/private-pensions/Pension-Markets-in-Focus-2014.pdf.

Painter, J. 2013. *Climate Change in the Media: Reporting Risk and Uncertainty*. University of Oxford.

Pelling, M., C. High, J. Dearing, and D. Smith. 2008. "Shadow Spaces for Social Learning: A Relational Understanding of Adaptive Capacity to Climate Change Within Organizations." *Environment and Planning A,* 40 (4): 867–884.

Peng, L. 2005. "Learning with Information Capacity Constraints." *Journal of Financial and Quantitative Analysis* 40 (2): 307–329.

Peng, L., and W. Xiong. 2006. "Investor Attention, Overconfidence and Category Learning." *Journal of Financial Economics* 80 (3): 563–602.

Pidgeon, N., and B. Fischhoff. 2011. "The Role of Social and Decision Sciences in Communicating Uncertain Climate Risks." *Nature Climate Change* 1: 35–41.

Pope, C., S. Ziebland, and N. Mays. 2000. "Qualitative Research in Health Care. Analysing Qualitative Data." *BMJ (Clinical research ed.)* 320 (7227): 114–116.

Reed, M. S., A. C. Evely, G. Cundill, I. Fazey, J. Glass, A. Laing, J. Newig, et al. 2010. "What is Social Learning?" *Ecology and Society* 15 (4): 1–10.

Rendell, L., L. Fogarty, W. J. Hoppitt, T. J. Morgan, M. M. Webster, and K. N. Laland. 2011. "Cognitive Culture: Theoretical and Empirical Insights into Social Learning Strategies." *Trends in Cognitive Sciences* 15 (2): 68–76.

Reserve Bank of Australia. 2015. *Recent Developments in Asset Management*. Reserve Bank of Australia, June Quarter Bulletin.

Rice, G. 2010. "Reflections on Interviewing Elites." *Area* 42 (1): 70–75.

Rotter, J. B. 1954. *Social Learning and Clinical Psychology*. Englewood Cliffs, NJ: Prentice-Hall.

Saldana, J. 2009. *The Coding Manual for Qualitative Researchers*. Thousand Oaks, CA: Sage.

Schoenberger, E. 1991. "The Corporate Interview as a Research Method in Economic Geography." *The Professional Geographer* 43 (2): 180–189.

Sievänen, R. 2014. "Practicalities Bottleneck to Pension Fund Responsible Investment?" *Business Ethics: A European Review* 23: 309–326.

Smith, E. R., and D. M. Mackie. 2007. *Social Psychology*. 3rd ed. Psychology Press.

Smith, H. A., and J. D. McKeen. 2003. "Creating and Facilitating Communities of Practice." In *Handbook on Knowledge Management: Knowledge Matters*, edited by C. W. Holsapple, 1st ed., 393–407. Berlin: Springer.

Srinivas, S. 2015. "Investors Ask Oil Companies to Disclose Refineries' Risks from Climate Change." February 27 ed. *The Guardian*.

Sterman, J. D. 2011. "Communicating Climate Change Risks in a Sceptical World." *Climatic Change* 108 (4): 811–826.

The Economist. 2015. "Hotter than August." *The Economist*. August 8th. Accessed March 2016. http://www.economist.com/news/united-states/21660548-new-rules-curb-emissions-power-plants-are-not-bold-they-seem-hotter.

Thomas, R. J. 1993. "Interviewing Important People in Big Companies." *Journal of Contemporary Ethnography* 22 (1): 80–96.

Towers Watson. 2012. *We Need a Bigger Boat: Sustainability in Investment*. London: Towers Watson

UNEP FI. 2009. *The Materiality of Climate Change: How Finance Copes With the Ticking Clock*. Geneva: United Nations Environment Programme Finance Initiative.

UNEP FI. 2014. *Financial Institutions Taking Action on Climate Change*. Geneva: UNEP Finance Initiative.

Voss, J. 2015. *Where to Find Valuable Investment Information*. CFA Institute. Accessed January 2016. https://blogs.cfainstitute.org/investor/2015/08/20/where-to-find-valuable-investment-information/.

Weigold, M. F. 2001. "Communicating Science: A Review of the Literature." *Science Communication* 23 (2): 164–193.

Wenger, E. 2011. *Communities of Practice: A Brief Introduction*.

Whitmarsh, L., I. Lorenzoni, and S. O'Neill. 2012. *Engaging the Public with Climate Change: Behaviour Change and Communication*. New York: Taylor and Francis; Earthscan.

Wolf, M. 2014. "A Climate Fix Would Ruin Investors." *The Financial Times*, June 17th.

World Bank. 2012. *Turn Down the Heat: Why a 4°C Warmer World Must Be Avoided*. The World Bank Group. Accessed May 2015. http://documents.worldbank.org/curated/en/865571468149107611/Turn-down-the-heat-why-a-4-C-warmer-world-must-be-avoided.

World Bank Database. 2015. *Carbon Emissions Per Capita*. Online: World Bank.

Ziebland, S., and A. McPherson. 2006. "Making Sense of Qualitative Data Analysis: An Introduction with Illustrations from Dipex (Personal Experiences of Health and Illness)." *Medical Education* 40 (5): 405–414.

Appendix 1. Climate change information sources

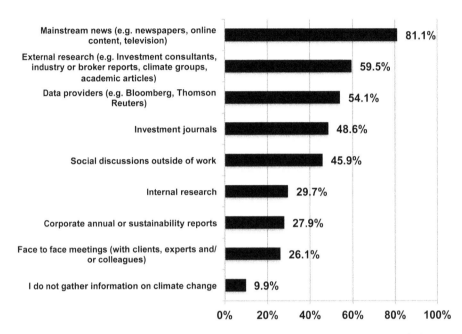

Figure A1. How do you gather information on climate change issues? Source: Research Survey.

Appendix 2. Investment decision information sources

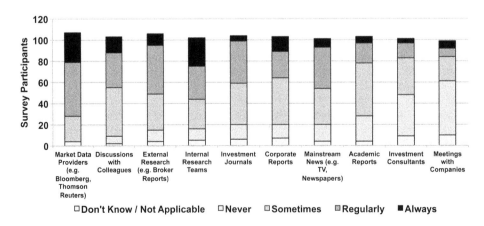

Figure A2. When making investment decisions, what forms of communication do you utilise? Source: Research Survey.

Assessing the sources of stranded asset risk: a proposed framework

Bob Buhr

ABSTRACT

Long-term investors, particularly bond investors, do not currently enjoy an efficient framework for assessing where stranded assets (SAs) might arise. Traditional risk categories currently embodied in credit research – Business Risk and Financial Risk – can capture a number of Environmental, Social and Governance (ESG) issues. However, there are some risks that are difficult to assess in this framework, primarily because many ESG categories themselves are not particularly efficient, or even meaningful, as analytical categories. We propose that a better analysis of these risks can be obtained by categorizing what are currently called ESG risks into three specific risk categories: (1) Operational or Management Risk; (2) Climate Risk, primarily related to climate mitigation and adaptation; and (3) Natural Capital Risks, a category intended to capture natural capital depletion, subsidy loss risks, and certain geopolitical risks – risks associated with water resources perhaps being the best example of a Natural Capital Risk. SAs can arise from all three sources, but those arising from Climate and Natural Capital Risk are more likely to be both significant and irreversible.

1. Introduction – expanding the typology of ESG credit risks

We have previously suggested (Buhr 2013, 2014) that Environmental, Social and Governance (ESG) issues would play an increasingly important role in credit research associated with medium- and long-term investment horizons, such as those required by pension funds. Most ESG issues can, in fact, be accommodated in a straightforward manner by simply expanding the range of issues to be monitored in traditional credit analysis. Moreover, there is accumulating evidence that incorporating ESG guidelines into credit analysis can have a positive performance effect (oekom research 2014). However, as useful as the ESG label is, for example, for portfolio screening purposes, it perhaps obscures a more meaningful analysis of some potential risks facing longer term investors. This may be the case in particular with reference to the concept of Stranded Assets (SAs). Under what research assumptions can SAs be best predicted?

'Traditional' credit analysis, such as that undertaken by credit rating agencies and by credit investors, typically relies on categorizing risks into two broad areas. The first, Business Risk, encapsulate a range of factors generally thought to fall under the following sub-categories: Industry Risk (including Regulatory Risk), Market Risk, Management Risk, Governance Risk (which may be a subset of Management Risk), Technological Risk, Competition Risk, Substitution Risk, and other risk categories pertaining to industry and company dynamics.

The second, Financial Risk, relates more specifically to events or situations that will have an impact on a company's balance sheet, income statement, or cash flows, and that may have an impact on a company's ability to service its debt (and other) obligations. These are not mutually exclusive categories. Financial Risk can also include issues such as governance practices and management's financial risk tolerance. Regulatory Risk has both business and financial risk aspects, and these can be interactive. Underlying this analysis is the assumption that certain credit ratios can capture credit trends of individual companies, and even sectors.

These categories embody a well-established analytical landscape with a long and largely successful track record for investors. All three major rating agencies – Moody's Investors Service, Standard & Poor's, and Fitch Ratings – essentially adopt some version of this framework for their analysis, as do non-agency analysts (both Buy-side and Sell-side) and portfolio managers. Note that credit investors, unlike equity investors, almost always have considerably more downside risk than upside risk – risk asymmetry is a characteristic of fixed income investing. Credit investors, then, pay considerably more attention to downside risks than to upside opportunities. Moreover, there is a very clear and well-established risk metric operating for credit investors – the risk of unanticipated rating agency downgrades.

While a consideration of ESG factors has some important uses, it also has some limitations. Specifically, many ESG-related categories are descriptive, but not necessarily explanatory, and are imperfect guides to a more detailed risk granulation. Consider Table 1, a version of which appeared originally in the generally useful *Corporate Bonds: Spotlight on Risk* (Principles for Responsible Investment 2013) prepared by the Fixed Income Steering Committee of the Principles for Responsible Investment (a shorter version appeared recently in the equally useful *Fixed Income Investor Guide* (Principles for Responsible Investment 2014)).

This typology, a fairly typical one in equity SRI/ESG circles and increasingly being adopted in the fixed income SRI/ESG sphere as well, displays a certain pattern. Specifically, nearly all the Social and Governance issues mentioned relate to management actions or policies – or inactions. Social and Governance Risk, such as those referenced above, are thus relatively straightforward to monitor. Whatever the form of Social or Governance

Table 1. Examples of ESG factors for corporate fixed income analysis.

Environmental	Social	Governance
Climate change	Employee relations	Shareholder rights
Biodiversity	Human rights	Incentives structure
Energy resources and management	Customer/stakeholder relations	Audit practices
Biocapacity and ecosystem quality	Product responsibility	Board expertise
Air/water/physical pollution	Health and safety	Independent directors
Renewable and non-renewable natural resources	Diversity	Transparency/disclosure
	Consumer relations	Financial policy
	Access to skilled labour	Business integrity
		Transparency/accountability

Source: Principles for responsible investment fixed income work stream (2013).

Table 2. Proposed ESG risk typology.

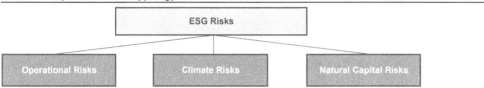

Source: SG cross asset research.

Risk, it generally arises either from actions that managements undertake, or from actions not taken by managements.

As such, these types of risks can be accommodated by, and are readily incorporated into, the fundamental approach to credit analysis promulgated by credit rating agencies. ESG investors (or the third parties they hire to screen for these issues) are increasingly tracking many of these factors, either to exclude poorly scoring companies, or to determine 'best-in-class' status in a particular sector.[1] From a risk perspective, there is nothing particularly unique about many of these risks. We refer to risks of this type – risks that are under the direct or indirect control of company managements – as 'Operational Risk.'

However, some of the issues intended to be encapsulated by an ESG analysis do not lend themselves to traditional business or financial risk analysis. Exactly how does global warming fit into this traditional analysis, for example? It is not at all clear that it does. This is because the concepts involved are at present only partially amenable to the sort of granulation that would allow these risks to be more readily categorized into business or financial risk categories. More broadly, climate change will generate a number of risks – there is no such thing as a single 'Climate Risk.' Climate Risk is actually a collection of risks, many of which remain uncertain in their scope and impact, but which are likely to be substantial.

Rather than attempting to characterize some of these risks as 'ESG risks,' characterizing these risks by their cause may provide a more appropriate analytical approach. Specifically, we propose that a tripartite division of ESG risks – Operational Risk, Climate Risk, and Natural Capital Risk, as shown in Table 2 – may represent a more useful approach to analysing what are broadly termed 'ESG' risks. It allows us to separate risks that can be reasonably tracked and assessed, against those where the assessment may be more speculative, particularly in terms of scope and timing. It allows us to disaggregate risks based on their causative source – water pollution and water depletion are both water 'risks' but derive from different causes.

2. Granulating ESG risk categories

2.1. Operational risk

We granulate Operational Risk into three further categories – Environmental, Social, and Governance – since those are the risks we are particularly interested in capturing. For each of these categories, we have three sub-categories: (1) Regulatory Compliance Risks, (2) Other Regulatory Risks; and (3) Litigation Risks. The lines between these categories can often get blurred. Nonetheless, we have classified these as Operational Risk because all three involve, either directly or indirectly, actions undertaken (or not taken) by managements in how they run their firms.

Our specific Operational Risk categories, shown in Table 3, are as follows:

Regulatory compliance risks – Regulatory compliance costs can affect operating costs, as regulated industries such as utilities and chemicals understand. The global regulatory environment will continue to evolve. For example, the REACH program (Registration, Authorization and Restriction of Chemicals), adopted by the EU to identify the potential health and environmental impacts of all chemicals currently in use in the EU, has added regulatory compliance costs to chemical producers,[2] but is also increasingly being looked at as a model for other regions.

The more general issue is whether these may be material enough to affect operating margins and other credit metrics sufficiently to cause concern. This already appears to be the case in some industries, such as the potential impact of regulations promulgated by the Obama administration on coal use by utilities – the Environmental Protection agency's Clean Power Plan (US Environmental Protection Agency 2014). Standard & Poor's has devoted some attention to this and other potential regulatory changes that would be likely to have negative credit impacts on the coal industry and a number of utilities (Standard & Poor's ratings Services 2014b) This report emerged several months after an earlier S&P report on the future of the coal industry specifically dealing with the potential risks of more stringent carbon regulations. (Standard & Poor's Rating Services 2014a)

There is another aspect to this category which merits consideration – that many companies, indeed industries, do not pay their full environmental costs. This is revealed in the data provided by Trucost (TEEB for Business Coalition 2012, 2013). Trucost analysed the environmental costs[3] of producers across 11 industries, and attempted to assess the potential impact of adjusting total EBITDA in those sectors for avoided environmental costs – in other words, how much would EBITDA be affected if companies paid those costs rather than externalizing them. The results of Trucost's analysis suggest that in a number of industries, including airlines, electricity generation, food producers, industrial metals,

Table 3. Operational risks.

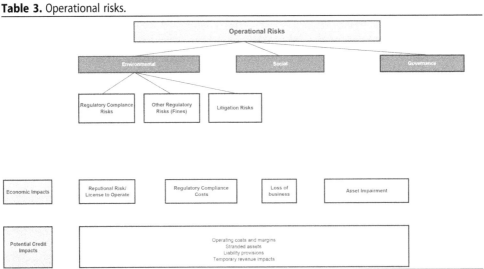

marine transportation and mining, unreported environmental costs can exceed 50% of reported sector EBITDA.

That a number of sectors would have their profitability significantly affected if full environmental costs (mostly associated with externalities and subsidies) were included in their operating performance should not be surprising. The more important point for our purposes is that these costs are, in fact, in the process of being internalized through increasing regulations (although slowly, and not uniformly across sectors) (KPMG International 2014). This trend is likely to continue. The regulatory area, and the potential compliance costs it represents, will remain perhaps the most important risk area for a number of industrial sectors, particularly energy, oil and gas producers, food producers, mining, industrial metals, and chemicals.

Other regulatory costs – These costs, particularly fines for regulatory compliance failures (including for criminal behaviour), can often result in non-trivial cash flow hits and, sometimes, substantial provisions. While there are few examples of such penalties being sufficiently onerous to result in rating downgrades, we note that these situations do present Reputational Risks (Deloitte 2014) and pose Social License to Operate (Ernst & Young 2014a) concerns. In some, albeit rare but potentially increasing, cases, operational failures such as BP's Deepwater Horizon oil spill and Shell's repeated embarrassments in the Gulf of Alaska (before its recent decision to withdraw potential drilling operations) have resulted in reputational damage that has had other impacts, such as the company's (or industry's) ability to receive new permits for proposed deep water drilling in US waters[4] (not to mention, in BP's case, continued uncertainty over possible financial penalties.) More recently, Volkswagen finds itself facing potentially significant regulatory penalties (not to mention increasingly significant litigation risk) following its September 2015 admission that it cheated on emissions tests in the US and, subsequently, elsewhere (Katz and Fisk 2016).

Litigation costs – Likewise, the same management failures that can lead to regulatory fines and other penalties can often entail litigation exposures, which, as the pharmaceutical and tobacco industry can testify, can result in substantial judgments against companies. A recent Bank of England report has even highlighted the potential impact of litigation resulting from climate change for financial institutions, particularly the insurance sector (Irwin 2015; Prudential Regulation Authority, Bank of England 2015). Such negative litigation judgments can often have substantial impacts on company cash positions, cash flow, and provisions – and can sometimes lead to credit rating downgrades, as seen from time to time in the tobacco and pharmaceutical industries. In the case of the asbestos industry in the 1980s, these judgments resulted in wholesale bankruptcies of nearly an entire industry (Ziffer 2012).

As previously indicated, nearly all social and governance risks, and many environmental risks as well, can be characterized as Operational (or Managerial) Risk. In addition to the Operational Risk category, two additional categories – Climate Risk and Natural Capital Risk – are necessary to encompass other, less-quantifiable (at present) risks.

2.2. Climate risks

As shown in Table 4, risks arising from climate change encompass a number of potential situations, basically (a) doing nothing or (b) doing something. While the former is not

Table 4. Climate risks.

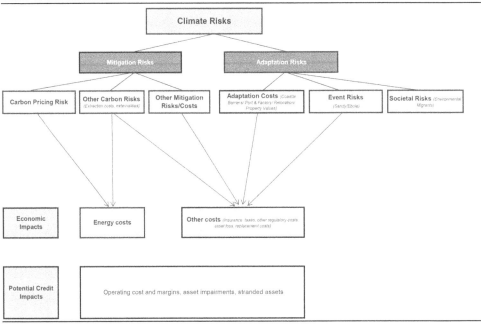

Source: SG Cross Asset Research.

generally a desired policy in most quarters, the lack of political unanimity on addressing these issues prior to the COP 21 meeting in Paris in December 2015 did not suggest a meaningful international effort would be successful. However, some significant positive momentum has come out of the Paris meetings, in which leaders of 195 countries adopted a global climate accord designed to reduce their carbon generation, with monitoring at regular intervals (Tollefsen and Weiss 2015). There is now some optimism that there may be some significant progress in addressing a number of climate-related risks (Liebreich 2015).

Alternatively, assuming that there will be concerted action on global warming at some point, we can subdivide Climate Risk into two broad categories that represent the possible responses to the threat of global warming – *Mitigation risk* and *adaptation risk*. Mitigation measures are designed to curtail the growth of greenhouse gas (GHG) emissions, principally CO_2 and methane. Adaptation responses deal with the probable physical, societal, and economic consequences of global warming on populations and regions.

Implementation of these measures, if enacted, will likely involve a combination of both mitigation and adaptation efforts. Some companies and industries will face high transition costs, or have business models that may be threatened, in the shift to a lower carbon economy. As previously mentioned, coal mining (Standard & Poor's Rating Services 2014a) has already fallen into this category. Moody's has provided an assessment of environmental risks and their potential impact across a wide range of sectors, with mining, power generation, oil & gas marketing and refining, building materials (including cement) and the commodity chemicals sectors bearing the highest near-term risks (Moody's Investors Service 2015). As Moody's notes, this is a medium- to long-term secular trend that will have broad impacts, including those on credit profiles of potentially affected companies. However, this knowledge is not particularly helpful for investors unless there is a further granulation of these risks in terms of their scope and, more particularly, their timing.

2.2.1. Mitigation risks

Unsurprisingly, most mitigation strategies that have been put forward by governments and NGOs, and the IPCC itself, have concerned the energy sector, or are directly concerned with controlling emissions from other sectors, such as transportation. We have subdivided mitigation risks into three sub-categories:

Carbon pricing risk – This category includes the risks posed by national and perhaps global attempts to price carbon, how these may evolve, and the differential effects such policies may have on different industrial sectors. This risk category has the potential to be the most serious potential near-term climate risk facing a number of sectors. These are essentially regulatory risks with a potentially significant financial impact, particularly on operating margins and asset valuations. Control of carbon discharge has been a regulatory goal for some time now, but there has been a significant lack of agreement regarding the most efficient means to achieve this.

At present, carbon pricing, the most desirable mechanism from a market perspective, has achieved little in the way of global carbon reduction, and has evolved into an unsatisfactory mix of national policies that are generally unconnected to each other. There is currently an increasing push under way to move towards regulating carbon on a global basis, with a uniform price (Litterman 2013). However, this is not the solution arrived at by the Paris COP21 negotiators, and the recent agreement provides counties with flexibility regarding meeting its carbon reduction goals, without the apparent need for a uniform global carbon price, or, for that matter, a global carbon budget (Arens et al. 2015; Liebreich 2015). Whether this approach will be successful remains to be seen.

It is possible to at least provide some preliminary assessment of where these mitigation efforts might fall by the simple method of seeing where GHGs come from. This approach assumes that these sectors are perhaps the most vulnerable if an aggressive carbon tax is implemented. The IPCC (2014) breakdown of GHGs by industry.

At present, there is considerable variability across industries in their voluntary adoption of lower carbon technologies. At times, trends can even appear contradictory – for example, while renewable energy appears to be being adopted rapidly in many parts of the world, coal remains a major source of power and electricity. National and international politics will continue to play a major role in how rapidly mitigation efforts develop, as will subsidy issues, which we discuss below. It seems clear that the less successful mitigation efforts are, the more ambitious adaptation measures will need to be.

Other carbon risks – There are also carbon risks associated with the continued use of fossil fuels, and risks associated with how carbon is extracted. With the (possibly temporary) exception of fracking for natural gas and oil in the US (where the long-term economics of fracking are still not well understood, but could be less positive than currently believed (Hughes 2014)), oil and gas, and in some regions coal, resources are generally less accessible than in past years. As a result, costs associated with extraction generally continue to rise (McKinsey Global Institute 2013a). While this is more specifically a Natural Capital Depletion risk (to be discussed in the next section), it is worth noting here because of its potential impact on energy costs in the future. There are also concerns associated with the increased potential for contamination of water resources (Payne, Dutzik, and Figdor 2009), among other issues.

Other mitigation risks – There is a broad range of potential mitigation efforts being considered at various government levels, and some are even being implemented. As a result, we leave open the possibility that other mitigation costs, including tax measures and insurance costs, will become increasingly used policy options. Some of these may be industry-specific – airlines, for example, are subject to a wide range of taxes for a variety of policy reasons already, and it is not difficult to envision that such policy measures may be used more aggressively in the future.

2.2.2. Adaptation risks

These risks relate to measures that will need to be adopted for adapting to the physical impacts of global warming. These impacts are generally regarded as including the following: (1) Sea-level rise; (2) Loss of glaciers, with attendant impacts on regional water availability; (3) Increased weather uncertainty and extreme weather; (4) Increased drought incidence; (5) Accelerated water depletion in some regions; and (6) Increased population migrations and possible social instability.

For example, one might guess that coastal property values might be strongly impacted by rising sea levels, and that large portions of current coastal property will be so negatively affected that its value in, say, 100 years will be worth essentially zero. But 100 years is a long time from an investing horizon – this is not necessarily anything that will have an impact on rating agencies' assessments of likely rating changes over the next three to five years, or, for that matter, provide a constraint to Real Estate Investment Trust (REIT) composition at present (although REITs with significant urban Florida exposure may wish to increase their monitoring of Miami's increasing flooding problems) (Goodell 2013; Kolbert 2015). So while pointing out this potential development might be stating the obvious, it is also not very relevant for investors at present.

Adaptation costs – This category refers to a broad range of costs, over a long time period, relating to the impacts of climate change. These risks encompass the impacts of climate change on the physical environment, and the potential financial impact such risks may carry for governments and corporations. Rising ocean levels and increased flooding will pose actual risks to coastal areas, for example, including port facilities and railroads, which left unmanaged have the potential to produce potentially significant SAs. At present, these costs are generally being borne by governments and insurance companies. For example, New York City has undertaken an aggressive $20 billion programme (Feuer 2014) to try to avoid a repeat of the flooding conditions that prevailed during Hurricane Sandy in 2012. Over the longer term these costs have the potential to be significant, and certainly have the potential to create SAs on a broad scale. At present, however, there are few near-term risks that are actually quantifiable, aside from those that may arise from extreme weather events. Moving a building's contents from a coastal location to higher ground is one thing; moving an entire railroad line is considerably more complex.

The US Gulf Coast offers a salutary lesson. It is the heart of the US energy complex, and also the mouth of the Mississippi River, which is fundamental to many parts of the US economy. As events of Hurricane Katrina indicated, it also is vulnerable to the effects of extreme weather. The economic consequences of Hurricane Katrina were significant because of multiple effects: disruption of traffic on the Mississippi River (a major transit conduit for the mid-American economy), the impact on US and chemical energy infrastructure, and the devastation of the real infrastructure of a major US city (Englund 2005). But the US Gulf Coast is but one among many global areas where significant assets are based on coasts. Nor are assets just based on coasts – significant assets are also based on rivers as well. Adaptation measures in these areas will be substantial, if not imminent.

Event risks – This category refers to the observed increase in natural disasters that are related to climate change impacts. Examples include Hurricane Sandy, increased flooding in parts of the world, and heat waves. What have traditionally been classified as idiosyncratic risks – natural disasters, for example – are becoming less idiosyncratic. While the number of natural disasters has declined from their high in 2005, they remain well above the levels of several decades ago – the number of extreme or catastrophic weather events continues to trend upwards, as does the amount of associated insured and uninsured damages (Swiss Re Sigma 2014).

Moreover, other Natural Capital risks continue to emerge – drought incidence, topsoil loss and desertification, resource exhaustion and scarcity, groundwater depletion, to name some of the more pressing. Many of these will be exacerbated by global warming. Moreover, these risks appear to be accelerating (Swiss Re Sigma 2014).

Societal risks – While this is the category least likely to have direct credit impacts, it nonetheless offers the prospect of increased societal costs over time. The most dramatic example of this is one that is currently occurring in various parts of the world – environmental migration. While Pacific islanders forced to leave their home islands has been well covered in the global media (Bawden 2015), few have noted the recent and ongoing turmoil in the Mideast in the context of severe sustained droughts in the region (Plummer 2013). These have contributed to political instability, and to the migration of entire regional populations, often to areas which cannot support those populations because they may be experiencing similar stresses. Environmental migration is one of several possible trends that have the potential for geopolitical destabilization, but at present it is difficult to granulate these potential impacts to specific economic sectors. Nonetheless, it is probably worth noting that civilizations have collapsed because of the occurrence of drought numerous times in human history (Conniff 2012).

2.3. Natural capital risk

The concept of Natural Capital Risk is relatively new, although the risks themselves are not. As put forward by the Chartered Institute of Management Accountants,

> Natural capital refers to the elements of nature that produce value, directly and indirectly, for people, such as forests, rivers, land, minerals and oceans. It includes the living aspects of nature, such as fish stocks, as well as the non-living aspects, such as minerals and renewable or non-renewable resources. Natural capital underpins all other types of capital and is the foundation on which our economies, societies and prosperity are built.

However, a number of forms of Natural Capital are being depleted more rapidly than they are being replenished, if they are renewable resources such as forests, fisheries, and farmland (Vangsbo, Bulmer, and Barrow 2014). Moreover, if we are referring to non-renewable resources such as minerals, the narrative becomes even more complex. Dependence upon Natural Capital is a fundamental fact of all economies, and risk assessment relating to Natural Capital Risk is likely to become more important over time as resources become more stressed (Chartered Institute of Management Accountants 2014).

'Natural Capital Risk' thus encompass risks to asset values, cash flows, or operating margins from events resulting from Natural Capital depletion or disruption. For example, the apparent increase in the number of droughts on a global basis is having an impact on water availability for some regions and industries – agriculture in California, for example. In fact, there is concern that some, indeed many, Natural Capital risks will arise in the next decades (TEEB for Business Coalition 2013). There are four in particular (as indicated in Table 5) that require some attention from investors, since these are the risks that are likely to have impacts on either the assets or the ability to economically sustain operations of various sectors: (1) Resource Depletion; (2) Climate change impacts; (3) Geopolitical event risks; and (4) Subsidy risks.

2.2.3. Resource depletion

Resource constraints provide a salutary example of how traditional analysis can lead to some complacency. For example, extraction of non-renewable resources has escalated sharply over the past several decades. Many of these resources are those reported on by companies in their corporate social responsibility or sustainability reports. Moreover, it is likely that commodity prices will continue to trend higher on a long-term basis, in spite of some recent (and painful) price breakdowns, such as iron ore and oil, and that the general commodity price increases we have seen since 2000 are unlikely to be broadly reversed over the longer term (McKinsey Global Institute 2013a, 2013b; Heck and Rogers 2014; KPMG International 2014). Note that what is at issue here is not necessarily the imminent depletion of resources. There apparently are few resources facing imminent depletion. More relevant is the increased difficulty and expense of recovering a range of resources. In many cases, even if the resource in question is not near depletion

Table 5. Natural capital risks.

Source: SG cross asset research.

levels, it is still likely to cost more than it used to for reasons laid out in a number of recent reports. As McKinsey has noted, commodity price increases since 2000 have erased the general decline of commodity prices in the twentieth century.[5]

Water risks represent the prime example of Depletion Risk. Aside from climate change, water is emerging as the dominant environmental issue of interest to investors and managements. The Water Resources Group of the World Bank has estimated that by 2030, global water demand looks set to exceed current supply by an estimated 40% without substantial efficiency gains (The 2030 Water Resources Group 2009). Water is a resource facing increasing – and often conflicting – demands, and water scarcity is becoming an increasingly important issue in a number of domains. There is already intense competition for water resources between agriculture, energy resources, and urban development in areas such as parts of China (Global Water Partnership 2015). And while the water cycle will continue to be a physical process, consumption trends appear to be running well ahead of the capacity of the water cycle to replenish adequate supplies.

All industries use water. But some use water much more intensively than others, and these industries are already, in many cases, engaging with the issues that surround concerns about longer term availability. The two industries dominating water consumption are the energy and agriculture industries. Other industries that are significant water consumers, in addition to metals and mining (which spent nearly $12 billion on water infrastructure in 2013 alone (Gordon 2013)), include the food and beverage industries (including both direct and indirect use), textiles, chemicals, steel, automobile manufacturing, and paper. The energy industry, from extraction to distribution (utilities), is an intensive water consumer – electric power generation is the single largest industrial use of water.

2.2.4. Climate risks
In the case of climate change, the concern here is with the impacts of those physical impacts described earlier on other Natural Capital trends – particularly the depletion of forests, agricultural land and other renewable resources, particularly water. Desertification of parts of the world may be accelerated under more draconian climate change scenarios. Again, we are dealing with uncertainties, but plausible uncertainties, and the uncertainty relates mainly to the scope and timing of these events. For industries affected – agriculture and forestry in particular – the impacts here will be tangible.

2.2.5. Geopolitical event risks
This category captures a certain aspect of resources – they are unevenly distributed globally, often in what some investors may regard as politically inconvenient countries. Two examples will suffice. First, demand for certain rare earth minerals is high, and is expected to remain so, because of its importance in the technology industry, particularly among handset manufacturers (International Electronics Manufacturing Initiative 2014). Most of these minerals are now mainly to be found in China. Second, phosphate fertilizer is a critical component of modern agriculture. Demand trends continue to rise, and supplies from the US and several other suppliers may be exhausted by 2040. Moreover, 70% of the required raw material – phosphorus – is found in one country – Morocco – and most other countries with some supply tend to be countries with unstable politics – Saudi Arabia, Algeria, Iraq and Syria (Rosemarin 2010). In recent years there have been numerous instances of supply-chain disruptions in the automobile and technology industries

following a warehouse fire, or a tsunami (Risk Response Network, World Economic Forum 2013) – recovery can often take several months. The belief that resources under the control of one or two countries could be immune to that sort of disruption should be resisted.

2.2.6. Subsidy risks

Subsidies generally enable economic producers and consumers to avoid paying the genuine economic costs of various resources. The fossil fuel industry, for example, benefits from a variety of subsidies on a global basis. The assessment of the value of these subsidies can vary, depending on where the assessment comes from (International Monetary Fund 2013; OECD 2013; US Department of Energy, Energy Information Administration 2014). One recent assessment, published by the International Monetary Fund, suggests that global energy subsidies (on a post-tax basis, reflecting environmental externalities associated with fossil fuels) may run as high as $5.3 trillion in 2015 (Coaty et al. 2015). Nor is the fossil fuel industry alone. The Worldwatch Institute has estimated that global agricultural subsidies in 2012 totalled about $486 billion, with OECD countries and seven others (Brazil, China, Indonesia, Kazakhstan, Russia, South Africa, and Ukraine) representing about 80% of the total (Potter 2014). Within the OECD, agricultural subsidies totalled about $257 billion in 2012. The steel industry in China (Wong 2014) continues to receive generous subsidies from the Chinese government – not an unusual situation in China, admittedly. The Australian mining industry (Grunhoff 2013), particularly coal, appears to benefit considerably from government largesse. The list here is potentially large.

From an ESG perspective, the subsidy issue is far from clear cut. If one's over-riding goal is global GHG emission reductions, then subsidies for renewable energy sources such as wind and solar seems an eminently sensible idea – and this is exactly the type of situation where subsidies should be encouraged. By the same token, the current US agricultural subsidies for the sugar industry (Rozental 2014), for example, appear to make little sense, and appear to be environmentally destructive as well.

If governments are forced to become more aggressive in acting on anthropogenic climate change, they will likely come under increasing pressure to remove a range of fossil fuel subsidies of various kinds. This process, in fact, has already begun in some regions, and may be expected to accelerate following the Paris accord (Mills 2016). A similar concern can be raised about agricultural subsidies in areas where water depletion risks are increasing.

3. SA risks – ESG risks as financial risks

The approach described above may prove of assistance to investors attempting to come to terms with the implications of climate change (and other ESG issues). SA Risks represent one of the few current examples of how ESG risks can get granulated to a level that fits into a traditional approach to credit analysis. In fact, SA Risks fit conveniently into the Financial Risk section of the typical S&P or Moody's approach. They are quantifiable, and, if crystallized, significant. They can have material impacts on asset valuations, earnings and cash flows. The question is whether various SA Risks (and risks of asset value deterioration in general) will crystallize, and, if so, when. Just because value has been impaired, this does not automatically result in an immediate adjustment to valuations, or to classification as a SA. Asset impairments can have negative credit consequences, as a number of German utilities were reminded in 2013 when the industry experienced substantial asset impairments and write-downs (Ernst & Young 2014b). In fact, the utilities sector has accommodated the notion of SA risk for a number of years – it is probably the corporate sector where these risks are best understood by investors.

There are clear implications here for credit investors. S&P, in conjunction with Carbon Tracker, analysed the potential impact of some hypothetical scenarios on the credit quality of some North American oil companies (Standard & Poor's Rating Services 2013), some of which were of moderate size and some of which were major oil and gas producers. S&P found generally negative implications under some scenarios over the longer term for the majors, and the nearer term for the smaller companies. S&P drew the conclusion that 'the financial models that use past performance and creditworthiness may be insufficient to guide investors looking to understand the possible effects of future carbon constraints on the oil sector.'

This raises an important point about SAs (and asset risks in general) and where they come from – *they can emerge from a number of different sources*. These include (but are not limited to) the following:

(1) Regulatory risk,
(2) Carbon pricing risk,
(3) Adaption risk,
(4) Depletion risk,
(5) Global warming impacts on natural resources (oceans, forests), and
(6) Subsidy loss risk.

There are some obvious business and financial risks that we have not listed here. Of these, technology risk is probably the most obvious. This is because we include technology risk in our list of Business Risks employed in traditional credit analysis discussed earlier. Technology risk is a fundamental risk often faced by many businesses on a regular basis, and we assume that this risk is dealt with in the normal way in company and sector analysis. So, for example, the potential disruptive risk of Tesla's Powerwall home battery for the grid and the utilities that run it (Fares 2015), while potentially significant, does not need to be encapsulated in an ESG analysis – it should already have been assessed through traditional credit analysis. Technology risk is perhaps the best example of 'traditional' risks that can lead to asset write-downs or SAs.

Regulatory risk: Companies in general are never surprised when new regulations emerge; in fact, they are often involved in a dialog with the responsible regulatory parties and policymakers while the regulations are being developed. Still, from time to time, regulations are adopted, both nationally and internationally, that can raise costs on various sectors – the REACH program in Europe, for example, which attempts to apply a preventive approach to the environmental impacts of a range of chemicals (McCann 2010).

Perhaps the best recent example comes from the impacts of the US government's Clean Power plan. While not a surprise, and resisted fiercely by a number of industry and utility groups, these regulations are now in effect. Unsurprisingly, these are already having some impact on affected industries, particularly coalmining and coal-based utilities, and an increase in SAs are now recognized as being one of the significant results of these policy changes, along with others (Parker 2015).

Carbon pricing risk: An even broader and more stringent carbon price, in a globalized carbon market, could also have a significant impact on a number of industries in addition to the energy industry. Following the COP accords, this now appears less likely on a global scale. However, the COP21 agreements shift more of this effort to nations themselves, which may have a comparable impact. Any industry which is highly energy intensive, such as the cement industry, or the steel industry, could see its cost dynamics altered sufficiently such as to potentially strand older facilities.

Adaptation risk: This category refers to a broad range of costs, over a long time period, relating to the impacts of global warming on the physical environment, and the potential financial impact such risks may carry for governments and corporations. At present, these costs are generally being borne by governments and insurance companies. Over the longer term these costs have the potential to be significant, and certainly have the potential to create SAs on a broader scale than figures in current discussion of SAs.

We note that the concerns here will be for assets in general, and not necessarily SAs. In some cases of longer term Adaptation risks, the assets in question may already have been fully depreciated, so that the risk of SAs in particular may be relatively minor, or indeed non-existent. This does not, however, mean that asset risks in general are modest – replacing assets at any time has the potential to be costly, irrespective of asset values in financial statements. This may be especially true in the case of infrastructure affected by global warming risks.

Depletion risk: Resource constraints provide a salutary example of how traditional analysis can lead to some complacency, as we discussed previously. Note that what is at issue here is not necessarily the imminent depletion of resources to the point of non-availability. More relevant is the increased expense of recovering resources that are more difficult, for whatever reasons, to extract. So are there resources in actual danger of depletion? This depends on several factors – not just the natural stock of whatever the resource is, but also whether that resource will be the subject of accelerating demand from emerging middle classes in Asia and Latin America.

Water risks represent an example of Natural Capital Risks where depletion concerns are escalating sharply. Consumption trends appear to be running well ahead of the capacity of the water cycle to replenish adequate supplies, particularly in regions where global warming is expected to exacerbate water availability problems. This is even discounting the impact of what appear to be increasingly frequent droughts on a global basis – the current and severe droughts in Brazil, California and the western US, Australia, Colombia, Pakistan, and China, amidst a host of others. These droughts have their own economic impacts, of course; the World Economic Forum estimates that worldwide drought costs the global economy about $8–$12 billion annually – a figure that is relatively small in terms of the global economy, but one which can have significant regional impacts. Some industries use water much more intensively than others, and these industries are already, in many cases, engaging with the issues that surround concerns about longer term availability.

Global warming impact on natural resources: Like Adaptation risk, this is a longer tail risk than several of the others being discussed. In the case of Global Warming, the concern here is with the impacts of those physical impacts on other Natural Capital trends – particularly the depletion of forest, agricultural land, and other renewable resources, particularly water. Desertification of parts of the world may be accelerated under more draconian global warming scenarios. Again, we are dealing with uncertainties, but plausible uncertainties, and the uncertainty relates more to the scope and timing of these events, rather than to whether they will actually occur. And again, we may be dealing with broader categories of Asset Risk than SA risks alone. But for industries affected – agriculture and forestry in particular – the impacts here will be tangible.

Subsidy loss risk: Additionally, loss of subsidies has the potential to create SAs as well. As we discussed, a number of industries benefit from support from a number of government subsidies, and this is likely to vary by country. Nonetheless, some subsidies may be at risk in coming years as government finances remain strained and pressure for less-carbon intensive energy continues to increase. Again, predicting the timing of any such subsidy withdrawals is difficult, and the political and economic interests benefiting from subsidies are not likely to be relaxed about losing these subsidies.

For all of these examples, we can make a direct linkage from an ESG risk and its financial impact in the form of potential asset impairment. While the scope and timing of that financial impact might be unclear, analysts can at least begin to sketch out possible scenarios in the event that it appears that any of the factors mentioned look likely to materialize and have some significant sector impacts.

Notes

1. It should be clear that these analyses generally apply only to public companies for which information on various operating metrics are divulged. This may not necessarily be the case for non-public companies, a constraint that may hamper high-yield investors looking to employ ESG criteria. These investors generally operate in a universe, particularly in the US, populated by a significant number of non-public companies.
2. European Commission, *Interim Evaluation: Functioning of the European chemical market after the introduction of REACH*, March 2013.
3. These costs represented a spectrum of environmental impacts, including greenhouse generation (carbon dioxide, HFCs, nitrous oxide, methane, perfluorocarbons, sulphur hexafluoride), air pollution, water consumption, waste generation (including land and water pollution).
4. Which turns out to be not difficult at all—after a drilling suspension and the adoption of new regulations, Gulf of Mexico offshore drilling is growing strongly – including for BP, although it took a couple of years.
5. Note that recent commodity price declines, while significant, still leave commodity prices well above levels seen in the 1980–2000 period.

Disclosure statement

No potential conflict of interest was reported by the author.

References

Arens, C., L. Hermwille, N. Kreibich, F. Mersmann, W. Obergassel, H. E. Ott, and H. Wang-Helmreich. 2015. *The Paris Agreement: Kick-off for True Global Climate Cooperation.* Wuppertal: Wuppertal Institute for Climate, Environment and Energy.
Bawden, T. 2015. "Global Warming: Thousands Flee Pacific Islands on Front Line of Climate Change." *The Independent,* December 2.

Buhr, B. 2013. *Getting There from Here: An ESG/SRI Primer for Credit Investors.* London: SG Credit Research.

Buhr, B. 2014. *ESG for Credit Investors: Operational, Climate and Natural Capital Risks.* London: SG Credit Research.

Chartered Institute of Management Accountants, Ernst & Young, International Federation of Accountants, and Natural Capital Coalition. 2014. *Accounting for Natural Capital: The Elephant in the Boardroom.* London: Chartered Institute of Management Accountants.

Coaty, D., I. Parry, L. Sears, and B. Shang. 2015. *IMF Working Paper: How Large Are Global Energy Subsidies?* Washington, DC: International Monetary Fund.

Conniff, R. 2012. *When Civilizations Collapse.* New Haven, CT: Environment Yale, Yale School of Forestry and Environmental Studies.

Deloitte. 2014. *2014 Survey on Reputation Risk.* London: Deloitte Touche Tohmatsu Limited.

Energy Information Administration. 2014. *World Energy Outlook.* Washington, DC: US Department of Energy.

Englund, M. 2005. "Katrina's 'Unique' Economic Impact." *Bloomberg Businessweek*, September 6.

Ernst & Young. 2014a. *Business Risks Facing Mining and Metals 2014–2015.* New York: Ernst & Young.

Ernst & Young. 2014b. *Benchmarking European Power and Utility Asset Impairments; Impairments at a High in 2013 as Utility Sector Transforms.* New York: Ernst & Young.

European Commission. 2013. *General Report on REACH.* Brussels: European Commission.

Fares, R. 2015. "What Does Tesla's Powerall Really Mean for the Grid?" *Scientific American*, May 14.

Feuer, A. 2014. "Building for the Next Big Storm." *New York Times*, October 25.

Global Water Partnership. 2015. *China's Water Resources Management Challenge: The Three 'Red Lines'.* Stockholm: Global Water Partnership (GWP) Secretariat.

Goodell, J. 2013. "Goodbye, Miami." *Rolling Stone*, June 20.

Gordon, J. 2013. "Water: Critical Resource and Costly Risk for Miners." *Mineweb*, May 30.

Grunhoff, M. 2013. "Pouring More Fuel on the Fire; The Nature and Extent of Federal Government Subsidies to the Mining Industry." The Australia Institute, Policy Brief No. 52, June 2013.

Heck, S., and M. Rogers. 2014. *Are You Ready for the Resource Revolution?* New York: McKinsey Quarterly.

Hughes, D. 2014. *Drilling Deeper: A Reality Check on U.S. Government Forecasts for a Lasting Tight Oil & Shale Gas Boom.* Santa Rosa: California Post Carbon Institute.

"International Electronics Manufacturing Initiative, iNEMI White Paper: Rre Earth Metals." Current Status and Future Outlook, Second Quarter 2014.

International Monetary Fund. 2013. *Energy Subsidy Reform: Lessons and Implications.* Washington: International Monetary Fund.

IPCC. 2014. "Climate Change 2014: Synthesis Report." Contribution of Working Groups I, II and III to the Fifth Assessment Report of the Intergovernmental Panel on Climate Change. Geneva: IPCC.

Irwin, N. 2015. "One of the World's Most Powerful Central Bankers Is Worried about Climate Change." *The New York Times*, September 30.

Katz, A., and M C. Fisk. 2016. "Volkswagen Faces Billions of Dollars in Penalties." Bloomberg Business, January 5.

Kolbert, E. 2015. "The Siege of Miami." *The New Yorker*, December 21.

KPMG International. 2014. *A New Vision of Value: Connecting Corporate and Societal Value Creation.* London: KPMG International Cooperative.

Liebreich, Michael. 2015. "We'll Always Have Paris." *Bloomberg New Energy Finance*, December 16.

Litterman, Bob. 2013. "What is the Right Price for Carbon Emissions?" *Regulation*, Summer, June 11.

McCann, R. 2010. "Reach Regulation: The 5 Most Commonly Asked Questions." *Environmental & Energy Management News*, September 2.

McKinsey Global Institute. 2013a. *Resource Revolution: Tracking Global Commodity Markets.* New York: McKinsey & Company.

McKinsey Global Institute. 2013b. *Reverse the Curse: Maximizing the Potential of Resource-Driven Economies*. New York: McKinsey & Company.

Mills, R. 2016. "The Energy Subsidies dam has Finally Broken in the Middle East." *Abu Dhabi: The National*, January 3.

Moody's Investors Service. 2015. *Environmental Risks Heat Map Shows Wide Variations in Credit Impact Across Sectors*. New York: Moody's Investors Service.

OECD. 2013. *Inventory of Estimated Budgetary Support and Tax Expenditures for Fossil Fuels 2013*. Paris: OECD.

oekom research. 2014. *The Importance of Sustainability Criteria in Assessing Opportunities and Risk of Investing in Corporate Bonds*. Munich: oekom research AG.

Parker, M. 2015. "Half of World's Coal Output is Unprofitable, Moody's Says." *Bloomberg Business*, October 1.

Payne, S., T. Dutzik, and E. Figdor. 2009. *The High Cost of Fossil Fuels*. Boston, MA: Environment America.

Plummer, B. 2013. "Drought Helped Cause Syria's War. Will Climate Change Bring More Like It?" *The Washington Post*, September 10.

Potter, G. 2014. *Agricultural Subsidies Remain a Staple in the Industrial World*. Washington, DC: Worldwatch Institute.

Principles for Responsible Investment. 2013. *Corporate Bonds: Spotlight on ESG Risks*. London: PRI Association.

Principles for Responsible Investment. 2014. *Fixed Income Investor Guide*. London: PRI Association.

Prudential Regulation Authority, Bank of England. 2015. *The Impact of Climate Change on the UK Insurance Sector*. London: The Bank of England.

Risk Response Network, World Economic Forum. 2013. *Building Resilience in Supply Chains*. Geneva: World Economic Forum.

Rosemarin, A. 2010. "Peak Phosphorus, the Next Inconvenient Truth?" – 2nd International Lecture Series on Sustainable Sanitation, World Bank, Manila.

Rozental, Andrés. 2014. *How Will a Fight Over Sugar Affect U.S.-Mexico Trade Ties?* Washington, DC: The Brookings Institute.

Standard & Poor's Rating Services. 2013. *What a Carbon-Constrained Future Could Mean For Oil Companies' Creditworthiness*. London: Standard & Poor's Rating Services.

Standard & Poor's Rating Services. 2014a. *Carbon Constraints Cast A Shadow Over The Future Of The Coal Industry*. London: Standard & Poor's Rating Services.

Standard & Poor's Rating Services. 2014b. *Carbon, Coal and Credit: What's Next for the US's Clean Power Plan*. London: Standard & Poor's Rating Services.

Swiss Re Sigma. 2014. *Natural Catastrophes and Man-Made Disasters in 2013*. Zurich: Swiss Re.

TEEB for Business Coalition. 2012. *Natural Capital at Risk: a Study of the Top 100 Business Impacts*. London: Trucost PLC.

TEEB for Business Coalition. 2013. *Natural Capital at Risk: The Top 100 Externalities of Business*. London: Trucost PLC.

The 2030 Water Resources Group. 2009. *Charting Our Water Future: Economic Frameworks to Inform Decision-making*. Washington, DC: The World Bank.

Tollefsen, J., and K. R. Weiss. 2015. "Nations Adopt Historic Global Climate Accord." *Nature* 528: 315–316.

US Environmental Protection Agency. 2014. "Clean Power Plan Proposed Rule." Washington, DC: Federal Register: 34829–34958.

Vangsbo, P. N., E. Bulmer, and L. Barrow. 2014. *The Basic Elements of Natural Capital*. Copenhagen: Worldwatch Institute Europe.

Wong, Fayen. 2014. "Steel Industry on Subsidy Life-Support as Chinese Economy Slows." *Reuters*, September 18.

Ziffer, L. B. 2012. *Bankruptcy Trusts and Asbestos Litigation*. Chicago, IL: American Bar Association.

Climate change and the fiduciary duties of pension fund trustees – lessons from the Australian law

Sarah Barker, Mark Baker-Jones, Emilie Barton and Emma Fagan

ABSTRACT

Leading financial market participants increasingly recognise that issues associated with climate change present significant – if not unparalleled – financial risks. Regulatory, technological and social responses present particular issues for investment strategy, asset valuation, risk assessment and disclosure by institutional investors. However, governance literature has historically characterised climate change as a non-financial issue, at least over mainstream investment horizons. Accordingly, there has been little academic analysis of whether trustee directors are compelled, rather than permitted, to have regard to climate change risks. This paper seeks to advance the literature by examining the obligations of pension (or 'superannuation') fund trustee directors in Australia. The analysis focuses on the obligation to apply due care, skill and diligence under section 52A of the Superannuation Industry (Supervision) Act 1993 (Cth) (SIS Act). It concludes that a passive or inactive governance of climate change portfolio risks is unlikely to satisfy their duties: whether the inactivity emanates from climate change denial, honest ignorance or unreflective assumption, strategic paralysis due to impact uncertainty, or a default to a base set by regulators or investor peers. Considered decisions to prevail with 'investment as usual' may also fail to satisfy the duty if they are based on outdated methodologies and assumptions.

1. Introduction

[D]evelopment of the common law, as a response to changed conditions, does not come like a bolt out of a clear sky. Invariably the clouds gather first, often from different quarters, indicating with increasing obviousness what is coming. (Lord Justice Nicholls, Re Spectrum Plus Ltd (in liq) [2005] 2 AC 680, [33])

Historically, climate change has often been regarded as an ethical issue for investors – a 'non-financial environmental externality' secondary to, and largely inconsistent with, the investment imperative to maximise financial returns. However, the relationship between climate change issues and wealth generation continues to rapidly, and radically, evolve.

Many leading market stakeholders now recognise climate change as a material financial issue for institutional investors.

This paper considers the implications of this evolution for the duties of pension fund trustee directors, using the exemplar of Australian law. It hypothesises a non-executive director of the corporate trustee of a defined contribution (or 'accumulation') pension fund, acting in good faith and without a conflict of interest.

The analysis is structured as follows. Following this *Section one: Introduction*, *Section two* provides background and context to the analysis, with an overview of directors' fiduciary duties and contemporary developments in climate change science, economics and law. *Section three* examines the duties of trustee directors under Australian law, focusing on the duties to act in beneficiaries' best interests, and due care, skill and diligence under the *Superannuation Industry (Supervision) Act 1993* (Cth) (*SIS Act*). *Section four* analyses a range of governance approaches to climate change by trustee directors against the legal standard of care. *Section five* considers the practical corollaries of the legal analysis for fund governance, and concludes.

Australian law has been chosen as an exemplar for analysis for a number of reasons. First, the Australian private pensions and superannuation sector is significant on a global scale, with the world's fourth largest pool of funds under management at USD1.8 trillion (See Sullivan et al. 2015, 26). Second, the Australian duties regime is relatively rigorous by global standards, with a *heightened* standard of care applied to trustee directors from 1 July 2013.[1] Third, the 'safe harbour' defence that commonly applies to directors' duties of due care and diligence in common law jurisdictions, the 'business judgement rule', does *not* apply to decisions made by trustee directors under the SIS Act. Where it does apply under the broader Australian corporate governance laws, it operates as a notoriously narrow defence rather than as a rebuttable presumption of competence (Austin 2014). Fourth, Australia has emerged as an attractive class action jurisdiction, with low 'class' threshold requirements coupled with a rise in specialist plaintiff law firms and professional litigation funders (Sutton and Hobson 2013). Fifth, the portfolios of Australian superannuation funds are heavily weighted towards domestic equities (Sullivan et al. 2015, 26), which are in turn heavily exposed to climate change risks (with more than two-thirds of capitalised value of companies listed on the Australian Stock Exchange concentrated in the resource, energy and financial sectors).[2] Finally, the Australian trustee directors' duties laws share a common foundation with those in other common law jurisdictions (including, for example, the UK,[3] the US,[4] Canada,[5] Singapore[6] and New Zealand)[7] – that of fiduciary obligations, requiring both loyalty and competence.[8] Whilst jurisdictional specificities prevail, it is indicative of the degree of similarity in the substance of the duties that both legal experts and courts in these jurisdictions often cite the law of another in support of articulated principles.[9] Accordingly, whilst it is acknowledged that the points of material difference between trustee directors' duties in each jurisdiction warrant specific future research, Australian law has broad precedential potential in testing the content of such duties with regard to climate change – a test that may have implications for fund governance and investment strategy globally.

2. Section two – background to fiduciary duties and climate change

2.1. The role of pension funds and their boards

Pension funds have the primary objective of investing members' funds to provide them with benefits upon their cessation of work. This usually occurs upon retirement, but may also be triggered by death, disability or other form of incapacity to generate income. Globally, pension funds manage over USD40 trillion of funds on behalf of their beneficiaries (Willis Towers Watson 2015).

In Australia, pension (or 'superannuation') funds are administered by corporate trustees, who are in turn governed by a board of directors. Trustee boards are ordinarily responsible for fund investment *strategy* (setting their fund's investment beliefs, strategy and objectives, and risk appetite) and *oversight* (supervision of executive implementation of the investment strategy, and of risk management frameworks).[10] The task of selecting assets within portfolio risk/return parameters is customarily delegated to managers acting within defined mandates (Donald 2009).

Trustee directors are 'fiduciaries' of the corporations of which they are a director and, in some jurisdictions, of the beneficiaries themselves.[11] A 'fiduciary' relationship exists where one party (the fiduciary) exercises power and/or holds property on behalf of, and for the benefit of, another (the principal).[12] The term 'fiduciary' derives from the Latin *fiducia*, meaning trust, confidence and reliance.[13]

As fiduciaries, trustee directors are subject to a number of duties in the discharge of their governance functions, directed to ensuring their single-minded pursuit of the best interests of their principal. The fiduciary duties owed by professional directors of institutional investment trustees, in particular, are amongst the highest known to corporations and securities' laws.[14]

As acknowledged above, the particular wording with which fiduciary duties are expressed in statute, regulatory instruments and case law differs by jurisdiction. However, the laws across common law countries are all based on the same fiduciary precepts – that a fiduciary must act to prioritise the interests of their principal, and so has obligations of *trust and loyalty* (including, for example, duties relating to avoidance of conflicts, honesty and good faith and proper purposes, and the fettering of discretions) and *competence* (including duties to act with prudence and/or due care, skill and diligence).[15] This universal origin means that fiduciary laws are amenable to general comparison and restatement across jurisdictions.

In Australia, trustee directors of corporate trustees owe their obligations *both* to the corporation and, pursuant to the covenants implied in the fund governing rules under section 52A of the SIS Act, directly to the beneficiaries themselves.[16]

2.2. The evolving relationship between financial interests and climate change

One of the seminal debates in fund (and indeed broader corporate) governance relates to the scope of the trustees' duty to act in beneficiaries' 'best interests'. More particularly, the debate centres on whether trustee directors must only pursue best financial interests of beneficiaries or a broader set of interests and, in doing so, the extent to which *environmental, social, governance* (ESG) factors can be taken into account.[17] Historically, climate change has been posited as an ethical issue – a 'non-financial environmental externality' secondary to, and largely inconsistent with, the commercial imperative to maximise financial returns for a fund and its beneficiaries.[18]

However, the relationship between climate change and financial wealth continues to rapidly – and radically – evolve.

With the solidification of the relevant science,[19] leading market stakeholders are warning that the *economic and financial* consequences of climate change are significant – if not unparalleled – and are increasingly relevant to investment risk and strategy over mainstream investment horizons. Such risks and opportunities arise not only from the physical impacts of climate change,[20] but associated regulatory, technological and societal responses. Such responses notably include:

- *technological developments* – such as the relative competitiveness of renewable energy generation, decentralised distribution and battery storage, carbon sequestration technologies and electric vehicles and
- *new laws or policy developments* that may result in rapid re-pricing of assets.

For example, as on 1 January 2016, carbon emissions trading schemes were in operation in 35 countries, 7 cities and 13 provinces – including the EU and California, and foreshadowed to commence in China in 2017.[21] The trend towards emissions controls is only set to increase as 196 nations seek to implement their commitments under the Paris Agreement settled at COP21[22] on 12 December 2015.[23] Under that Agreement, the parties committed to (amongst other measures):

- a goal of limiting the 'increase in the global average temperature to well below 2°C above pre-industrial levels' and to pursue 'efforts to limit the temperature increase to 1.5°C above pre-industrial levels',[24] with provision for a 'five year review and ratchet' of the emissions reduction commitments pledged by each signatory country[25] and
- 'net zero' global emissions (i.e. where the anthropogenic emission of greenhouse gases is equally offset by their removal by sinks) in the second half of the century.[26]

The achievement of these goals will require a significant reduction to 'business as usual' emissions (which the IPCC estimates would result in warming of up to 4.8°C by 2100)[27] – even beyond the post-2020 emissions mitigation pledges made by the parties to the Paris Agreement (which, if implemented, would hold global warming to approximately 2.7°C).[28] Those reductions will, in turn, necessitate a significant transformation in the global economy to a low-carbon paradigm. The impacts will be both systemic and differentiated across all asset classes and industrial sectors, with particular risks of asset stranding in carbon-intensive industries.[29]

These developments have the potential to significantly impact on the investment strategy, asset valuation, risk assessment and disclosure activities of institutional investors. This has been recognised by such significant market stakeholders as, for example:

- the United Nations,[30] the International Monetary Fund,[31] the World Bank,[32] the World Economic Forum,[33] the Organisation for Economic Co-operation and Development[34] and the World Federation of Exchanges;[35]

- investor signatories to the Principles of Responsible Investment (representing USD59 trillion in assets under management, or close to half the total global institutional asset base),[36] the CDP (formerly the Carbon Disclosure Project),[37] and international investor groups on climate change in North America,[38] Oceania[39] and Europe;[40]
- leading mainstream financial sector participants such as French-based global insurance giant AXA,[41] the world's largest sovereign wealth fund, the Norwegian Government Pension Fund Global,[42] Standard & Poors,[43] BlackRock,[44] Mercer,[45] Schroders,[46] Boston Common Asset Management,[47] Willis Towers Watson[48] and Citi[49] and
- prominent scholars from academic institutions such as Cambridge University (Cambridge Institute for Sustainability Leadership, 2015), the University of Oxford[50] and Columbia University.[51]

This paper investigates the legal corollaries of the evolution of climate change from an 'ethical environmental issue' to material financial risk for the trustee directors of pension funds, by reference to their primary fiduciary duties.[52]

2.3. Prevailing literature and extensions offered by this paper

The question of 'liability' for climate change damages has historically revolved around responsibility for mitigation of emissions and its costs.[53] Australian Courts have yet to consider such a case.[54] A number of claims have been pursued in the US[55] and Europe[56] in tort (primarily alleging damage caused by the defendant's negligent failure to take reasonable precautions against the emission of greenhouse gases) and under the public trust doctrine. However, no claims again non-government defendants have yet been successful, or even proceeded to substantive hearing.[57] Claimants have faced significant barriers to standing and justiciability. Beyond this, duty and causation have been considered near 'insurmountable' evidentiary hurdles due to the disconnect between the global nature of emissions and their collective, cumulative effect, versus the localised nature of their impacts.[58]

More recently, however, the attention of litigants – and regulators – has begun to broaden from responsibility for emissions and their mitigation, to liability for a failure to adapt or safeguard against, climate change-induced harms. In September 2015 the Bank of England Prudential Regulation Authority (PRA) released its report on *The Impact of Climate Change on the UK Insurance Sector* (Prudential Regulation Authority 2015, 5). The report, which had a high-profile launch by Bank Governor Mark Carney at Lloyds of London, specifically warned of 'liability risk' exposures for the insurance industry under third-party liability policies (such as Directors' and Officers' insurance), including where: 'insured parties have not sufficiently accounted for climate change risk factors in their acts, omissions or decision-making … [including in the] governance of economic or financial issues that are material to corporate risk or return.'(Prudential Regulation Authority 2015, 59).

The PRA's warning is being borne out in practice. Damages claims for losses suffered due to a third party's failure to manage risks associated with climate change are beginning to emerge in the US. For example:

- In 2014 a subsidiary of global insurance giant Zurich issued a claim against local municipalities in the Chicago area, seeking compensation for business and residential policy holder payouts following Super Storm Sandy.[59] The claims essentially alleged that the municipalities had negligently failed to prevent flood-related damage by upgrading their stormwater and sewerage networks, despite their knowledge that climate change would cause more frequent and intense rainfall. The cases were later withdrawn.

- In June 2015, employee beneficiaries of the employee pension plans of the world's two largest publicly traded coal companies, Peabody Energy and Arch Coal, filed complaints against the trustee directors of the plans (amongst other defendants).[60] The claims, which do not actually use the terms 'climate change' or 'global warming', allege that the fiduciaries breached their duty of competence under the *Employee Retirement Income Security Act of 1974* (ERISA) – the duty of 'prudence' (amongst other duties) – by failing to consider financial risks that may be driven (at least in part) by climate change. Those risks are alleged to include a decline in the US coal industry, attributed to factors including increased competitiveness of renewable energy technologies, clean energy policies and more stringent emissions regulations.

- On 4 November 2015, the New York Attorney-General issued a subpoena to oil producer ExxonMobil as part of an investigation into whether its regulatory filings had misrepresented the financial risks to their business from climate change (ExxonMobil 2015). By the end of April 2016, no less than 20 State Attorneys-General had joined the investigation.

- On 9 November, the New York Attorney-General announced the resolution of similar investigations into Peabody Energy. The Attorney-General determined that Peabody had contravened State misleading disclosure laws[61] by filing annual reports that misrepresented the potential impact of emissions regulations on its business, and selectively disclosing only favourable International Energy Agency energy and fuel-mix projections from a range of scenarios.[62] The Attorney-General's investigation was settled pursuant to an 'Assurance of Discontinuance', in which Peabody Energy did not admit or deny the allegations of breach.

These claims, whilst untested before the courts, provide a stark demonstration of the potential capacity of prevailing tort and securities laws to apply in relation to corporate governance of risks associated with climate change. The scrutiny of this issue by the New York Attorney-General and Bank of England Prudential Regulation Authority is especially significant, for two reasons. First, it provides an authoritative recognition that issues associated with climate change can give rise to material financial risks and opportunities – of such breadth and significance that their negligent governance or misrepresentation to the market warrants regulatory intervention. Second, regulators' enforcement activities are not necessarily constrained by the need to prove causation, reliance and loss – factors commonly cited as significant barriers to private litigants claiming damages under similar causes of action.[63]

Despite these practical examples, the legal literature is only now beginning to interrogate the implications of climate change's evolution to a material financial issue under corporations and securities laws.[64] This paper adds to the emerging commentary in this area in the specific context of the duties of pension fund trustee directors. It is distinguishable from, and seeks to advance, the extant literature on trustee directors' duties in a number of important respects.

First, the extant academic analysis of trustee directors' duties with regard to environmental, social or governance issues has largely been focused on the scope of beneficiaries' 'best interests', and the extent to which those interests may include 'non-financial' concerns.[65] Historically, the literature has framed climate change as an 'ethical' or 'environmental' issue, whose impact on financial risk/return is largely immaterial.[66] Accordingly, its focus has been on the extent to which trustee directors are *permitted* to consider this issue (e.g. in 'tie-breaker' circumstances or when mandated under the fund's governing rules), rather than the circumstances in which they may be in *breach* of their duties for a failure to do so. Whilst this paper does reflect on the scope of the 'best interests' duty in Section Three, it takes a somewhat antithetical perspective on the intersection between climate change and wealth-based objectives. In particular, it posits climate change as a squarely *financial* concern: not only consistent with, but *prerequisite to*, portfolio wealth generation, and therefore imperative to discharge trustee directors' duties in pursuit of beneficiaries' best financial interests.

Second, having framed climate change as a material financial issue, this paper goes on to analyse the obligations of fund trustee directors under the duty of 'due care, skill and diligence'. Whilst the application of this duty to climate change issues has been flagged by some commentators, to date this has been at a high level and, in the academic literature, without consideration of the *heightened* standard of care applicable from 1 July 2013 pursuant to section 52A of the SIS Act.[67] The contribution of the paper to the trustee duties literature is further extended in Section Four, with its unique interrogation of those circumstances in which governance inaction on climate change may contravene directors' due diligence obligations.

3. Section three – the codification of trustee directors' duties under Australian law

3.1. Overview

In Australia, the primary duties of company directors are prescribed under the *Corporations Act 2001* (Cth) (*Corporations Act*). These duties reflect the universal fiduciary principles of both trust and loyalty (including the duty to act in good faith in the best interests of the corporation, and for a proper purpose (section 181)) and competence (the exercise of due care and diligence (section 180(1)). Additional statutory obligations apply to fund trustee directors under the SIS Act, again reflecting the primary fiduciary precepts. In particular, section 52A of that Act sets out a series of 'covenants' that are taken to be implied in the fund's governing rules.[68] These covenants include requirements to:

- '*perform the director's duties and exercise the director's powers as director of the corporate trustee in the best interests of the beneficiaries*' (section 52A(2)(c)) and
- '*exercise, in relation to all matters affecting the entity, the same degree of care, skill and diligence as a prudent superannuation entity director would exercise in relation to an entity where he or she is a director of the trustee of the entity and that trustee makes investments on behalf of the entity's beneficiaries*' (section 52A(2)(b)).[69] (emphasis added)

Trustee directors have concurrent duty obligations under the general law (including the significant bodies of trust law and equity), statute (including the Corporations Act and

State and Territory *Trustee Acts*) – although the obligations implied under the SIS Act generally prevail in the case of inconsistency.[70] These concurrent bodies of law are instructive in the interpretation of the SIS Act covenants.[71]

The application of each of these duties in the context of issues associated with climate change is considered below.

3.2. Climate change and best interests

Section 52A of the SIS Act implies a covenant in the fund's governing rules requiring trustee directors to exercise their powers in the 'best interests of the beneficiaries'.

Although yet to be specifically considered by the Australian courts, the 'best interests' of the fund (and beneficiaries) are ordinarily considered to be *financial* in nature.[72] This is for a number of reasons. First, there are consistent references throughout the SIS Act to 'contributions' and 'benefits'. One such reference is contained in the oft-cited 'sole purpose' test in section 62, which requires the trustee to ensure that the fund is maintained solely for the purpose of providing benefits to members (or their dependants) upon their retirement (or attainment of a specified age, or death).[73] Second, it would seem incongruous if a fund's outputs were of an inconsistent nature to the financial inputs contributed by its beneficiaries.[74]

The notion that such 'interests' are singularly financial is also supported by the 'authoritative exposition'[75] in *Cowan v Scargill*,[76] in which Megarry VC held that trustee governance should be directed to the pursuit of beneficiaries' financial wealth, and not motivated by the personal agendas of the directors. *Cowan v Scargill* is often cited as an authority for the proposition that trustee directors cannot have regard to environmental, social or political issues in their pursuit of beneficiaries' interests. However, as has been recognised in an extraordinary extra-curial comment on the case by Megarry VC himself (Rt Hon Sir Robert Megarry (1989), Chapter 6), such an interpretation is selective and incomplete without reference to later parts of the judgement. Those parts made clear that the single-minded pursuit of financial interests does not preclude the consequential achievement of extraneous social outcomes, and that environmental, social or political factors may themselves have a material impact on investment risk, strategy and performance.[77]

Governance of issues associated with climate change will therefore be consistent with the pursuit of a fund's best interests where, at a minimum, the issue presents a potentially material financial risk or opportunity for a fund, its operations or investments. In considering those interests, trustee directors cannot disregard the longer-term time horizon inherent in the function of its funds as vehicles for retirement savings.[78] Given the balance of significant stakeholder views on the economic risks and opportunities associated with climate change outlined earlier in this paper, it is increasingly clear that climate change is a material issue relevant to financial risk and return – and one whose impacts only compound over a longer-term time horizon. Of course, whether or not a particular issue associated with climate change has potentially material *consequences* in the circumstances, such that it warrants a strategic or risk management-based response, will be a matter that necessarily varies in each unique case. However, with the balance of economic authority summarised in Section Two, it is now arguable that a conclusion that the consequences for a fund were *not* materially financial would need to be based on specific, robust analysis, rather than assumption or default to historical norms.

Accordingly, a consideration of the risks (and opportunities) associated with climate change, driven by a concern for the fund's financial interests, is squarely consistent with the purposes for which trustee directors must apply their governance activities. The fact that the pursuit of those financial interests is associated with, or results in, an incidental positive environmental or social outcome, does not negate a purposive pursuit of wealth-based interests.[79]

Of course, consistent with Megarry VC's judgement in *Cowan v Scargill*, it would be a different matter if the governance conduct were directed to the achievement of interests that are extraneous to beneficiaries' best financial interests in retirement, such as a desire to support a particular environmental or social outcome. Subject to any relevant gloss in the fund's trust instruments, governance conduct that has such extraneous objectives (rather than as a secondary benefit in the pursuit of financial interests) may be beyond trustee directors' powers, and itself risk contravening their duties to act in the best interests of the fund.[80]

With climate change evolving to a material financial *issue*, trustee directors must then apply due care, skill and diligence in considering its impact on their fund – and, if a determination is made that the *impact* of the issue is material in a particular context, in overseeing the fund's strategic and risk management response.

3.3. Competence: due care, skill and diligence

As outlined above, the SIS Act requires that trustee directors exercise, in relation to all matters affecting the entity, the same degree of care, skill and diligence as a *prudent superannuation entity director* would exercise in the circumstances.[81] 'Prudent' in this context is not to be equated with an inherent conservatism *per se*, but a wise, careful and astute exercise of sound judgment.[82] A 'superannuation entity director' is defined as '*a person whose profession, business or employment is or includes acting as director of a corporate trustee of a superannuation entity and investing money on behalf of beneficiaries of the superannuation entity*'[83] – in other words, as a prudent *professional trustee*. This standard of care, which has applied since 1 July 2013, has yet to be judicially considered. Nor has its scope been subject of specific guidance from the relevant regulator, the Australian Prudential Regulation Authority.[84] However, the Explanatory Memorandum makes it clear that Parliament's intention was to *heighten* the standard of conduct expected of superannuation fund directors above that expected of the 'ordinary' prudent person – and above that of a director of an 'ordinary' trading company.[85] This is reinforced by the Courts' view that a '*more exacting*' standard of care is imposed on the 'reasonable' directors of registered schemes (as against that of 'ordinary' company directors) under the Corporations Act – by virtue of both their particular professional expertise, and the specific vulnerabilities of fund members.[86] Section 52 also contains additional covenants that require the corporate trustee to (amongst other things) formulate, review regularly and give effect to:

- an *investment strategy* for the whole of the entity and for each investment option offered, and to exercise due diligence in doing so (sub-section (6)). The trustee must have regard to factors such as risk (of making, holding and realising the investments in the strategy) and likely return in the context of the fund's investment objectives, cash flow and liquidity requirements, diversification, availability of reliable valuation information and other relevant matters and

- a *risk management strategy* that relates to the trustee's activities in the exercise of its powers or the performance of its duties and functions (sub-section (8)).

The covenants in relation to investment strategy and risk management apply to the corporate trustee itself, rather than its directors. However, the duties implied under section 52A(2)(f) of the SIS Act require trustee directors to exercise due care and diligence in ensuring that the corporate trustee discharges those obligations.

3.4. Content of the standard of care

In broad terms, a director's duties of due care and diligence hold them to a standard of competence that a *reasonable* person would apply in the particular circumstances. The Courts apply the subjective characteristics of the director and their corporation (including the type of company involved, the size and nature of its business or businesses, its Constitution, the composition of the board and its reserved powers, and whether the company is public or private)[87] to an objective assessment of whether the director has taken 'all reasonable steps to be in a position to guide and manage the company'.[88] This, in turn, requires a balancing of the magnitude of the relevant risk (its gravity, frequency and imminence) and the probability that it will crystallise, as against the expense, difficulty and inconvenience of any countermeasures, and the defendant's conflicting responsibilities.[89]

The Australian Courts are yet to specifically consider the import of pension fund trustee directors' 'heightened' standard of care implied under section 52A of the SIS Act – that of a prudent professional trustee director. However, guidance as to its requirements can be found in cases determined under the 'general' duty of due care and diligence in section 180(1) of the Corporations Act, along with those determined under the duty of due care and diligence applicable to directors of managed investment vehicles under section 601FC and 601FD of that Act.[90] Indeed, given both the particular responsibilities to which fund trustee directors are entrusted,[91] and the fact that their duties were *heightened* by introduction of section 52A, it is likely that any general conclusion regarding the application of the 'general' due care and diligence standard would apply *a fortiori* to fund trustee directors.[92]

The Courts have emphasised that there are certain minimum obligations inherent in the duty of care.[93] Applying those obligations in a pension fund governance context, the taking of 'all reasonable steps' in strategy and oversight requires trustee directors to:

(a) *educate*: proactively acquire and maintain an 'irreducible core' of knowledge and understanding of the fundamentals of their corporation (fund), including in relation to its activities, its financial position and regulatory environment. Relevant issues must be identified and understood to facilitate properly informed consideration. In the words of the High Court in *Finch v Telstra*:
   'If the consideration is not properly informed, it is not genuine';[94]

(b) *inquire*: proactively inquire into relevant matters: 'take a diligent and intelligent interest in the information available to them or which they might appropriately demand from the executives or other employees and agents of the company'.[95] Fund trustee directors may be obliged to make (or procure the making of) further inquiries where a 'dearth of material' on a relevant issue,[96] or a conflicting body of material,[97] is otherwise placed before them. This may include obtaining legal advice where they are unsure of the scope of their powers[98] and

(c) *critically evaluate*: bring this knowledge to bear in a process of active, 'careful', 'real and genuine consideration':[99] an independent and critical evaluation of the matters for which they are responsible.[100]

The discharge of trustee directors' duty of care must be both *dynamic and timely*. Contemporary circumstances may require that previous decisions are monitored and, where appropriate, reconsidered in the context of contemporary investment norms.[101] Such reconsideration is in fact directly contemplated in the language of section 52 of the SIS Act, under which corporate trustees are required to (amongst other things) 'regularly review' the investment strategy for the fund and each product offered, and the risk management framework. And relevant information must be acted upon with reasonable dispatch.[102]

In short, the critical inquiry into whether a trustee director has satisfied their duty of due care and diligence relates to the *process* of information gathering and deliberation, rather than a retrospective assessment of whether an optimum financial outcome was achieved.[103] In the words of Lord Nicholls, 'Not every error of judgment is regarded as a breach of trust or a failure to act reasonably'.[104] The fact that a fund underperforms – or even suffers a loss in value – is not in and of itself a breach of duty.[105] And whilst the process applied must be robust, it is not a 'counsel of perfection'.[106] Even under the 'lower' standard of care applicable prior to 1 July 2013, in *Alcoa* Nettle JA stated that the standard:

> does not mean that a trustee is required to do the impossible. Nor is it to suggest that a trustee is expected to go on endlessly in pursuit of perfect information in order to make a perfect decision. The reality of finite resources and the trustee's responsibility to preserve the fund for the benefit of all beneficiaries according to the terms of the deed means that there must be a limit.[107]

However, directors must identify, understand and carefully consider issues that are relevant to their fund in the pursuit of beneficiaries' financial interests upon retirement. Suffice that such issues must, at a minimum, include those relevant to investment strategy and risk management– activities for which corporate trustees are expressly responsible, and which trustee directors must ensure have been discharged by the trustee, with due care, skill and diligence.

So, within the general framework of this standard of care, what does the exercise of due care, skill and diligence by trustee directors in relation to climate change look like in practice?

4. Section four – due care and diligence on climate change

The question of whether a trustee director has satisfied their duty of care and diligence will, of course, turn on the facts of each case. The particular material risks and opportunities associated with climate change, and appropriate risk management treatments, will vary across asset classes, between funds, within particular portfolios and between different investment objectives. And they will need to be weighed against conflicting obligations (which may, for example, include diversification and liquidity requirements) and expenses.

It is therefore difficult to set out a universal 'checklist' of governance processes or actions that will satisfy the duty (or, conversely, that are unlikely to do so).[108] Conduct can, however, be considered across broad themes. This paper considers five categories of passivity or inactivity in relation to climate change risks as a proxy for conduct across the governance spectrum.[109] These include:

(a) *Denial* – overt denial or climate change scepticism;[110]
(b) *Honest ignorance* – a failure to consider the financial risks and/or opportunities for their portfolio presented by climate change (in general, or in relation to specific projects such as large direct investments);[111]
(c) *Uncertainty paralysis* – honest uncertainty regarding the speed, scope and scale of climate change impacts and its consequences for portfolio risk and strategy;[112]
(d) *Conscious cost/benefit* – an active decision to continue with 'investment as usual' where that decision is based on methodologies or assumptions that are not fit for purpose in the contemporary investment environment;[113]
(e) *Standards-based* – default to compliance with regulatory requirements, or industry standards/norms.[114]

The duty of due care and diligence is applied to each of these categories in turn, below. In each case, it is presumed that the directors are acting honestly, with a genuine subjective belief that their actions are directed to the pursuit of the best financial interests of the fund's beneficiaries.

4.1. Denial

A director may argue that they maintain a genuine view of climate change denial or scepticism which is both honestly held and based on robust information gathering and analysis.

However, such robust systems would also necessarily inform the director that key market stakeholders, including regulators, insurers, creditors, credit ratings agencies and analysts, are increasingly accepting of the financial risks associated with climate change. This presents, at a minimum, indirect stakeholder risks, and direct regulatory, litigation, market and insurance risks, that must be actively considered in the pursuit of wealth-based interests. Accordingly, a 'reasonable' trustee director simply cannot ignore the risks and opportunities presented by climate change or presumptively dismiss them as insignificant or improbable – *regardless of whether the prevailing consensus conflicts with their genuine personal ideologies.*[115] In fact, to do so may also contravene the trustee director's duty to act in the best interests of their fund and its beneficiaries under the principles set out by Megarry VC in *Cowan v Scargill.*[116]

4.2. Honest ignorance

It is increasingly difficult to argue that ignorance of climate change and its potential impacts on financial risk and return[117] is consistent with the conduct of any 'reasonable' trustee director. Directors have a positive obligation to apply an inquiring mind to their role, bringing to bear knowledge that they reasonably ought to have known about the fund and its investment and operational context.[118] It has been clearly established that the duty to exercise care and diligence is not limited by the director's subjective knowledge on material issues (or, by extension, any deficiencies in the breadth, depth or currency of that knowledge) – even where they are acting with subjective honesty and in good faith.[119] This may include 'failing to make relevant inquiries or raise matters which ought to have been raised'[120] or a failure to 'join the dots'.[121] And their knowledge and inquiry must be continuous and dynamic in the context of contemporary investment and market norms – with previous decisions monitored and, where appropriate, reconsidered.[122]

It is clear that an issue of such high-profile and potential economic significance as climate change – one that receives regular prominence in the mainstream financial press – would put a reasonable, yet uninformed, trustee director on notice that further inquiries were warranted.[123]

If analysis of the relevant risks and strategic opportunities were not being presented to the board, it would be incumbent upon the trustee directors to inquire of management (and/or relevant experts), and to query issues such as the impact on the fund's investment strategy, valuation methodologies and response capacity of the fund's risk management systems.[124]

4.3. Uncertainty paralysis

Pervasive *uncertainty* regarding the speed, magnitude and distribution of climate change impacts may cause paralysis in the formulation of an appropriate strategic response, leading to a 'wait and see' perseverance with 'investment as usual' until the way forward becomes clearer.[125]

A defendant trustee director would essentially submit that the magnitude and probability of the relevant risks were too difficult to estimate, and were outweighed by the competing resource demands of more quantifiable risks.

However, to adopt the language of Lord Nicholls:[126]

> Inertia is a comfortable pillow … Trustees … must positively consider what is the sensible course for them to adopt … it must be doubtful whether today they discharge their duty simply by letting matters be until some disquieting event happens.

More particularly, difficulty in quantifying relevant risks does not mean that trustee directors are relieved of their obligation to manage them. It is unlikely that pervasive uncertainty, *without more*, would justify 'investment as usual' (or doing very little) as 'all reasonable steps' in fund governance and oversight in the context of the evolving climate change risk landscape. Whilst the scope, scale and speed of climate change impacts remains inherently uncertain, the scientific, economic and political context has significantly evolved – particularly in a 'post-Paris' world with political consensus that global emissions must be radically reduced to keep average warming well below 2°C. It is no longer reasonably arguable that it is remote or 'unforeseeable' that issues associated with climate change will have a material impact on portfolio risk and return over mainstream investment horizons. And these risks only compound over the longer-term investment horizons inherent in retirement vehicles. Any argument that action on mitigation or adaptation is premature, or the range of potential climate futures so vast to be effectively 'unmanageable', may actually strengthen the imperative for investor action. The wealth-maximising response in such circumstances cannot be to 'do nothing', but to reduce exposure and vulnerability by proactively developing resilience, flexibility and adaptive capacity within portfolio management structures.

There are in fact a number of recognised economic methodologies that can be applied to augment traditional cost–benefit analysis under conditions of pervasive uncertainty. These include sensitivity analysis, stress testing and scenario planning, which allow the modelling of risks, opportunities and resilience across the range of plausible potential futures. Climate future scenarios that may reasonably be applied include, for example, the 'Representative Concentration Pathways' promulgated by the United Nations Intergovernmental Panel on Climate Change and emissions scenarios published by the International Energy Agency in its annual World Energy Outlook.[127]

4.4. Conscious cost/benefit

The 'conscious cost/benefit' scenario considers the situation where trustee directors, appreciating the range of potential climate futures and the risks and opportunities to their fund, make a *considered decision* that 'doing nothing' (or doing little) to adjust investment beliefs and objectives, asset allocations, risk management frameworks and manager mandates et cetera is the most advantageous investment strategy in pursuit of beneficiaries' best financial interests. In the context of the relevant legal test, the trustee director would submit that they had made an independent judgement after informing themselves as to the magnitude and probability of the relevant risks and opportunities, and having critically evaluated them in the context of available treatments and competing resource demands. Indeed, trustees must also consider conflicting obligations such as diversification and liquidity requirements. Factors such as the need for adequate diversification and historical growth and/or yield-based outperformance of equities in fossil fuel-intensive industries, are in fact commonly advanced as reasons as to why a fund should stay invested in such stocks.[128] For a given fund, it may be that the costs of current action on climate change adaptation measures are wholly disproportionate to the risk and expected benefits. This may be particularly relevant for passively managed products where cost containment is a key consideration.

The fact that trustee directors determine that the costs of a proactive investment strategy or risk management treatment on climate change outweigh their benefits is not a breach of duty. The law is not concerned with substantive judgements or outcomes *per se*, but the robustness of the information gathering and deliberation process on which they are based. But it does mean that judgements must be defensible on the basis of robust, sophisticated and fit-for purpose modelling, based on the unique forward-looking risks and opportunities associated with climate change. In short, 'investment as usual' *methodologies* may now themselves be insufficient to demonstrate that a trustee director was adequately informed and took 'all reasonable steps' in their assessment and governance of future climate change risks.[129] For example, such analysis is likely to be open to challenge if it does not consider factors such as: the limitations of historical data as a predictor with climatic and economic scenario modelling; the risks of *maladaptation* from short-term investment strategies – that is, strategies that may deliver short-term economic gains but exacerbate vulnerability to expected climate change impacts in the medium to long term (such as direct investment in carbon-intensive infrastructure with no regard to treatment of 'stranded asset' risks); and the likelihood that climate change impacts will not be incremental or gradual, but occur in dramatic 'step-changes' (which may result in the rapid re-pricing, and decline in liquidity, of assets in carbon-intensive industries – a disorderly market response leading to a 'rush for the exit').[130] The contention that passively managed investments cannot be 're-risked' for issues associated with climate change is also increasingly open to challenge. Leading providers of indexed fund management services such as MSCI and Amundi now offer low-carbon passive investment options, with performance competitive with (and in fact often exceeding) that of general indices.[131] Similarly, green bonds are commonly offered at the same coupon (or rate of return) as 'standard' debt instruments.[132]

Accordingly, it is unlikely that a decision to persevere with an 'investment as usual' strategy would be considered duly diligent if that conclusion is a product of conventional methodologies and assumptions that are increasingly inappropriate for their forward-looking purpose.

4.5. Standards-based

The duty of due care and diligence is not a counsel of perfection. Nor does it 'occur in a vacuum'.[133] With the standard of conduct tested against the hypothetical 'reasonable prudent professional trustee', trustee directors may assert that their actions conform with 'custom' or institutional investor norms (or, crudely: 'we did no less than any other mainstream fund'). Similarly, they may argue that climate change is a *policy* matter within the exclusive remit of government, and that their duty of care was discharged by ensuring corporate adherence to relevant statutory obligations. In the context of the duty of due care and diligence, this would equate to an argument that a response *beyond* that mandated by law, or in advance of their peers, would be so expensive, difficult or inconvenient as to outweigh the magnitude of the relevant risks.

Governance conduct (or inaction) that proceeds on this basis alone is unlikely to discharge the trustee directors' duty of due care and diligence, for a number of reasons. First, 'acceptable' or 'usual' practice will be relevant, but not decisive, in determining the conduct of a 'reasonable' trustee director. And whilst necessary, it will not be sufficient. In any event, it is not that the legal, corporate governance or management literature sanctions a weak governance response to climate change risks. To the contrary, the significant – and ever-increasing – literature outlined in this paper supports a proactive approach to the management and exploitation of environmental risks (including climate change), and warns of the economic consequences of the failure to do so. Second, industry customs and norms are inherently dynamic. There can be no doubt that the trajectory of investment risk from the impacts of climate change is trending upwards, commensurate with the solidification of the science and the physical and economic consequences of global mitigation inaction to date. The *extent* of the strategic response it demands must therefore continue to increase accordingly, such that reliance on historical benchmarks – or even current industry norms – will not necessarily suggest that 'all reasonable steps' have been taken. Third, to satisfy their duty of care and diligence a trustee director will also need to establish that they formed an independent judgement, borne of their own critical evaluation of the relevant information in the context of their *own fund's* portfolios, products, investment beliefs, asset allocations, risk appetite and investment objectives. It will not be sufficient to point to the actions of other funds alone to establish that the directors were active in their engagement with the relevant material risk to *their* fund. Risks and risk treatments are highly context-specific, and therefore unique to each portfolio and product. This is not to say that trustee directors should not observe the adaptation actions and experiences of other leading funds, and learn and build from them. Rather, the inaction of others is unlikely to provide an adequate justification for their fund's own lack of strategic progress.

Finally, even if a rigid delineation between 'public policy' and private responsibilities was conceptually robust or practically feasible, trustee directors do not discharge their statutory duties by merely ensuring that the fund invests 'legally'. A strategy to 'comply with minimum legal obligations' is not a good proxy for the pursuit of beneficiaries' best financial interests: necessary in a *conformance* context, but not sufficient in relation to performance.

4.6. A note on the 'business judgement rule' defence

The duty of care and diligence does not render trustee directors liable for every mistake or error of judgement. Courts are reluctant to second-guess the merits of commercial decisions that are made in good faith, which inherently involve the exercise of judgement and the taking of calculated risks.[134] This gives rise to one of the seminal tensions in corporate governance law: that between the desirability to hold directors accountable for their failures, and judicial reluctance to second-guess good faith commercial decisions.[135] A balance for this tension appears in the form of the 'business judgement rule' defence to breach of directors' duties of competence. Such rules are intended to provide directors with a 'safe harbour' from personal liability in relation to honest, informed and rational decisions relating to their corporation's business.[136] In Australia, this principle has been codified as a defence to the duty of due care and diligence under section 180(2) of the Corporations Act. However, *the SIS Act contains no equivalent defence for fund trustee directors.*

In any event, this oft-raised, but rarely successful,[137] defence would be unlikely to assist defendant directors whose governance of climate change falls within the categories discussed above, under Australian law. This is because those failures can generally be categorised as *procedural* in nature – either a failure to consider a material issue, to remain appropriately informed, or to apply appropriate methodologies.[138] In contrast, the business judgement rule only applies to protect governance failures of a *substantive* nature – where the director makes an active decision that a matter relating to the performance of the corporation is in its best interests, having formed a rational belief upon critical evaluation of appropriate information.

4.7. Conclusion – due care, skill and diligence

The sharp evolution in the relationship between climate change and wealth-based interests suggests that, as with any material financial risk, an inactive or passive approach to its governance may be inadequate to satisfy trustee directors' SIS Act duty of due care, skill and diligence. This includes inactivity emanating from climate change denial, honest ignorance or unreflective assumption, paralysis caused by the inherent uncertainty of the magnitude and timing of relevant impacts, or a default to a base set by regulators or investor peers. Even considered decisions to prevail with 'investment as usual' are increasingly unlikely to satisfy the duty, particularly if they are the product of a conventional methodology that fails to recognise the unprecedented investment challenges presented by an erratically changing climate, and the market responses it provokes.

The practical corollaries of this analysis for fund governance, and related areas warranting future research, are considered below.

5. Section five – corollaries and conclusion

5.1. Practical corollaries for fund governance

The analysis above suggests that trustee directors are duty-bound to proactively engage with the issue of climate change in their governance of the fund. Climate change has a direct impact on the strategy and oversight functions for which trustee directors are responsible – from the setting of fund investment beliefs, investment strategies and objectives, to the supervision of the policies and procedures by which they are implemented, and risk management frameworks.[139] Although the nature of 'all reasonable steps' in the governance of climate change issues will depend on the specific context of each fund, a 'reasonable prudent professional trustee director' may be expected to inquire into, actively consider and constructively evaluate issues including:

- current portfolio climate change risk exposures (including carbon reserve exposures, risk exposures of portfolio assets to the physical, transition and liability risks associated with climate change);
- climate change impacts on, and corollaries for, fund investment beliefs and policies, investment strategy (including in stress testing scenarios and diversification), strategic asset allocation and portfolio construction, risk/return objectives, fund valuation methodologies and assumptions, manager mandates and asset selection processes/criteria;
- the existence and effectiveness of fund processes directed to ensuring that the fund (and its advisors) appropriately considers material climate change risks and opportunities and
- appropriate risk management responses in the context of the fund's unique circumstances. Such responses range far beyond a blunt 'invest–divest' from companies with high absolute or relative stranded asset exposures, to active stewardship and engagement (both pre- and post-investment), hedging and tilts. And they may differ across products with active versus passive management, and across or within asset classes.[140]

Even if the operational aspects of these functions are delegated to management or external advisors, trustee directors must demonstrate diligence in their *oversight*.[141] A mere presumption that any material financial issues associated with climate change will be covered off by managers under existing delegations or mandates is unlikely to be sufficient.[142] Rather, trustee directors must proactively monitor delegates' adherence to, and the integrity and effectiveness of, board-approved policies, processes, systems and frameworks.[143] The board must receive, and interrogate, reports from management delegates on point.[144] And if it is not clear from those reports whether and how the frameworks have responded to the evolution of climate change into a material financial issue, the duty of due care and diligence makes it incumbent on directors to *inquire*.

This does *not* mean, however, that fund trustee directors are duty-bound to decarbonise their portfolios, or that environmental sustainability must be universally prioritised. The conduct of trustee directors must remain directed towards a pursuit of beneficiaries' best interests – the provision of benefits upon their retirement. And, in pursuing those interests, the risks and opportunities associated with climate change must be balanced against other relevant considerations, such as liquidity and cash flow requirements, adequate diversification, taxation consequences and cost.

Nor does it mean that the mere fact that a fund, or particular product offered by it, sustains loss – even catastrophic loss – will not be sufficient to establish a breach of duty by its trustee directors.[145] Trustee directors will not be liable merely because the passage of time and/or benefit of hindsight reveals a particular investment strategy to be poor. Rather, the relevant examination is of their conduct in the *context* of that governance decision – deficiencies in the information systems applied, manager mandates or supervision, methods of evaluation or quality of monitoring and oversight – that may bring into question whether their heightened standard of care has been discharged.

5.2. A note on related areas of further research

In addition to their governance of risk and strategy, trustee directors are also ultimately responsible for *disclosures* made by their funds. There is a significant body of authority holding that directors may breach their duty of care and diligence where they cause,[146] permit[147] or fail to take reasonable steps to prevent[148] their corporation from making misleading statements to the market (including misrepresentation by silence or non-disclosure).[149] Although yet to be tested in a fund context in Australia, it is not inconceivable that a material misstatement of a fund's management of the risks and opportunities associated with climate change (e.g. in its annual reports to members or statutory documents such as 'Product Disclosure Statements') would be actionable against its trustee directors as a failure to exercise due care, skill and diligence. Such claims in fact form part of the complaints against the trustee directors of the Arch Coal and Peabody Coal employee pension funds on foot in the US.[150] The liability of trustee directors for misleading fund disclosure on exposure to, or management of, risks associated with climate change is a subject that warrants significant additional research beyond the scope of this paper.

Finally, despite the conclusions of this paper in relation to conduct that is unlikely to satisfy trustee directors' statutory duties, barriers to *enforcement* of breach, such as class standing and leave, proof of causation, reliance and loss must be acknowledged, and warrant significant further research. As a preliminary observation, these issues may present far lower barriers for a claim alleging breach of trustee directors' duties (whether under statute or common law) than those faced by claims based on harm caused by a failure to mitigate emissions. In short, this is because the claim's focus 'shift[s] … from the overwhelming complexity and non-justiciability of global warming science to a single [fiduciary's] preventable creation of foreseeable harms' (Cosman 2008). The potential for enforcement may also be assisted by the preparedness of regulators such as the New York Attorney-General to take action, as discussed in Section Two above.

5.3. Conclusion

> [There is a] bias to retrospection amongst regulators, policy makers, and academics – focus-
> ing on near-term data and clinging to the notion that markets [are] perfectly efficient, despite
> a wealth of evidence to the contrary. Any system built on a mismatch between expectations
> and actual outcomes is inevitably going to be prone to crisis.
> Edward Waitzer and Douglas Sarro, 'Fiduciary Society Unleashed: The Road Ahead for the
> Financial Sector'. (The Business Lawyer, 9 August 2014, 1083–1084)

Leading market stakeholders increasingly recognise that climate change presents unparalleled risks and opportunities across the global economy. As its impacts intensify, the portfolios of reactive funds will be far more vulnerable to tail losses in the inevitable market
realignment. An inactive or passive governance stance increasingly compromises investors'
ability to take advantage of potential opportunities whilst managing material climate
change risks, and is thus inimical to the maximisation members' retirement benefits.

A consideration of the risks (and opportunities) associated with climate change, driven
by a concern for beneficiaries' financial interests, is squarely consistent with trustee directors' statutory (and broader fiduciary) duties. The fact that the pursuit of those financial
interests is associated with, or results in, a positive environmental or social outcome does
not negate a purposive pursuit of wealth-based interests.

In considering particular implications of this material issue for their fund, trustee directors must exercise due care, skill and diligence. With the particular vulnerabilities of beneficiaries' retirement savings, it is appropriate that the SIS Act standard to which trustee
directors are tested – that of a prudent professional trustee – is particularly intense. The
duty of due care and diligence is concerned with robust governance process, to which
proactivity and engagement are central. At a minimum, trustee directors must maintain
an awareness of material issues, and inquire of relevant experts as appropriate. Their independent judgement must be brought to bear in the process of critical evaluation. The effectiveness and implementation of associated policies and delegations must be overseen. And
that process must be dynamic and continuous.

Within this framework, passive or inactive governance of climate change portfolio risks
by trustee directors is unlikely to satisfy the covenant of due care, skill and diligence
implied under section 52A of the SIS Act. This includes inactivity emanating from
climate change denial, honest ignorance or unreflective assumption, paralysis caused by
the inherent uncertainty of the magnitude and timing of relevant impacts, or a default
to a base set by regulators or investor peers. In addition, even considered decisions to
prevail with 'investment as usual' are increasingly unlikely to satisfy the duty, particularly
if they are the product of a conventional methodology that fails to recognise the unprecedented investment challenges presented by an erratically changing climate, and the market
responses it provokes.

Investment strategies and risk management, by their nature, are not functions that can
be optimised post-facto. They are complex issues, and unique to each fund, each portfolio
and each asset. It should therefore come as no surprise that a prudent, professional 'diligence' in their governance requires more than a blunt, disengaged, uninformed response.
Investment beliefs can only be set, strategy determined and risk managed, on the best
information currently available. And the best strategy is not, and cannot be, to fail to
actively govern pension fund portfolios for the reality of a changing climate.

Notes

1. See, for example, discussion in Ford and Lee (2015) [9.510].
2. Including 28% metals and mining, 17% other materials and industrials and 25% financials: ASX, *Listing on ASX – Gateway to the resource capital of Asia*, Sydney, 2013. This includes many companies listed in the Forbes 'Global 50', including BHP Billiton, the Commonwealth Bank, Westpac and NAB. See also discussion in The Climate Institute (2015, 11).
3. See sections 172 and 174; *Pensions Act 1995*, sections 33(1), 35, 36(2); *Trustee Act 2000*, section 1.
4. See Delaware General Corporation Law and In re Caremark International Inc. Derivative Litigation, 698 A.2d 959 (Del. Ch. 1996); Uniform Prudent Investor Act §§2(b), (f), 7B U.L.A. 20 (2006); Employee Retirement Income Security Act 29 U.S.C. § 1104(a).
5. See the *Canada Business Corporations Act* R.S.C. 1985, c. C-44; provincial Trustee Acts – for example, *Trustee Act* R.S.O. 1900, c.T23, s27(1) (Can), amended by S.O. 1998, c.18, sched. B, s16(1); and provincial Pension Benefit Acts – for example, *Pension Benefits Standards Act* 2015, section 35(3)(b). It is noted that the legal system in Quebec province is based on the French civil law, although federal statutes based on common law precepts do apply in that province. See generally Waitzer and Sarro (2014), 1081–1116; Gold and Scotchmer (2015).
6. See *Companies Act*, Cap 50 section 157(1); *Securities and Futures Act*, Cap 289.
7. See *Companies Act 1993*.
8. See, for example, Hansell and Hazell (2004); Gregory, Grapsas, and Powell (2013); Sheehy and Feaver (2014) 347; Sheehy (2015). For a discussion of the points of difference between Australian duties laws and those in other common law jurisdictions, see Redmond (2012).
9. See, for example, Law Commission of England and Wales, *Fiduciary Duties of Investment Intermediaries* (2014) Law Com 350 (at 30, 34, 35, 37, 40, 42, 43, 44, 46, 105, 114, 171, 186, 187, 190,191 and 196) in which the Commission's review and report on the fiduciary duties of investment intermediaries in the UK was informed by statutory and judicial authorities from the US, New Zealand, Australia and Canada; *Hospital Products Ltd v United States Surgical Corporation & Ors* (1984) 55 ALR 417 (at 431, 433, 436 and 466) in which the High Court of Australia cites authorities from the UK, the US, New Zealand and Canada in support of the content of fiduciary obligations (albeit not in a pension fund context) (including UK decisions *Phipps v Boardman* [1967] 2 AC 46 at 123 and *NZ Netherlands Society "Oranje" Inc v Kuys* [1973] 1 WLR 1126 ; [1973] 2 All ER 1222 and *Tate v Williamson* (1866) 2 Ch App 55 at 61, United States decision *Flexitized, Inc v National Flexitized Corporation* (1964) 335 F (2d) 774, New Zealand decision *Coleman v Myers* [1977] 2 NZLR 225 and Canadian decisions *Canadian Aero Service Ltd v O'Malley* (1973) 40 DLR (3d) 371), *McLeod and More v Sweezey* [1944] 2 DLR 145 and *Jirna Ltd v Mister Donut of Canada Ltd* (1971) 22 DLR (3d) 639; affirmed (1973) 40 DLR (3d) 303; *Nestle v National Westminster Bank PLC* [1993] 1 WLR 1260, at 1268–69, in which the UK Court of Appeal cited the Canadian case of *Guerin v The Queen* (1984) 13 D.L.R. (4th) 321 as authority in relation to trustee obligations to follow a proper investment policy; and the seminal UK case of *Cowan v Scargill* [1985] Ch 270, 286–287, in which Megarry VC drew from two US cases in considering the duties of public pension fund trustees: *Blankenship v Boyle* 329 F Supp 1089 (1971) and *Withers v Teachers' Retirement System of the City of New York* 447 F Supp 1248 (1978). It is also notable that when section 52 (applicable to the trustee itself) was introduced, the Treasurer expressed an intention to follow the standard of the 'prudent expert' set by the United States under the Employment Retirement Income Security Act – see *Strengthening Super Security: New Prudential Arrangements for Superannuation* (AGPS, Canberra, October 1991), 10.
10. For a general overview of the role of boards in the governance of institutional investors, see a recent speech by Andrew Bailey, Chief Executive Officer of the Bank of England Prudential Regulation Authority: Andrew Bailey, *Governance and the Role of Boards*, transcript of speech given to the Westminster Business Forum, London, 3 November 2015. See also, for example, Amado and Adams (2012); Bainbridge 2012, 43.

11. See, for example, Wolters Kluwer CCH, *Australian Master Superannuation Guide,* (at 31 March 2015) ¶3–100; Wolters Kluwer CCH, *Australian Superannuation Commentary* (at 23 November 2015) ¶2–810.

12. See, for example, under Australian law Murphy JA (with whom McLure P and Buss JA agreed on this point) in *Streeter v Western Areas Exploration Pty Ltd [No.2]* (2011) 29 ACLC ¶11–012, at 364–365: 'The critical feature of a fiduciary relationship is that the fiduciary under-takes or agrees to act for or in the interest of another person. The fiduciary acts in a repre-sentative character', applying *Hospital Products Ltd v United States Surgical Corporation* [1984] HCA 64; (1984) 156 CLR 41, 96–97; *Pilmer v The Duke Group Ltd (in liq)* [2001] HCA 31; (2001) 207 CLR 165, 196–197 [71]; *John Alexander Tennis Club v White City Tennis Club* (2010) 241 CLR 1, [87] (French CJ, Gummow, Hayne, Heydon, and Kiefel JJ). Under United States law, see REST 3d TRUSTS § 2, comment b: '[A] person in a fiduciary relationship to another is under a duty to act for the benefit of the other as to matters within the scope of the relationship.'

13. See, for example, Morwood 2001, 56; Edelman 2014.

14. *Australian Securities Commission v AS Nominees* [1995] 133 ALR 1, 13–14; *Bartlett v Bar-clays Bank Trust Co Ltd (No's 1 and 2)* [1980] Ch 515, per Brightman LJ at 534; *Finch v Telstra Super Pty Ltd* (2010) 271 ALR 236 at 254. See generally Noel Davis and Michael Chaaya, LexisNexis Butterworths, *The Law of Superannuation in Australia,* vol 1 (at Service 28) [13–120]; Tennent (2009); REST 3d TRUSTS § 2, comment b, see §§ 70–84, and Restatement Second, Trusts §§ 169–185.

15. See, for example, *Invensys Australia Superannuation Fund Pty Ltd v Austrac Investments* (2006) 198 FLR 302 at 324. See generally discussion in Richardson 2012, Chapter 5.

16. See also discussion of the direct liability of trustee directors to beneficiaries prior to the enact-ment of section 52A in Hanrahan (2008).

17. See, for example, discussion in Clark and Viehs (2014); Donald, Ormiston, Charlton 2014; Drummond (2010); Langbein and Posner (1980); Leigh (1997); Nicholls of Birkenhead (Lord) (1996); Richardson (2007); Richardson 2012, 69; Solomon 2009; Margaret Stone (Justice) (2007); Thomas (2008); Thornton (2008).

18. Notable exceptions include Clark and Viehs (2014); and Richardson 2007, 2012, 162–163 and 69.

19. See, for example, United Nations, Intergovernmental Panel on Climate Change (IPCC), AR5, *Climate Change 2013: The Physical Science Basis – Headline Statements from the Summary for Policymakers,* Working Group I Contribution to the IPCC Fifth Assessment Report (IPCC, 27 September 2013); International Energy Agency, *International Energy Agency* (2015) http://www.iea.org/; World Meteorological Organisation (2013); NASA, *Natural Aeronautics and Space Administration,* https://www.nasa.gov/

20. The physical impacts of climate change include both 'catastrophic events' such as the increased variability and extremity in weather patterns (including in the frequency, distri-bution and duration of extreme weather events) and 'gradual onset' impacts such as the increase in global average temperatures, rising sea levels due to water expansion and ice melt, and alteration of regional precipitation patterns. These impacts, in turn, can cause inun-dation of coastal and estuarine areas, regional droughts, ocean acidification, shifts in pro-ductive and habitable lands, and extinction of species of flora and fauna – see, for example, the scientific authorities set out in n19 above.

21. International Carbon Action Partnership, *Emissions Trading at a Glance* (2015) https://icapcarbonaction.com/en/?option=com_attach&task=download&id=289. China has announced plans for nation-wide emissions trading from 2017 (UNFCCC, *Moving towards national wide domestic emissions trading scheme in China,* (2015) https://cdm.unfccc.int/filestorage/e/x/t/extfile-20151005182716706-P7_2_ETS_in_China_SinoCarbon_Tang_Jin.pdf/P7_2_ETS%20in%20China_SinoCarbon_Tang%20Jin.pdf?t=bFd8bzBxMWp0 fDByDZ6G8qAcBBFTzpFnb4na)

22. 'COP21' refers to the 21st Conference of the Parties to the United Nations Framework Con-vention on Climate Change.

23. *Paris Agreement (FCCC/CP/2015/L.9/Rev.1).*
24. *Id.,* Article 2(1)(a).
25. *Id.,* Article 4(3) and (9).
26. *Id.,* Article 4(1).
27. IPCC, Climate Change 2014 Synthesis Report, *Summary for Policy Makers,* 10.
28. Framework Convention on Climate Change, Conference of the Parties, Paris, 12 December 2015 http://unfccc.int/resource/docs/2015/cop21/eng/l09r01.pdf.
29. Association for Sustainable and Responsible Investment in Asia (*ASRIA*) and Chubb Insurance Group (*Chubb*), *Climate Governance in Asia: Considerations for Corporate Directors and Officers*, 2015, 20–29, 32–33; Boston Common Asset Management, (2015); Carbon Tracker and the Grantham Research Institute, (2013); Rick Stathers and Alexia Zavos, (2015), 4.
30. See, for example, Sullivan et al. 2015; United Nations, 'PRI Climate Change Strategy Project' (Discussion Paper: Reducing Emissions Across the Portfolio, United Nations, July 2015).
31. See, for example, International Monetary Fund, *Climate, Environment, and the IMF*, Factsheet, 16 September 2015.
32. See, for example, World Bank, *Economics of Adaptation to Climate Change: Synthesis Report,* (2010) https://openknowledge.worldbank.org/handle/10986/12750.
33. See, for example, World Economic Forum, *The Global Risks Report 2015* http://reports. weforum.org/global-risks-2015/, in which six out of the top ten 'Global Risks in Terms of Likelihood and Impact' were associated with climate change – including a failure of climate change adaption, water crises, biodiversity loss and ecosystem collapse, extreme weather events, natural catastrophes and energy price shocks.
34. See, for example, OECD 2015.
35. See World Federation of Exchanges, *World Federation of Exchanges Visions,* World Federation of Exchanges http://www.world-exchanges.org/home/index.php/about/about-wfe-vision.
36. Principles of Responsible Investment, *About the PRI Initiative*, http://www.unpri.org/about-pri/about-pri/; Friede, Busch and Bassen (2015), 210.
37. CDP works with 822 institutional investors holding USD95 trillion in assets to help reveal the risk in their investment portfolios – see https://www.cdp.net/en-US/Pages/About-Us.aspx.
38. The Investor Network on Climate Risk represents 110 institutional investors with more than USD13 trillion in assets under management – see http://www.ceres.org/investor-network/incr.
39. The Investor Group on Climate Change Australia/New Zealand, which represents 60 institutional investors with more than USD1 trillion in assets under management – see http://www.igcc.org.au/about.
40. The Institutional Investors Group on Climate Change represents 120 institutional Investors with more than €13 trillion under management – see http://www.iigcc.org/.
41. See, for example, AXA, *AXA and Climate Risks* (July 2015) https://cdn.axa.com/www-axa-com%2F1b503ed0-104e-4fe1-9b4f-cf6ea62844ae_axa_and_climaterisks_2014.pdf.
42. See, for example, Norges Bank, *Financial Risks Associated with Climate Change* (February 2015) http://www.nbim.no/en/transparency/submissions-to-ministry/2015/financial-risk-as-a-consequence-of-climate-change/.
43. See, for example, Standard & Poors, *How Environmental and Climate Risks Factor Into Global Corporate Ratings* (October 2015) https://www.globalcreditportal.com/ratingsdirect/renderArticle.do?articleId=1467885&SctArtId=348528&from=CM&nsl_code=LIME&source ObjectId=9373730&sourceRevId=1&fee_ind=N&exp_date=20251020-17:15:34.
44. See, for example, Black Rock Investment Institute, *The Price of Climate Change: Global Warming's Impact on Portfolios* (October 2015) https://www.blackrock.com/corporate/en-mx/literature/whitepaper/bii-pricing-climate-risk-international.pdf.
45. See, for example, Mercer, *Investing in a Time of Climate Change* (June 2015) http://www.mercer.com.au/services/investments/sustainable-growth/climate-change-report-2015.html.
46. See, for example, Stathers and Zavos (2015).

47. Boston Common Asset Management 2015.
48. See, for example, Willis Towers Watson Thinking Ahead Group, *We Need a Bigger Boat: Sustainability in Investment* (1 August 2012) https://thinkingaheadinstitute.org/Document/List?categoryId=231&categoryName=Major publications.
49. See, for example, Citigroup, *Global Darwinism II: Why a Low Carbon Future Doesn't have to Cost the Earth* (August 2015) https://ir.citi.com/hsq32Jl1m4aIzicMqH8sBkPnbsqfnwy4Jgb1J2kIPYWIw5eM8yD3FY9VbGpK%2Baax.
50. See, for example, Caldecott, Dericks, and Mitchell (2015); Clark, Feiner, and Viehs (2014).
51. See, for example, Hart 2015.
52. The debate regarding whether duties of due care and diligence owed by Australian directors are 'fiduciary' in nature is acknowledged, although not pursued in this paper. That debate centres on whether the duties are *prescriptive* (i.e. requiring positive action) or confined to the proscriptive (requiring restraint). This debate was prompted by the decision of the High Court of Australia in *Breen v Williams* (1996) 186 CLR 1 that a duty can only be 'fiduciary' in nature if it is proscriptive, not prescriptive. See, for example, discussion by Austin J in *Australian Securities and Investments Commission (ASIC) v Rich* (at 7190), and in the *Bell Group* cases in their consideration of the Australian common law duty to act in good faith in the best interests of the company. For a general discussion of the issue see, for example, Collins (2014); Langford (2013). For a discussion of this issue under US and Canadian law, see Waitzer and Sarro (2014), 1090. For the purposes of this paper, the duty (and the statutory covenants under the SIS Act) in relation due care and diligence are referred to as 'fiduciary' duties.
53. See, for example, Gerrard and Freeman (2014); McDonald (2011); Lord et al. 2012; Fisher (2013); Faure and Peeters (2011); Shearing 2010; Peel and Osofsky (2015); Vanhala and Hilson (2013); Zahar, Peel, and Godden (2012).
54. Peel and Osofsky 2015.
55. See, for example, *California v General Motors Corporation et al*, Case No. C06-05755 MJJ, Order granting Defendants' Motion to Dismiss (N.D. Cal. 2007), p.2 and *Native Village of Kivalina v ExxonMobil Corp., et al*, 2009 WL 3326113 (N.D. Cal.) (*Kavilina*) – cf. the appeal in *Comer et al v Murphy Oil USA Inc et al*, Third Amended Complaint, Case No., 1:05-CV-436 LTD-RHW, (2006 WL 1066645 (S.D. Miss. 2006)) (*Comer*) and *Connecticut, et al. v American Electric Power Company Inc., et al*, 2009 WL 2996729 (C.A.2 (N.Y.)) and, more recently, *Washington Environmental Council; Sierra Club, Washington State Chapter v Bellon* (9th Circuit, 17 October 2013). See generally discussion in Colares and Ristovski (2014). Claims for breach of the public trust doctrine have also recently been successful against Washington State in the United States (*Zoe & Stella Foster v. Washington Department of Ecology*, 14-2-25295-1 (Ct App, 2015) and the Federal government in *Juliana et al v.the United States of America et al*, 6:15-cv-1517-TC, Order, Findings & Recommendation, (D.C. Oregon, 8 April 2016). See discussion in Tuhus-Dubrow (2015); Castillo (2015).
56. In Europe, public interest litigants have pursued national governments for alleged negligence in climate change policy setting. In one high-profile example, in June 2015 The Hague District Court found in favour of Dutch non-government organisation Urgenda in its claim that the Dutch Government had negligently failed to implement emissions controls consistent with the Netherlands' proportionate contribution to emissions reductions aimed at limiting global warming to <2°C above pre-industrial levels (see The Hague District Court, *Urgenda v Netherlands*, Case number C/09/456689/HA ZA 13-1396. For an English translation of the judgment on 24 June 2015, see http://www.urgenda.nl/documents/VerdictDistrictCourt-UrgendavStaat-24.06.2015.pdf). The Government is appealing the decision. Similar claims, based either in negligence or the public trust doctrine, were also on foot at the time of writing in Norway, Belgium and New Zealand.
57. For a general discussion of potential causes of action against government entities, see Klein 2015.

58. See, for example, the obiter comments of the District Court on the merits of the plaintiff's claim in *Comer* (2006 WL 1066645 (S.D. Miss. 2006)) and those of the Court in *Kivalina* (2009 WL 3326113 (N.D. Cal.)), 8:

[T]he harm from global warming involves a series of events disconnected from the discharge itself. In a global warming scenario, emitted greenhouse gases combine with other gases in the atmosphere which in turn results in the planet retaining heat, which in turn causes the ice caps to melt and the oceans to rise, which in turn causes the Arctic sea ice to melt, which in turn allegedly renders Kivalina vulnerable to erosion and deterioration resulting from winter storms.

59. *Illinois Farmers Insurance Co. et al. v. Metropolitan Water Reclamation District of Greater Chicago et al.*, case number 1:14-cv-03251; *Illinois Farmers Insurance Co. et al. v County of McHenry*, case number 1:14-cv-03282; *Illinois Farmers Insurance Co. et al. v. County of Dekalb et al*, case number 2014L31; *Illinois Farmers Insurance Co. et al. v. Country of DuPage el al.*, case number 2014L000385; *Illinois Farmers Insurance Co. et al. v County of Kane et al.*, case number 2014L153; *Illinois Farmers Insurance Co. et al. v. County of Kendall et al.*, case number 2014L034; *Illinois Farmers Insurance Co. et al v. County of Lake*, case number 14L281; *Illinois Farmers Insurance Co. et al. v. County of LaSalle*, case number 2014L63; *Illinois Farmers Insurance Co. et al. v. County of Will*, case number 14L00314.

60. See *Roe v Arch Coal Inc et al*, Case: 4:15-cv-00910-NAB, United States District Court, Eastern District of Missouri, 9 June 2015 (consolidated class action complaint filed 11 December 2015, proceedings stayed on 15 January 2016 following Arch Coal's filing for Chapter 11 bankruptcy protection) and *Lynn v Peabody Energy Corporation et al*, Case: 4:15-cv-00916-AGF, United States District Court, Eastern District of Missouri, 11 June 2015 (second amended complaint filed 11 March 2016). Although Peabody also filed for Chapter 11 protection in April 2016, as at 29 April 2016 the defendants' Notice seeking a stay of the proceedings has been contested by the plaintiffs on the basis that the claim against individually-named defendants should not be impacted.

61. Article 23-A, Section 352 *et seq.* of the New York General Business Law (the '*Martin Act*') and Section 63(12) of the New York Executive Law.

62. Attorney General of the State of New York Environmental and Investor Protection Bureaus, *In the Matter of Investigation by Eric T Schneiderman, Attorney General of the State of New York of Peabody Energy Corporation, Respondent*, Assurance 15–242.

63. It is noted that the Full Federal Court of Australia recently found that a market-based approach to causation (i.e. generally, that does not require a plaintiff to demonstrate specific reliance on a misleading statement or conduct by the defendant where loss manifests due to a decline in market price) is reasonably arguable under Australian law – see *Caason Investments Pty Ltd v Cao* [2015] FCAFC 94.

64. For early explorations on point, see, for example, Baker & McKenzie, (2012, 16); Barker 2013; Barker and Girgis (2015); Gold and Scotchmer (2015); Pam McAllister, 'Climate Change Risk', Mercer Legal Consulting, November 2015, http://proxywatch.com/wp-content/uploads/2015/11/151117_INV19481_Super-trustee-liability_Pams-Article_4-pager-2.pdf; Nina Hart, 'Legal Tools for Climate Adaptation Advocacy: Securities Law'(Paper, Sabin Center for Climate Change Law, Columbia Law School, University of Columbia, May 2015); Sullivan et al. 2015; Waitzer and Sarro (2014).

65. Donald and Taylor (2008); Donald, Ormiston and Charlton (2014); Drummond (2010); Langbein and Posner 1980; Leigh 1997; Nicholls 1996; Shearing 2010; Stone 2007; Thomas 2008.

66. Richardson (2007, 2012, 162–163) acknowledges that a failure to have regard to climate change may be in breach of duty, but does not interrogate the issue further:

fiduciary investors who utterly ignore environmental and social considerations arguably may also contravene their fiduciary obligations. Some ecological and human rights issues are becoming so pervasive and serious that few investors can continue to be indifferent to their impact. Climate change is an example.

67. See, for example, Butler (2008); Collins 2014; Donald 2009; Donald, Ormiston and Charlton 2014; Langbein and Posner 1980; Leigh 1997; Thornton 2008. See also commentary referred to in n64 above.

68. Section 52A(6) provides that the covenants in section 52A 'operate as if the director were a party to the governing rules'.

69. As these covenants are implied into the trusts' governing rules under section 52A(2) of the SIS Act, they are effectively duties *owed directly to beneficiaries* as well as the corporate trustee. However, the analysis in this paper presumes that the interests of the corporate trustee and its beneficiaries are materially aligned. This is not to suggest that the strategic objective of a particular *member* may not be to maximise short-term returns (e.g. given impending retirement), or even of the fund itself in particular circumstances (e.g. of a defined benefit fund to meet current pension payment requirements). However, this paper focuses on the objective of a solvent fund in the ordinary course of its business. See, for example, Gold and Scotchmer (2015), 11–12.

70. An exception to this general proposition applies in relation to the trustee's covenants regarding the avoidance, disclosure and management of conflicts under sections 52(2)(d) and 52A (2)(d) which, under sections 52(4) and 52A(3), prevail over any obligations to the contrary under Part 2D.1 of the Corporations Act. See generally discussion in Davis and Chaaya, ¶13,102, ¶81,060-81-080, Chapter 48.

71. *ASIC v Australian Property Custodian Holdings Ltd (recs and mgrs apptd) (in liq) (controllers apptd) (No 3)* [2013] FCA 1342, 525; *ASC v AS Nominees* (1995) 62 FCR 504, 517. See also general discussion in *Australian Superannuation Commentary*, ¶2–810, ¶2–835.

72. See, for example, Donald and Taylor (2008); Tennent 2009.

73. This is consistent with the 'sole purpose test' for registrable superannuation entities under section 62(1) of the SIS Act, which provides that the 'core purpose' for which the fund is maintained must be for the provision of benefits for (or in respect of) each member upon their retirement, attainment of a specified age or death. See also *Scott v Federal Commissioner of Taxation (No 2)* (1966) 10 AITR 290; 14 ATD 333, which considered the forerunner to section 62 of the SIS Act, section 23(j) of the *Occupational Superannuation Act*. Windyer J held (at 278): ' … a fund bona fide devoted as its sole purpose to providing for employees who are participants money benefits … upon their reaching of a prescribed age' (emphasis added). Whilst Donald, Ormiston and Charlton 2014 (at 543–544) suggest that in its interpretation of the sole purpose test in section 62 in *Superannuation Circular No.III.A.4: The Sole Purpose Test* (February 2001), the Australian Prudential Regulation Authority 'envisages a less exacting test of "sole purpose" than a literal reading of the section would impose … [with] a more accommodating attitude to the presence of "incidental advantages" in the exercise of a trustee's power', an examination of the wording of that circular (at [34]) reveals that it does not disturb the primacy of the financial objective in driving trustees' exercise of power: '*the provision of retirement benefits for members is the overriding consideration behind the investment decision*'. The consistency of incidental environmental and social benefits with the pursuit of financial benefits is discussed further in relation to *Cowan v Scargill*, below.

74. See, for example, Nicholls 1996, at 211: '*the money in the fund represents part of the overall pay package of the members, in the form of deferred remuneration*'; *Sutherland v Woods* [2011] NSWSC 13 at [115].

75. Collins 2014, 632.

76. *Cowan v Scargill*, 286–287.

77. See, for example, discussion of *Cowan v Scargill* in *Harries v The Church Commissioners for England* [1992] 1 WLR 1241. For discussion of its frequent mis-interpretation, and application in a modern investment context, see, for example, Law Commission of England and Wales and Gold and Scotchmer (2015), 14–18.

78. See, for example, Gold and Scotchmer (2015), 11–12. This is not to suggest that the strategic objective of a particular *member* may not be to maximise short-term returns (e.g. given impending retirement), or even of the fund itself in particular circumstances (e.g. of a defined benefit fund to meet current pension payment requirements).
79. See, for example, Thornton 2008, 411.
80. See also discussion in Leigh 1997, 348.
81. Section 52A(2)(b), emphasis added. Section 52A(2)(f) also requires fund trustee directors to exercise a reasonable degree of care and diligence for the purposes of ensuring that the corporate trustee carries out *its* (similar) covenants set out in section 52. The general fiduciary obligations of the trustee and its directors continue to apply in addition to the covenants prescribed under the SIS Act – as do the directors' duties prescribed under Part 2D of the *Corporations Act* (except in relation to the trustee's covenants regarding the avoidance, disclosure and management of conflicts under sections 52(2)(d) and 52A(2)(d) of the SIS Act which, under sections 52(4) and 52A(3), prevail over any obligations to the contrary under Part 2D.1 of the *Corporations Act*.)
82. See generally Davis and Chaaya, ¶81,060; Donald 2009, n16 at 56; *Re VCA and APRA* (2008) 105 ALD 236; [2008] AATA 580, 347, 50, [347].
83. SIS Act, section 29VO(3).
84. Section 34C of the SIS Act empowers APRA to promulgate binding prudential standards. It also issues (non-binding) statements of expectation in the form of prudential practice guides. APRA's Prudential Practice Guide on Investment Governance (SPG 530), issued in 2013, states that a trustee may adopt an 'ethical investment option' with an ESG focus, subject to appropriate supporting analysis that demonstrates that the same will not expose beneficiaries' interests to undue risk. ESG factors are referred to in SPG530 as 'non-financial'.
85. *Superannuation Legislation Amendment (Trustee Obligations and Prudential Standards) Bill 2012*, Explanatory Memorandum, paragraph 1.42: '[The reform] also heightens existing requirements in relation to the degree of care, skill and diligence required of trustees. The overall effect of these changes [introducing the covenants in section 52] … will be to hold trustees to a higher standard.' See also *ASIC v Australian Property Custodian Holdings Ltd (recs and mgrs apptd) (in liq) (controllers apptd) (No 3))* [2013] FCA 1342 at [542] re the higher standard of care owed by trustee directors (as against directors of 'ordinary' corporations). *Trustee Act 1958* (Vic), section 6(1); *Trustee Act 1925* (NSW), section 14A (2); *Trustee Act 1973* (Qld), section 22(1); *Trustee Act 1936* (SA), section 7(1); *Trustee Act 1898* (Tas), section 7(1); *Trustee Act 1925* (ACT), section 14A(2); *Trustee Act 2007* (NT), section 6(1). The only decided case that has considered the content of these duties is *Gardner & Anor v Mattila* [2015] NTCA 1, in which the Court of Appeal of the Supreme Court of the Northern Territory considered the content of the duty in the second limb of the test of due care and diligence under section 6(1)(b), *viz*, the duty owed by *non-professional* trustees to exercise 'the care, diligence and skill that a prudent person of business would exercise in managing the affairs of other people'. Even in respect of this *lower* standard of care (one arguably akin to the 'ordinary prudent person' standard that applied under the *SIS Act* until 2013), their Honours held that the appellant had breached his fiduciary duty of care:

[35] Unfortunately for those with little education and skill who take on the duties of a trustee, the standard is an objective one, independent of the skill and prudence the trustee in question personally possesses … [36] … Mr Gardner discharged none of these duties. … no consideration was given by Mr Gardner to the best use of Mr Mattila's money, no alternative use or investment was considered, no business plan was prepared, no legal or financial advice was sought on Mr Mattila's behalf, and the risk of overcapitalization (which eventuated) was not considered.

Prior to 2013, the trustee directors' SIS Act duties did not materially add to those applicable under the general law – see, for example, *Manglicmot v Commonwealth Bank Officers Superannuation Corporation Pty Ltd* [2011] NSWCA 204. See also discussion in Collins 2014; at 645–46 and Donald 2009, at 51.

86. See the mirror provisions to section 180(1) in sections 601FC(1)(b) and FD(1)(b) of the Corporations Act; *ASIC v Australian Property Custodian Holdings Ltd (recs and mgrs apptd) (in liq) (controllers apptd) (No 3))* [2013] FCA 1342 at [643]: [536] I consider that the standard of care applicable where a corporation is a professional trustee, holding itself out to the public and being paid as such, will often be more exacting. The requirement that a professional trustee exercise a higher standard of care and take a cautious approach was discussed by Finn J in *ASC v AS Nominees* at 516–517 where his Honour usefully set out and considered the relevant authorities: see *Speight v Gaunt* (1883) 9 App Cas 1; *King v Talbot* (1869) 40 NY 76; *Re Whiteley*; *Whiteley v Learoyd* (1886) 33 Ch D 347 at 355 per Lindley LJ; Scott, The Law of Trusts (4th ed, Little Brown & Company, 1988) at 432 … .[643] The Explanatory Memorandum (at para 8.8) indicates that these duties are intended to reflect the fundamental duties of a fiduciary and the special nature of the relationship between an RE and the members of a scheme. The duties exist largely for the protection of the members.

87. *ASIC v Rich* (2003) 44 ACSR 341, [35]; *ASIC v Rich* (2009) 75 ACSR 1, [7201], citing *Commonwealth Bank of Australia v Friedrich* (1991) 5 ACSR 15, 123; *ASIC v Vines* (2005) 55 ACSR 617, [1067]; *Daniels v Anderson* (1995) 37 NSWLR 438, 505.

88. *ASIC v Healey & Ors* [2011] FCA 717 (hereafter *Centro*), [16], [143] and [162]. See also *ASIC v Rich* (2009) 75 ACSR 1, [7205-6].

89. *Wyong Shire Council v Shirt* (1980) 146 CLR 40, 47, applied in *ASIC v Rich* (2009) 75 ACSR 1, [7231, 7236] and *ASIC v Vines* (approved by the Court of Appeal in *Vines v ASIC* (2007) 25 ACLC 448); *ASIC v Ingleby* (2012) 91 ASCR 66, 69.

90. See *ASIC v Australian Property Custodian Holdings Ltd (recs and mgrs apptd) (in liq) (controllers apptd) (No 3))* [2013] FCA 1342 at [532].

91. See, for example, authorities above n84 and 85.

92. The difference in the language used to express the duty of competence under the *Corporations Act* ('due care and diligence') and the SIS Act ('due care, *skill* and diligence') is noted. However, the addition of the word 'skill' has not been regarded as material 'other than as attempt to add emphasis to the application of effort or utilising the skill necessary to discharge the requirement of due care and diligence' – Collins 2014; at 644. See also Butler 2008, at 227.

93. See generally *Centro* [2011] FCA 717, [16], [143] and [162]. See also *ASIC v Rich* (2009) 75 ACSR 1, [7205-6].

94. See *Finch v Telstra* above n20, at 254; *ASIC v Australian Property Custodian Holdings Ltd (recs and mgrs apptd) (in liq) (controllers apptd) (No 3))* [2013] FCA 1342 at [571]; applied in *Sharp v Maritime Super Pty Ltd* [2013] NSWSC 389 at [33].

95. *Centro* [2011] FCA 717, [16], [143] and [162]. See also *ASIC v Rich* (2009) 75 ACSR 1, [7203].

96. *Alcoa of Australia Retirement Plan Pty Ltd v Frost* [2012] VSCA 238, Nettle JA at [47–48], in relation to the determination of a fund member's entitlement to TPD benefits. Section 56(3) of the SIS Act specifically contemplates that trustee directors should seek advice, and be indemnified out of the assets of the trust in doing so In the words of Deputy President Forgie in *Re VBN and APRA*:

As essential as professional advice is, the trustees' obligation goes beyond merely seeking, accepting and following professional advice … the trustee [must] use their own acumen, knowledge and judgment in weighing all the relevant factors, including professional advice – '*VBN and Ors and Australian Prudential Regulation Authority and Anor* [2006] AATA 710; (2006) 92 ALD 259 (25 July 2006), 469.

97. *Finch v Telstra*, at 254.

98. *Nestle v Westminster Bank*, 1270.

99. See, for example, *Tuftevski v Total Risks Management Pty Ltd* [2009] NSWSC 1021, where a question arose as to what was required by way of enquiry on the part of a trustee in the context where the trustee had received material adverse to the employee's claim. Smart AJ held [at 16]:

In my opinion bona fide enquiry and genuine decision making where these are required constitute an integral part of performing a fiduciary obligation. … The process followed by the Trustee … must involve deciding a question of fact in good faith and giving it real and genuine consideration. This often cannot be done without conducting some investigation and making relevant inquiries … .

See also *ASIC v Australian Property Custodian Holdings Ltd (recs and mgrs apptd) (in liq) (controllers apptd) (No 3))* [2013] FCA 1342 at [571]; *Finch v Telstra*, 254; *Sharp v Maritime Super Pty Ltd* [2013] NSWSC 389 at [33], [39].

100. *Centro* [2011] FCA 717.
101. See *ASIC v Australian Property Custodian Holdings Ltd (recs and mgrs apptd) (in liq) (controllers apptd) (No 3))* [2013] FCA 1342 at [567]–[574] (*cf Gilberg v Stevedoring Employees Retirement Fund Pty Ltd* [2008] NSWSC 1318 where trustees did not have legal discretion (power) under the trust deed to reconsider a decision in relation to total and permanent disablement benefits); *Nestle v National Westminster Bank*, where the Court of Appeal held that a trustee bank had a duty to review investments of a beneficiary regularly, and that a changing investment environment during the life of the trust should have prompted consideration of a variation in the content of the portfolio. The position under Australian and UK law is consistent with that in the United States, wherein the Supreme Court recently held in *Tibble et al v. Edison International et al* S. Ct., No. 13-550, 2015 WL 2340845 (May 18, 2015) that the duty of due care and diligence (prudence) under §1104 of ERISA requires on-going monitoring and, where appropriate, reconsideration, of previous decisions. See generally discussion in Thornton 2008.
102. *Apostolovski v Total Risk Management Pty Ltd* (2010) 79 NSWLR 432.
103. See, for example, discussion in Collins 2014; 634 and Thornton 2008; 410.
104. See Nicholls 1996, at 210.
105. See, for example, *Nestle v Westminster*, at 1275, 1284.
106. *ASIC v Australian Property Custodian Holdings Ltd (recs and mgrs apptd) (in liq) (controllers apptd) (No 3))* [2013] FCA 1342 at [571]; applied in *Sharp v Maritime Super Pty Ltd* [2013] NSWSC 389 at [33].
107. *Alcoa of Australia Retirement Plan Pty Ltd v Frost* [2012] VSCA 238, Nettle JA at [60].
108. Waitzer and Sarro (2014), 1090–1091.
109. Whilst there is a significant body of literature examining the motivations for *positive, voluntary* corporate adaptation to climate change, the reasons for governance *inaction* remain under-researched in the recent literature – see, for example, Peer C Fiss and Edward J Zajac, 'The Symbolic Management of Strategic Change: Sensegiving via Framing and Decoupling' 49 *Academy of Management Journal*, 1173; Solomon 2009 and United Nations Environment Program Finance Initiative (*UNEPFI*), *Climate risk to the Global Economy*, CEO Briefing on Climate Change, 2002, 1 http://www.unepfi.org/fileadmin/documents/CEO_briefing_climate_change_2002_en.pdf. These categories of governance inaction on climate change were originally synthesised by lead author Sarah Barker 2013.
110. See, for example, Greg Liddell, *Fiduciary duty and climate change* (24 May 2015) Investment Operations & Custody http://ioandc.com/fiduciary-duty-and-climate-change/; Loechel, Hodgkinson, and Moffat (2013); Solomon 2009, 19.
111. See, for example, Loechel, Hodgkinson, and Moffat (2013), 473; Rouse, (2 July 2013); Solomon 2009, 13.
112. See, for example, Claudia Delpero, *Is your pension fund safe from climate change? Fiduciary duty is the key* (30 October 2015) Road to Paris: Science for Smart Policy http://roadtoparis.info/2015/10/30/is-your-pension-fund-safe-from-climate-change-fiduciary-duty-is-the-key/; Fischman and Rountree 2012; Loechel, Hodgkinson, and Moffat (2013); Trexler and Kosloff 2012.
113. Solomon 2009, 21; Trexler and Kosloff (2012).
114. Amado and Adams (2012), 12; Solomon 2009, 13; Trexler and Kosloff (2012); UNEPFI.

115. *H v Royal Alexandra Hospital for Children* (1990) Aust Torts Reports ¶81-000, SC (NSW). In a climate change context, see also Gold and Scotchmer (2015), 23:

> Given the overwhelming scientific consensus about the causes and implications of global climate change, climate change denial is not an option for pension fiduciaries. Per Scargill, it is not permissible for a fiduciary to bring personal or ideological views to bear on fiduciary decision-making; rather the duty of prudence requires a thorough, [on-]going and rational evaluation of relevant information to support fiduciary decision-making.

116. *Cowan v Scargill*; 286–287.

117. Solomon 2009, 22:

> Despite a general interest in climate change issues among the trustees, and a general understanding of what would result from climate change, they seemed to display little understanding of a direct link between climate change and financial return. Many commented that the 'connection' between climate change and financial return was unclear. When asked whether they thought climate change was an important factor affecting financial return and shareholder value, most of the interviewees claimed that it had very little, if any impact.

> See also UNEPFI.

118. *Centro* [2011] FCA 717.

119. *ASIC v Lindberg* (2012) 91 ACSR 640, [30]. See also *ASIC v Ingleby* (2012) 91 ACSR 66; *AWA v Daniels* (1992) 7 ACSR 759; *Centro* [2011] FCA 717, [189].

120. *Centro* [2011] FCA 717, [189]; *Alcoa of Australia Retirement Plan Pty Ltd v Frost* [2012] VSCA 238, Nettle JA at [47–48].

121. *ASIC v Ingleby* (2012) 91 ACSR 66 (appeal to the CAVSC upheld in relation to quantum of penalty, but not liability); *ASIC v Lindberg* (2012) 91 ACSR 640; *Shafron v ASIC* (2012) 286 ALR 612.

122. See authorities in n 101 above.

123. *ASIC v Ingleby* (2012) 91 ACSR 66 (appeal to the CAVSC upheld in relation to quantum of penalty, but not liability); *ASIC v Lindberg* (2012) 91 ACSR 640; *Shafron v ASIC* (2012) 286 ALR 612.

124. *ASIC v Ingleby* (2012) 91 ACSR 66; *ASIC v Lindberg* (2012) 91 ACSR 640; *Centro* [2011] FCA 717; *Alcoa of Australia Retirement Plan Pty Ltd v Frost* [2012] VSCA 238, Nettle JA at [47–48].

125. See e.g. Fischman and Rountree 2012; Loechel, Hodgkinson, and Moffat 2013; Celeste K Young and Roger N Jones, *Building Bridges: Supporting Adaptation in Industry*, VCCAR Think Tank Policy Paper, Victorian Centre for Climate Change Adaptation Research, Melbourne, September 2013; 3.

126. Nicholls 1996 at 214–215.

127. See United Nations IPCC; International Energy Agency, *World Energy Outlook 2015*, November 2015, www.worldenergyoutlook.org. It is noted that prevailing scenarios may also now be updated to account for the 1.5°C target included in the COP21 Paris Agreement.

128. See, for example, Cornell (2015).

129. The Courts have previously held that non-executive directors can be in breach of their duty of care and diligence where misleading statements are made to the market, where the directors have failed to query the assumptions or methodologies on which the actuarial reports underlying the statements are based – see *ASIC v Macdonald (No 11)* [2009] NSWSC 287, 325. The findings on liability in this matter were confirmed on appeal to the High Court of Australia – see *ASIC v Hellicar* [2012] HCA 17.

130. See, for example, The Climate Institute 2015, 8.

131. See MSCI, *Environment Agency Pension Fund Selects MSCI as Low Carbon Equity Index Provider,* (2015) https://www.msci.com/documents/10199/b1235841-4cde-4645-8614-c799c57701d7 and ETF, *Amundi launches Europe's Second Low Carbon ETF,* (2015)

http://europe.etf.com/europe/sections/features-a-news/10823-amundi-launches-europes-second-low-carbon-etf.html.

132. See, for example, KPMG, *Gearing up for green bonds,* (2015) https://www.kpmg.com/Global/en/IssuesAndInsights/ArticlesPublications/sustainable-insight/Documents/gearing-up-for-green-bonds-v2.pdf and Allens, *Green bonds: emergence of the Australian and Asian markets,* (2015) https://www.allens.com.au/pubs/pdf/baf/report-baf23oct15.pdf.

133. *Centro* [2011] FCA 717, [182].

134. *ASIC v Lindberg* (2012) 91 ACSR 640; *Harlowe's Nominees Pty Ltd v Woodside (Lakes Entrance) Oil Co NL* (1968) 121 CLR 483, 493, per Barwick CJ, McTiernan and Kitto JJ:

> Directors in whom are vested the right and duty of deciding where the company's interests lie and how they are to be served may be concerned with a wide range of practical considerations, and their judgment, if exercised in good faith and not for irrelevant purposes, is not open to review in the courts.

> See also *Howard Smith Ltd v Ampol Petroleum Ltd* [1974] AC 821 at 832, where the Privy Council held: 'There is no appeal on merits from management decisions to courts of law: nor will courts of law assume to act as a kind of supervisory board over decisions within the powers of management honestly arrived at.'

135. See, for example, *ASIC v Maxwell* (2006) 59 ACSR 373, 397 [102]; *ASIC v Lindberg* (2012) 91 ACSR 640, 654 [72].

136. Explanatory Memorandum, *Corporate Law Economic Reform Bill 1999*, [6.1], [6.4].

137. *ASIC v Mariner Corporation Limited* [2015] FCA 589.

138. See, for example, discussion in Solomon 2009.

139. ASRIA and Chubb, 4.

140. For a discussion of functions inherent in the assessment of climate change risks, and the range of responses thereto, see, for example, ASRIA and Chubb; PRI, *Developing an Asset Owner Climate Strategy*, December 2015; Stathers and Zavos (2015); The Climate Institute (2015); UNEP FI and 2C Investing Initiative, *Climate Strategies and Metrics: Exploring Options for Institutional Investors,* UNEPFI http://2degrees-investing.org/IMG/pdf/climate_targets_final.pdf.

141. Section 52A(2)(f) of the SIS Act specifically requires trustee directors to exercise due care and diligence in ensuring that the corporate trustee carries out its own obligations – which in turn specifically include investment strategy and risk management. See also the preamble to APRA SPS 510 Governance pursuant to section 34C of the SIS Act states: 'The ultimate responsibility for the sound and prudent management of [a superannuation fund's] business operations rests with its Board of directors.' Paragraph 10 states:
The Board, in fulfilling its functions, may delegate authority to management to act on behalf of the Board with respect to certain matters, as decided by the Board. This delegation of authority must be clearly set out and documented. **The Board must have mechanisms in place for monitoring the exercise of delegated authority. The Board cannot abrogate its responsibility for functions delegated to management.** (emphasis added)

142. See, for example, AODP, *Climate Change Investment Initiative: Funds Survey Results*, report for the AIST and the Climate Institute, March 2010, 11; UNPRI, *Developing an Asset Owner Climate Strategy*, December 2015, 5.

143. See, for example, *ASIC v Adler* (2002) 41 ACSR 72, in which a CEO contravened his duty to exercise due care and diligence (amongst other breaches) due to his failure to ensure that proper safeguards were implemented for the appraisal of investments against company policies (appeal largely dismissed: *Adler v ASIC* (2003) 46 ACSR 504).

144. See *ASIC v Macdonald (No 11)*.

145. See, for example, *ASIC v Maxwell* (2006) 59 ACSR 373, 397 [102]; *ASIC v Lindberg* (2012) 91 ACSR 640, 654 [72]; *Nestle v Westminster Bank*, 1284. In a US context, see, for example, *Fifth Third Bancorp v Dudenhoeffer*, 134 S. Ct. 2459 (2014).

146. *ASIC v Citrofresh International Ltd (No.2)* (2010) 77 ACSR 69.
147. *ASIC v Sydney Investment House Equities Pty Ltd & Ors* (2008) 69 ACSR 1.
148. *ASIC v Elm Financial Services Pty Ltd* [2005] NSWSC 1033; *ASIC v MacDonald (No. 11)* (2009) 256 ALR 199.
149. As was alleged in the *Fortescue* series of cases against its managing director, Andrew 'Twiggy' Forrest, in which the High Court of Australia ultimately found that the company had not made a misleading disclosure to the market: see *ASIC v Fortescue* (2011) 274 ALR 731, *Forrest v ASIC* [2012] HCA 39.
150. See discussion in Section Two, above.

Disclosure statement

No potential conflict of interest was reported by the authors.

Notes on contributor

Sarah Barker (B.Com LLB (Hons) M.Env (Hons) MAICD) is a Special Counsel in the corporate group at international law firm Minter Ellison. She is a non-executive director of the Emergency Services & State Superannuation Fund, the Responsible Investment Association Australasia and NRCL Ltd, and teaches directors' duties and responsibilities for the Australian Institute of Company Directors.

References

Amado, Jean-Christophe, and Peter Adams. 2012. "Value Chain Climate Resilience: A Guide to Managing Climate Impacts on Companies and Communities." Report prepared for Partnership for Resilience and Environmental Preparedness, Montreal, July, 11.
Austin, Robert. 2014. "Time to lift the grey cloud of litigation." Australian Financial Review (Melbourne), 21 March, 33.
Bainbridge, Stephen M. 2012. *Corporate Governance After the Financial Crisis*. New York: Oxford University Press, 1–3: 43.
Baker & McKenzie. 2012. Pension and Superannuation Trustees and Climate Change Report, Sydney.
Barker, Sarah. 2013. "Directors Duties in the Anthropocene: Personal Liability for Corporate Inaction on Climate Change." University of Melbourne, December.
Barker, Sarah, and Maged Girgis. 2015. 'Institutional investment, corporate governance and climate change: what is a trustee to do?' Minter Ellison, 27 January. http://www.minterellison.com/publications/articles/Institutional-investment-corporate-governance-and-climate-change-what-is-a-trustee-to-do/.
Boston Common Asset Management. 2015. Are Banks Prepared for Climate Change? Impact Report 2015, October.
Brian Cosman. 2008. "Green Derivatives: Extorting Reductions in Greenhouse Gas Emissions via Shareholder Derivative Suits." *Arizona State Law Journal* 40: 743–774.
Butler, Lisa. 2008. "The Super Standard of Care – How High Should Superannuation Trustees Jump?" *Journal of Equity* 2: 225–244.
Caldecott, Ben, Gerard Dericks, and James Mitchell. 2015. "Stranded Assets and Subcritical Coal: The Risk to Companies and Investors." Report of the Stranded Assets Program, Smith School of Enterprise and the Environment, University of Oxford, March.
Cambridge Institute for Sustainability leadership. 2015. 'Unhedgeable Risk: How Climate Change Sentiment Impacts Investment,' Report, University of Cambridge, November. http://www.cisl.cam.ac.uk/publications/sustainable-finance-publications/unhedgeable-risk.
Carbon Tracker and the Grantham Research Institute. 2013. *Unburnable carbon 2013: Wasted capital and stranded assets.*

Castillo, Kassandra. 2015. "Climate Change & The Public Trust Doctrine: An Analysis of Atmospheric Trust Litigation." *San Diego Journal of Climate & Energy Law* 6: 221–235.

Clark, Gordon, and Michael Viehs. 2014. "Corporate Social Responsibility for Investors: An Overview and evaluation of the Existing CSR Literature." Working Paper, Smith School of Enterprise and the Environment, August.

Clark, Gordon, Andreas Feiner, and Michael Viehs. 2014. "From the Stockholder to the Stakeholder: How Sustainability Can Drive Financial Outperformance." SSEE Research Report sponsored by Arabesque Asset Management.

Colares, Juscelino, and Kosta Ristovski. 2014. "Pleading Patterns and the Role of Litigation as a Driver of Federal Climate Change Legislation." *Jurimetrics: The Journal of Law, Science & Technology* 54 (4): 329–373.

Collins, Paul. 2014. "The Best Interests Duty and the Standard of Care for Superannuation Trustees." *ALJ* 88 (9): 632–647.

Cornell, Bradford. 2015. *The Divestment Penalty: Estimating the Costs of Fossil Fuel Divestment to Select University Endowments*. Los Angeles: California Institute of Technology. September 3, 2015.

Donald, M Scott. 2009. "The competence and diligence required of trustees of a 21st century superannuation fund." *Australian Business Law Review* 27: 50–62.

Donald, M Scott, and Nicholas Taylor. 2008. "Does "Sustainable" Investing Compromise the Obligations Owed by Superannuation Trustees?" *Australian Business Law Review* 36: 47–61.

Donald, M Scott, J. Ormiston, and K. Charlton. 2014. "The Potential for Superannuation Funds to make Investments with a Social Impact." *Company and Securities Law Journal* 32 (8): 540–551.

Drummond, Stanley. 2010. "SIS Act Obligations to Beneficiaries." *Journal of Equity*, 4: 54–164.

Edelman, James. 2014. "The Role of Status in the Law of Obligations." In Andrew S Gold and Paul B Miller, Philosophical Foundations of Fiduciary Law. Oxford Scholarship Online, 23.

ExxonMobil. 2015. 'ExxonMobil to Hold Media Call on New York Attorney General Subpoena'. News release, 5 November.

Faure, Michael, and Marjan Peeters, eds. 2011. *Climate Change Liability*. Maastricht: Edward Elgar.

Fischman, Robert L., and Jillian R. Rountree. 2012. "Adaptive Management." In *The Law of Adaptation to Climate Change – US and International Aspects*, edited by Michael B. Gerrard, and Katrina Fischer Kuh, vol. 19, 23–24. Chicago: American Bar Association.

Fisher, Elizabeth. 2013. "Climate Change Litigation, Obsession and Expertise: Reflecting on the Scholarly Response to *Massachusetts v EPA*." *Law & Policy* 35 (3): 236–260.

Ford, Harold, William Lee, and Thomson Reuters. 2015. *Ford and Lee: The Law of Trusts*. 3rd ed. London: Sweet and Maxwell.

Friede, Gunnar, Timo Busch, and Alexander Bassen. 2015. "ESG and Financial Performance: Aggregated Evidence From More than 2000 Empirical Studies." *Journal of Sustainable Financial and Investment* 5 (5): 210–233.

Gerrard, Michael, and Jody Freeman, eds. 2014. *Global Climate Change and US Law*. 2nd ed. Chicago: ABA Book Publishing.

Gold, Murray, and Adrian Scotchmer. 2015. "Climate Change and the Fiduciary Duties of Pension Fund Trustees in Canada." Koskie Minksy LLP, 18 September, http://kmlaw.ca/wp-content/uploads/2015/10/KM_Climate_Change_Paper_06oct15.pdf.

Gregory, Holly J., Rebecca C. Grapsas, and Reid Powell. 2013. "International Comparison of Selected Corporate Governance Guidelines and Codes of Best Practice." Weil Gotshal & Manges LLP, New York, February.

Hanrahan, Pamela. 2008. "Directors' Liability in Superannuation Trustee Companies." *Journal of Equity* 2: 204–224.

Hansell, Carol, and Laurence Hazell. 2004. "Corporate Governance and Fiduciary Duties – A Multi-Jurisdictional Review of the Directors' Relationship to the Corporation." Working Paper, American Bar Association.

Hart, Nina. 2015. "Legal Tools for Climate Adaptation Advocacy: Securities Law." Paper, Sabin Center for Climate Change Law, Columbia Law School, University of Columbia, May.

Klein, Jennifer. 2015. "Potential Liability of Governments for a Failure to Prepare for Climate Change." Paper, Sabin Center for Climate Change Law, Columbia Law School, University of Columbia.

Langbein, John, and Richard Posner. 1980. "Social Investing and the Law of Trusts." *Michigan Law Review* 79 (1): 72–112.

Langford, Rosemary Teele. 2013. "Solving the Fiduciary Puzzle – the Bonafide and Proper Purposes of Company Directors." *Australian Business Law Review* 41: 127–141.

Leigh, Andrew. 1997. "'Caveat Investor': The Ethical Investment of Superannuation in Australia." *Australian Business Law Review* 25: 341–350.

Loechel, Barton, Jane Hodgkinson, and Kieran Moffat. 2013. "Climate Change Adaptation in Australian Mining Communities: Comparing Mining Company and Local Government Views and Activities." *Climatic Change* 119: 465, 473–477.

Lord, Richard, Silke Goldberg, Lavanya Rajamani, and Jutta Brunnee, eds. 2012. *Climate Change Liability: Transnational Law and Practice.* Sydney: Cambridge University Press.

Margaret Stone (Justice). 2007. "The Superannuation Trustee: Are Fiduciary Obligations and Standards Appropriate?" *Journal of Equity* 1: 34–181.

McDonald, Jan. 2011. "The Role of Law in Adapting to Climate Change." *Wiley Interdisciplinary Reviews: Climate Change* 2 (2): 283–295.

Morwood, J., ed. 2001. *Pocket Oxford Latin Dictionary.* Oxford: Oxford University Press.

Nicholls of Birkenhead (Lord). 1996. "Trustees and their Broader Community: Where Duty, Morality and Ethics Converge." *Australian Law Journal* 70: 205–216.

OECD. 2015. *The Economic Consequences of Climate Change.* Paris: OECD Publishing.

Peel, Jacqueline, and Hari M. Osofsky. 2015. *Climate Change Litigation: Regulatory Pathways to Cleaner Energy.* Cambridge: Cambridge University Press.

Prudential Regulation Authority. 2015. 'The impact of climate change on the UK insurance sector: A Climate Adaptation Report by the Prudential Regulation Authority'. Report, Prudential Regulation Authority. September, 5.

Redmond, Paul. 2012. "Directors' Duties and Corporate Social Responsiveness." *UNSWLJ* 35: 317–340.

Richardson, Benjamin. 2007. "Do the Fiduciary Duties of Pension Funds Hinder Socially Responsible Investment?" *Banking and Finance Law Review* 146 (22): 162–163.

Richardson, Benjamin. 2012. "Fiduciary and Other Legal Duties." In *Socially Responsible Finance and Investing: Financial Institutions, Corporations, Investors, and Activists,* edited by H Kent Baker, and John Nofsinger, 69–86. Hoboken: John Wiley & Sons.

Rouse, Louise. 2013. "Pensions Funds and Climate Change: Can't Act, Won't Act." *The Guardian,* 2 July http://www.theguardian.com/sustainable-business/pension-funds-climate-change-inaction.

Rt Hon Sir Robert Megarry. 1989. In *Equity, Fiduciaries and Trusts,* edited by T. D. Youdan, i–xxix. Carswell: The Carswell Company Limited.

Shearing, Susan. 2010. "Climate Change Governance and Corporations: Changing the Way 'Business Does Business'?" In *In the Wilds of Climate Law,* edited by Robyn Lyster, 175–195. Bowen Hills: Australian Associated Press.

Sheehy, Benedict, and Donald Feaver. 2014. "Anglo-American Directors' Legal Duties and CSR: Prohibited, Permitted or Prescribed?" *Dalhousie Law Journal* 37 (1): 345–395, 347.

Sheehy, Benedict. 2015. "Defining CSR: Problems and Solutions." *Journal of Business Ethics* 131 (3): 625–648.

Solomon, Jill. 2009. "Pension Fund Trustees and Climate Change." Research Report No 106, Association of Certified Chartered Accountants, http://www.accaglobal.com/content/dam/acca/global/PDF-technical/climate-change/rr-106-001.pdf, 7, 22.

Stathers, Rick, and Alexia Zavos. 2015. *Responding to Climate Change Risk in Portfolio Management,* Schroders, February. http://www.schroders.com/staticfiles/Schroders/Sites/global/pdf/Portfolio-Climate-Change-Risk-April-2015.pdf.

Sullivan, Rory, Will Martindale, Elodie Feller, and Anna Bordon. 2015. "Fiduciary Duty in the 21st Century." Global Compact Report, United Nations, September 9.

Sutton, Randy, and Tricia Hobson. 2013. "A Global Perspective on Securities Class Actions: A Comparative Analysis." The International Comparative Legal Guide to Class& Group Actions 2014, Report, the Global Legal Group Ltd, London. October 12–20.

Tennent, Doug. 2009. "Ethical Investment in Superannuation Funds; Can it Occur without Breaching Traditional Trust Principles?" *Waikato Law Review* 17: 98–114.

The Climate Institute. 2015. Australia's Financial System and Climate Risk, July, 11.

Thomas, G. W. 2008. "The Duty of Trustees to Act in the Best Interests of their Beneficiaries." *Journal of Equity* 2: 177–202.

Thornton, Rosy. 2008. "Ethical Investments: A Case of Disjointed Thinking." *Cambridge Law Journal* 67: 396–422.

Trexler, Mark C., and Laura H. Kosloff. 2012. *The Changing Profile of Corporate Climate Change Risk*. Kindle ed. Bradford: Do Sustainability.

Tuhus-Dubrow, Rebecca. 2015. "Climate Change on Trial." *Dissent* 62 (4): 152–158.

Vanhala, Lisa, and Chris Hilson. 2013. "Climate Change Litigation, Symposium Introduction." *Law & Policy* 35 (3): 141–149.

Waitzer, Edward, and Douglas Sarro. August 2014. "Fiduciary Society Unleashed: The Road Ahead for the Financial Sector." *The Business Lawyer* 9: 1081–1116.

Willis Towers Watson. 2015. "Global Pension Assets Study." February, 3.

World Economic Forum. 2013. "Testing Economic and Environmental Resilience." In *Global Risks 2013, An Initiative of the Risk Response Network*, edited by Lee Howell, 8th ed, 19.

World Meteorological Organisation. 2013. *A Summary of Current Climate Change Findings and Figures*, WMO Information Note, March, http://www.wmo.int/pages/mediacentre/factsheet/documents/ClimateChangeInfoSheet2013-03final.pdf.

Zahar, Alexander, Jacqueline Peel, and Lee Godden. 2012. *Australian Climate Law in a Global Context*. Melbourne: Cambridge University Press eBook.

Game theory and corporate governance: conditions for effective stewardship of companies exposed to climate change risks[†]

Lucas Kruitwagen, Kaveh Madani, Ben Caldecott and Mark H. W. Workman

ABSTRACT

Engagement between investors and corporate boards has been suggested as a pathway to mitigate stranded asset and climate change risks. Debate is ongoing as to whether divestment or active ownership strategies are more appropriate to deliver long-term value and environmental sustainability. The paper tests the effectiveness of owner engagement strategies by studying the conditions for cooperation between investors and their companies. Characteristics of investors and companies are modelled in game theoretic frameworks, informed by semi-structured interviews with professionals from the energy and finance industries, and academia, NGO, and regulatory sectors. Conditions for mutual cooperation between investors and companies are characterized as prisoners' dilemmas. A number of parameters are examined for their impact on the development of sustained cooperative equilibria, including: the benefits and costs of cooperation; the degree of strategic foresight; individual discount factors; and mutual history. Challenges in the formation of investor coalitions are characterized and solutions are proposed.

1. Introduction

Climate change is rapidly becoming a material investment risk. Recent work by the Carbon Tracker Initiative (CTI) (e.g. 2013, 2014), McGlade and Ekins (2015), the University of Oxford Smith School of Enterprise and the Environment (e.g. Caldecott, Horwath, and McSharry 2013, 2015), HSBC (e.g. Spedding, Mehta, and Robins 2013), Standard & Poor's (2013, 2015), Kepler Cheuvreux (Lewis and Voisin 2014), and others has made stranded assets and misallocated capital a key concern of owners of fossil fuel companies. Universal owners are also gaining awareness of undiversifiable climate change value-at-risk (Covington and Thamotheram 2015; The Economist Intelligence Unit 2015). Investors must employ stewardship strategies to mitigate climate change risk on behalf of their beneficiaries. The Kay Review (2012) observes that investors have only two options in their relationships with companies: divestment and engagement. Shareholder engagement and

---

[†]Prepared for the 1st Global Conference of Stranded Assets and the Environment September 24 and 25, 2015; Oxford, UK.

active ownership is becoming a popular tool for shareholders wishing to influence the behaviour of their companies (e.g. Orsagh 2014; Kim and Schloetzer 2013 from PWC 2015; Goodman and Fields 2015). A common application of shareholder engagement is the mitigation of Environmental, Social, and Governance (ESG) risks of portfolio companies, such as those arising from climate change (Clark, Feiner, and Viehs 2014).

In July 2012, climate activist Bill McKibben popularised fossil fuel divestment with an article in the *Rolling Stone* (2012). McKibben called on university endowments and pensions to divest from fossil fuel holdings, on the logic that these funds exist to allow their benefactors to enjoy a prosperous future free of the impacts of climate change. Modelled on the divestment campaign which placed economic pressure on apartheid South Africa, more than 501 institutions with collective assets worth over US$3.4tn have joined the Fossil Free divestment campaign, pledging either full or partial divestment of fossil fuel assets (gofossilfree.org 2015). Ansar, Caldecott, and Tilbury (2013) argue that the greatest impact of the divestment campaign might be the stigmatisation of fossil fuel companies.

In their dissenting opinions on fossil fuel divestment, Harvard University (Faust 2013), The Wellcome Trust (Farrar 2015), and the Expert Group of the Norwegian Ministry of Finance (Skancke et al. 2014) all cite active ownership as their preferred management strategy for climate change risks. Divestment and engagement strategies now stand at odds with one another. Central to this debate is the question of what effect, if any, divestment (i.e. exclusion from a universe of investible securities) might have on the actions or outcomes of a company or class of companies. Alternatively, what effect might shareholder engagement and active ownership have on a company's actions or outcomes? Under what conditions might shareholder engagement be effective?

Despite a growing interest from investors in climate change risk management, approaches to these questions have been unsophisticated so far. Divestment decisions have been made largely on the grounds of ethics and mission-alignment of funds, belied by the prominence of faith-based groups and charitable foundations among divesters (gofossilfree.org 2015). Engagement on climate change risk has either focussed on supplementary disclosure (e.g. CDP) or targeted initiatives with extractive companies (e.g. the Aiming for A coalition). There is a demonstrated need for investors to be able to identify conditions for effective stewardship, to make intelligent and systematic engagement and disinvestment decisions corresponding to underlying environment-related risks.

This study examines the relationship between the management and equity owners of companies exposed to climate change risks. Characteristics of companies and shareholders which are deterministic in divestment or engagement decisions over carbon risk are identified and parameterized. In doing so, the paper proposes certain psychological factors (e.g. memory and foresight) and situational factors (e.g. multiplicity of investors, benefits, and costs), which may inform the development stewardship theory (e.g. Davis, Schoorman, and Donaldson 1997) and its relationship to agency theory (e.g. Ross 1973). Game theory concepts are applied to the relationship between companies and equity owners, and elementary models are developed to explore dynamics of engagement strategies. The work is informed by semi-structured interviews with professionals in the oil and gas industry, the financial industry, and NGO, regulatory, and academic sectors.

2. Method

The paper examines how investors and companies might interact with each other to mitigate climate change risks. The subject of study is the decision-making processes of both oil and gas companies and their investors, and critically how their decisions influence each other. The study of how individuals or organizations (hereafter called *agents*) make decisions is called *decision theory*.

Decision theory is the study of how a single rational agent maximizes their outcome, especially under uncertainty, and has found application among engineers, economists, psychologists, computer scientists, and policy-makers (Hansson 2005). Decision theory has its origins in Expected Utility Theory proposed by Daniel Bernoulli in 1738 (translated 1954). Mesterton-Gibbons (2000) provides a high-level overview of decision theory domains based on the number of agents and the number of rewards they receive, adapted in Figure 1. As the decisions and outcomes of investors and their companies are clearly interrelated, game theory tools will be used to examine the decision-making of various agents.

Game theory is the mathematical study of strategic decision-making. Classical Forms are those first described by Von Neumann and Morgenstern (1944) and bolstered substantially by Nash (e.g. 1950), and a number of other economists writing in the 1950s and 1960s. Metagame analysis was invented by Howard (1971), citing a need to develop strategic analysis tools which are easier to understand and are more descriptive of real agent behaviour. Axelrod in the 1980s (e.g. 1980, 1984) rekindled an interest in the field by realizing its potential to study problems of social coordination and cooperation. Smith (1982) was influential in introducing the subject to evolutionary biology. Game theory and its derivative disciplines now span diverse fields ranging from policy (Madani 2013) to transport planning (Rouhani et al. 2013) to project management (Asgari, Afshar, and Madani 2013).

Game theory is used to identify equilibria solutions from which no player is likely to deviate. Various equilibrium concepts exist, differing, for example, in their treatment of rationality, their stability in repeated play, and robustness to diverse agent beliefs (Madani and Hipel 2011). In the following section, classical normal form games are used to examine conditions for effective stewardship. The equilibria developed provide insight into effective engagement strategies between investors and their companies. Challenges of coalition formation among investors are also explored. Table 1 describes equilibria forms used in this paper.

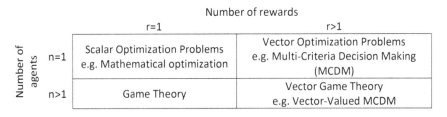

		Number of rewards	
		r=1	r>1
Number of agents	n=1	Scalar Optimization Problems e.g. Mathematical optimization	Vector Optimization Problems e.g. Multi-Criteria Decision Making (MCDM)
	n>1	Game Theory	Vector Game Theory e.g. Vector-Valued MCDM

Figure 1. Decision Theory Fields. Adapted from Mesterton-Gibbons (2000).

Table 1. Selected equilibria for classical form games. Adapted from Gibbons (1992).

Solution concept	Description
Nash Equilibrium	Nash equilibria are a set of strategies chosen by agents wherein no agent can strictly improve their utility by choosing any other strategy given the strategies of the other agents; all agents are playing best responses to each other
Bayesian Nash Equilibrium	Bayesian Nash Equilibrium are a set of strategies chosen by agents which are best responses to the *expected* strategies of the other agents

3. Game theory models

3.1. Social dilemmas between an investor and a company

Engagement between an investor and a company on an ESG issue is characterized as a social dilemma. A social dilemma occurs when agents individually seek higher payoffs for antisocial behaviour to the detriment of their collective interests (Dawes 1980). Stewardship theory seeks to identify when agents are intrinsically 'pro-organisational' and 'collectivist' (Davis, Schoorman, and Donaldson 1997). The prisoner's dilemma is the canonical social dilemma and is used in this paper to explore agent choices between cooperation and defection.

A 1v1 iterated prisoner's dilemma (IPD) is developed as a representation of the interaction between an investor (or a coalition of investors) and a company. In such a scenario, a cooperative outcome is one in which an investor engages on an ESG issue of interest, and the company delivers a corresponding change in behaviour. This is the socially optimal outcome wherein the investor and the company management both benefit from the financial outperformance of successful engagement, as demonstrated by Dimson, Karakas, and Li (2012) and Eccles, Ioannou, and Serafeim (2012). A non-cooperative outcome is one in which the company, the investor, or both fail or refuse to deliver on their engagement. An investor may lose interest in the subject or even divest from the company, and a company board may defect from its commitment to the investor. Characteristic of the IPD, the reward of mutual cooperation vests continually over time, whereas the temptation to defect delivers immediate utility to that agent followed usually by less cooperative future outcomes (e.g. Gibbons 1992). A brief development of the IPD parameterization follows. An extensive mathematical description of the methodology used is available in Appendices A and B.

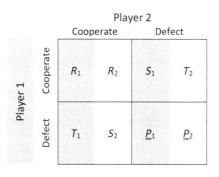

Figure 2. 1v1 Prisoner's dilemma payoffs in matrix form with Nash Equilibrium underlined.

The prisoner's dilemma was introduced by Dresher & Flood in 1950 to model strategic options during the cold war (Aumann and Maschler 1964). It is reproduced in its familiar form in Figure 2. Among other 2×2 games, the prisoner's dilemma is described by its ordered preferences: $T > R > P > S$, leading to the non-cooperative Nash Equilibria (*defect, defect*).

The uncooperative Nash Equilibria is dissatisfying for its failure to predict the cooperative equilibria regularly observed between real individuals and organizations (e.g. Fehr and Fischbacher 2003; Pothos et al. 2011). Repeated interactions between agents have the potential to create conditions of trust and mutual cooperation, resulting in improvements in both private outcomes and the overall system efficiency (Kreps et al. 1982; Axelrod 1984).

As an IPD of indeterminate length, no closed-form solution exists, and no deterministic strategy is dominant (Gibbons 1992). To develop a solution, a mixed-strategy IPD simulation is used to develop Bayesian Nash Equilbrium, per Harsanyi (1973), with Bayesian inferences and evolutionary decision-making as in Goeree and Holt (1999). The simulation was developed in MATLAB according to the methodology developed in Appendix B.

Variables examined in this model include the benefits and costs of cooperation, discount factors of the agents, and foresight and memory horizons. Table 2 describes how these parameters may be interpreted as conditions for cooperation between companies and investors and how IPD payoffs are simplified to a cost and benefit framework. Costs and benefits in this framework capture the business benefits (e.g. firm financial and operating performance (Clark, Feiner, and Viehs 2014)) and associated costs (e.g. personnel salaries (Wong 2010)).

In the simple model developed, payoffs are considered to be symmetrical – which does not reflect the separation and distinction of investor and firm interests, as held by typical agency problems (e.g. Davis, Schoorman, and Donaldson (1997)). As the intention of this paper is to explore conditions for mutual cooperation only, and because the payoffs are arbitrary and relative, this simplification is appropriate. Mutual cooperation would otherwise simply be limited by the less cooperative party (Kruitwagen 2015).

Further, this model considers the relationship of an investor and company management in isolation from other exogenous factors. These exogenous factors, such as changing exposure to risk, or changing opportunity cost for the investor's capital allocation, may

Table 2. IPD parameterization.

Parameter	Symbol	Interpretation
Benefit	BEN = [1 … 10]	Benefit of cooperation, for example, financial outperformance of company, mitigation of asset and reputation risk, talent attraction, social licence to operate
Cost	$COS = \left[0 \ldots {}^{BEN}/_2\right]$	Cost of cooperation, for example, engagement personnel salaries, opportunity costs
IPD Payoffs	Temptation	$T = BEN$
	Reward	$R = BEN - COS$
	Punishment	$P = 0$
	Sucker	$S = -COS$
Discount factor	$\delta_i = [0\% \ldots 100\%]$	Decreased value of future payoffs relative to present payoffs, or probability of game termination on subsequent round
Memory	$Q_i = [1 \ldots 10]$	Horizon of significance for past activity on which agents base present beliefs
Foresight	$L_i = [1 \ldots 10]$	The number of iterations an agent foresees in the future for which they calculate future-value payoffs

disrupt both the magnitude and ordinality of the payoffs proposed in this model. Environment-related risks in particular have the potential to manifest rapidly (e.g. Caldecott, Horwath, and McSharry (2013)), changing payoffs and resulting in different equilibria. These intricacies are outside the scope of this paper.

3.2. Social dilemmas between multiple investors

An N-agent IPD (NIPD) is developed as a representation of the coordination between multiple investors. NIPD models are commonly used to examine challenges of free-riding and coordination in social dilemmas (e.g. Ray and Vohra 1999). The NIPD is used here to examine the interest of investors in forming coalitions in their engagements with companies. See Appendix C for the full development of the NIPD.

It is more difficult to develop cooperative equilibria in an NIPD than in the 2-agent IPD, with the challenge increasing with the number of agents (e.g. Komorita 1976). In the NIPD, cooperative rewards are socialized to all agents, sanctions against non-cooperative agents have social externalities, and often elements of anonymity prevent agents from identifying cooperators and defectors (Dawes 1980). Example uses of the NIPD are to describe *tragedy of the commons* resource problems (Hardin 1968), endogenous coalition formation (Ray and Vohra 1999), and energy and climate policy free-riding problems (Nordhaus 2015).

Investors seeking to form coalitions in their interactions with companies face a typical free-riding problem. Collectively they benefit from strong engagement with the company, but individually they would benefit from neglecting their responsibilities and free-riding on the efforts of others. Solutions to the NIPD must overcome both the short-termism temptation of the IPD and the free-riding temptation. Many solution models (i.e. structures of strategies and payoffs that lead to cooperative equilibria) for the NIPD exist, including asymmetric payoffs (e.g Vyrastekova and Funaki 2010), side payments (e.g. Ray and Vohra 1999; Nordhaus 2015), spatial and personality interactions (e.g. Axelrod 1984; Manhart and Diekmann 1989), and social network theories (e.g. Rezaei, Kirley, and Pfau. 2009). The *relaxed* NIPD presented in this paper adds to these solution concepts. The payoff structure of Manhart and Diekmann (1989) is adapted by relaxing the strict dominance of defection payoffs and by giving agents unique weightings, allowing agents to have asymmetric payoffs. As in the IPD, agents use Bayesian inferences and evolutionary decision-making (Goeree and Holt 1999) to develop Bayesian Nash Equilibria (Harsanyi 1973). The simulation was developed in MATLAB according to the methodology developed in Appendix C.

This solution is well suited to investors who have different ownership portions of a company, and thus varying interests in the company's performance. Table 3 develops and interprets the parameters of the NIPD. Weighting and payoffs are again assigned arbitrarily for relative significance only.

Table 3. NIPD parameterization.

Parameter	Symbol	Interpretation
Weighting	$U_i = 0.5 + \text{RAND}[0\ldots1]$	Equity ownership of a shareholder, that is, how much weight they might add to a coalition
Payoffs	$R_i = \alpha K_i^{\gamma}$ $\alpha = [0\ldots1], \gamma = [0\ldots1]$	Benefit of cooperation, that is, joining the coalition
	$T_i = K_i + DD = [0\ldots0.2]$	Benefit of defection, that is, free-riding on the coalition

4. Results

4.1. Social dilemmas between an investor and a company: the IPD

The IPD is resolved in order to examine how parameters in Table 2, which are proxies for the attributes of companies and investors, lead to mutual cooperation. Mutual cooperation is interpreted as a proxy for effective stewardship. The sustained mutual cooperation of investors and companies leads to long-term management of environment-related risks and financial outperformance.

4.1.1. Dependence on payoffs and discount factors

The first parameters examined as conditions for effective stewardship are payoffs and discount factors. The payoffs for effective stewardship generally capture the benefits of stewardship (for example, the financial outperformance of the company and the mitigation of environment-related risk) less the costs of engagement. The defection of either the company or the investor allows them to capture the benefit of stewardship without the costs but may lead to less cooperative outcomes in the future.

Holding other factors constant, payoffs and discount factors are varied to explore their influence on conditions of mutual cooperation, shown in Figure 3. Benefits and costs need only be defined relative to each other; integer values are chosen on a range of 1–10. Discount factors are chosen on intervals between 0% and 100%.

The discount factor is used as a proxy for the discount rate used in discounted cash flow analysis by investors or companies (up to approximately 20% (Haldane and Davies 2011)). As a proxy however, the discount factor can also be used to capture excessive discounting and short-termism (an additional 5–10%, Haldane and Davies 2011) or the likelihood that an investor will sell their position within the year (>100% for the USA and UK, based on average stock holding time (Bogle 2010)).

Conditions for cooperation are strongest between an investor and a company when the benefit of cooperation is large, and the cost of cooperation is small. The social dilemma aspect of the game makes costs much more deterministic in cooperative outcomes than benefits. In engagements between companies and investors, it is critical, therefore, that both parties feel a strong benefit from engaging with each other and have minimal costs for doing so.

Low discount factors for both investors and companies encourage mutual cooperation. Agents with low discount factors place larger weights on future payoffs. For investors and companies in shareholder engagements, it is crucial that they have a low discount factor as the benefit of their engagement activities must vest continually to exceed the short-term payoff of defection.

Section 5 develops a more critical discussion of these findings.

4.1.2. Dependence on memory and foresight horizons

Keeping other factors constant at conditions for high mutual cooperation, horizons of memory and foresight are varied to explore their influence on the development of mutual cooperation, shown in Figure 4.

With a low foresight horizon, it is difficult to establish conditions of mutual cooperation. Closely related to discount factor, the foresight of investors and companies is deterministic in whether they engage or not. While a discount factor examines the

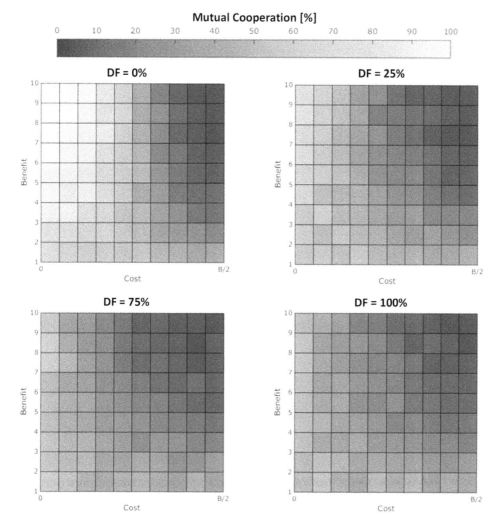

Figure 3. Modelled dependence of mutual cooperation on payoff and discount factors.

weight that agents give to future payoffs, foresight determines whether they consider the value of those future payoffs at all.

Even with longer foresight horizons, mutual cooperation may be hindered by long memories of past history. A longer memory in this sense allows agents to recall past defections which quickly eliminate any potential for present cooperation. Memory horizons indicate the significance of consistency in cooperation, showing that past defections can be deterministic in present cooperation.

4.2. Social dilemmas between multiple investors: the NIPD

The NIPD is resolved in order to examine how parameters in Table 3, which are proxies for the attributes of investors, lead to mutual cooperation, which is used as a proxy for coalition formation. The sustained mutual cooperation of investors leads to the

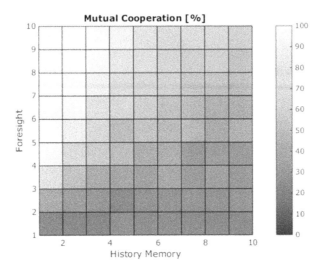

Figure 4. Modelled dependence of mutual cooperation on degree of foresight and history memory.

long-term formation of a coalition to engage on the management of environment-related risks.

4.2.1. Free-riding temptation
In traditional solution models, mutual cooperation diminishes rapidly with the number of agents, reaching a stable non-cooperative asymptote in the neighbourhood of 20–30 agents (Komorita 1976). In the relaxed NIPD, Figure 5 shows mixed free-riding and cooperation among 50 agents over successive iterations.

The left plots map the defector and cooperator payoffs dependent on the proportion of agents cooperating. The right plots are the probability density distributions of cooperating agents. The diminishing returns of cooperation are expressed by equations of payoffs for cooperation and defection. Even under these relaxed conditions, cooperative equilibria remain elusive. The smaller the difference between payoffs for free-riding and cooperating, the higher the participation in the cooperative coalition.

4.2.2. Cooperation dependence on weighting
Figure 6 shows the simulation of 50 mutually cooperating agents based on the size of the *defection* payoff and agent weighting. For a number of *defection* payoffs (D), the larger-weighted agents (i.e. investors with larger holdings) are more likely to cooperate with one-another. This reflects how large institutional investors have been the first to join ethical-based investors in engaging on climate change risks. The 'Aiming for A' coalition, for example, includes 23 pension funds in addition to 32 charity, foundations, and church groups (Aiming for A 2015). It must be noted that diminishing the defection payoff bonus (D) results in the violation of the strict ordinality of the temptation payoff (T) and the reward payoff (R), as required by Equation (18), Appendix C.

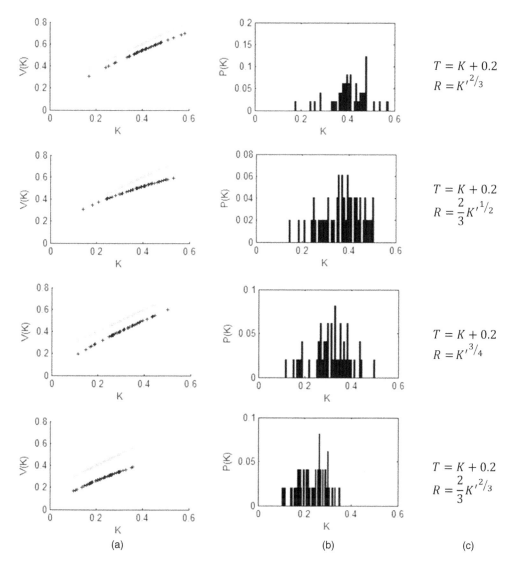

Figure 5. (a) Freerider and cooperator payoffs (V) dependent on the portion of cooperators (K). (b) Population density (P) of cooperating agents (K). (c) Payoff functions for freeriders (T) and cooperators (R).

5. Discussion

Discussion topics in this section are supported by interview testimony collected in July and August 2015. Thirteen semi-structured interviews were conducted with experts from the finance and energy industries, and the NGO, regulatory, and academic sectors (collectively 'NGO'). Interviews were conducted during a period of dramatically falling oil prices and significant shareholder engagement on carbon asset risk. The interviews were thus timely, but the interests and opinions of experts may have shifted significantly since a few years prior.

The success of recent shareholder resolutions with extractive companies is indicative of how engagement on climate change risk is currently conducted. In 2015, shareholder

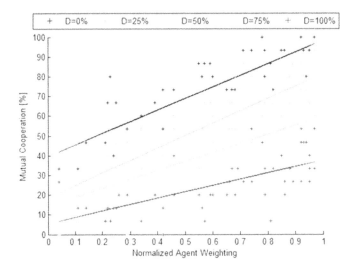

Figure 6. Cooperation dependence on agent weighting subject to various defection payoffs.

resolutions to examine and disclose carbon asset risk were submitted with Shell, BP, and Statoil (LAPFF 2015). Coalitions of investors (such as 'Aiming for A') engaged directly with company management on performance and disclosure objectives. Certain investors also delegated stewardship responsibility to firms who engaged with companies on their behalf (e.g. Hermes Equity Ownership Services). As a result of the multi-year engagement processes, the climate change risk shareholder resolutions with Shell, BP, and Statoil passed with over 98% of the shareholder vote (LAPFF 2015).

However, the vast majority of shareholders are unsophisticated with their stewardship practices – most delegate the decision-making of their votes to company management or to proxy advisory services (McCall and Larker 2014). Where climate change risk resolutions do not have broad coalition and management support, their success has typically been limited to approximately 20% of the vote (CERES 2015). It was the management's support of the resolutions at Shell, BP, and Statoil that led to their resounding success. Company management thus has sufficient agency in the company's action on climate risk to warrant their own representation in the social dilemmas considered.

In social dilemmas, costs are shown to dominate potential benefits in the development of cooperation. By preparing for engagement on climate change risk, company directors reduce their own costs at the time of engagement and thus are more likely to cooperate. As one energy industry contributor notes:

> If one or other party is not [conducting engagement] as a matter of routine … that's where the marginal cost related to the interaction creeps into significant value.

Likewise, investors can demand incremental progress which is not as immediately burdensome to company directors. The dominance of costs in cooperative equilibria may help explain why passive investors, who operate tight business models, have been reluctant to join stewardship efforts (Wong 2010; Johnson 2015). One finance industry contributor suggests:

> I think [engagement is] a challenge for the passives because they're pressed hard on fees.

The IPD shows how the long memories of agents diminish the chance for cooperative equilibria. This indicates that prior defections can be detrimental to current engagement efforts. Investors should then seek consistent small improvements from their companies with sustained engagement over successive years, rather than rapid change and adaptation. This was the strategy employed by Aiming for A, whose landmark shareholder proposals regarding climate change risk passed in 2015 after years of engagement (PIRC 2015). One finance industry contributor describes their engagement approach:

> It's been a very strategic approach, the resolutions didn't come out of the blue, we built extremely good relationships, [the companies] know us, they know where we're coming from.

Large foresight horizons are shown to be necessary for cooperative equilibria. Foresight horizons are related to discount factors, but represent instead the horizon beyond which a decision-maker has no ability or interest to foresee a payoff. Oil and gas company executives have an average tenure of 4.5 years (Reinsvold 2015), with performance incentives usually vesting three years after (Alvarez & Marsal Taxand LLC 2015). It is possible that the reluctance of companies to engage on climate change risks is explained by the bounded near-term foresight horizon of company executives. NGO and finance industry contributors describe executive preoccupation with short-term results:

> The company is so tied to that quarterly earnings call … which makes it really hard to think long term and strategically.
> We're not just interested in value over the next three months- we're interested in multiple decades of owning some of these key holdings. We need bring this perspective to companies and CEOs who may have a much shorter cycle.

The existence of a foresight horizon may also help explain why passive investors are reluctant to engage in stewardship activities. Their belief in efficient or near-efficient markets may preclude their interest in any foresight horizon as part of their investment strategy.

The NIPD is known to be a more frustrating social dilemma than the IPD, and increases in difficulty with the number of agents (Komorita 1976; Dawes 1980). Shareholders may have a large potential influence with companies, but only when they are coordinated. Per one energy industry contributor:

> Shareholders are incredibly powerful … what you need to see is a significant weight of shareholders getting behind [this view].

Even with the enhanced cooperation payoffs of the NIPD model above, wide-spread cooperation of the agents is rare. Oil and gas companies in particular have massive disparate shareholder bases numbering in the hundreds of thousands of holders (e.g. BP plc 2014). However, the number of significant shareholders is much less. Less than 10 individual shareholders often control a disproportionate amount of oil and gas companies – over 20% (e.g. BP (2014), Total (2015), Shell (2015), ExxonMobil (Yahoo! Finance 2015b) and Chevron (Yahoo! Finance 2015a)). An engageable number of shareholders might control a dominating interest in an oil and gas company.

Additional NIPD mechanisms may present concepts for the formation of coalitions among shareholders. Resource allocation and side payment mechanisms (e.g. Shenoy 1979; Nordhaus 2015) are familiar game theory subjects which allow agents to come to terms among each other for increased cooperation. This is already in practice by investors, for instance the UN Principles for Responsible Investment's (PRI's) use of a clearing house mechanism to allocate support and resources to engagements by fellow investors (PRI 2015). One interviewee involved in an engagement coalition described the use of shared costs and responsibilities to maximize impact across a portfolio of companies in a structure similar to a social network game. These coalitions are still subject to free-riding, but cost sharing among cooperative investors enables easier coalition formation.

6. Conclusion

In this work, non-cooperative social dilemma games were used to develop insight into the conditions for effective stewardship of companies by their investors. Iterated prisoners' dilemmas were used to explore conditions for mutual cooperation between pairs and groups of agents. The games and insights developed were informed by semi-structured interviews with energy and finance industry professionals and NGO/regulator/academic sector professionals.

Several barriers to mutual cooperation and coalition formation in engagements were identified, including the disproportional impact of costs relative to benefits, low discount factors, short foresight horizons, and sensitive memories. Free-riding temptations increase in larger groups, making coalition formation among large groups of shareholders difficult. Novel solution models like side payment and social network mechanisms can inform the development of structures for stable coalitions of investors.

The long-term interests of asset owners are driving sustainability performance in their investee companies in order to mitigate exposure to environment-related risks. For investors interested in influencing company behaviour, challenges remain in overcoming short-term defection between investors and company boards. Conditions for mutual cooperation have been developed in this paper to give investors insight as to when their engagements of sustainability issues will be more effective. Investors seeking to build stable coalitions with other investors must overcome free-riding incentives to wield stronger influence with companies.

This work offers investors additional insight for making engagement, disinvestment, and divestment decisions. The ultimate significance of this work is that engagement and divestment decisions may eventually be made empirically, based on underlying environment-related risks and the effectiveness of investor stewardship and engagement.

Acknowledgements

The authors extend their sincere thanks to the 13 interviewees who informed the development of this work. Constructive comments from the two anonymous reviewers are also appreciated.

Disclosure statement

No potential conflict of interest was reported by the authors.

References

Aiming For 'A' Investor Coalition. 2015. BP Shell AGM 2015 Institutional Co-Filing Group 2nd Feb 2015 Final. Accessed January 24, 2016. http://www.churchinvestorsgroup.org.uk/system/

files/documents/James%20Corah/BP%20Shell%20AGM%202015%20Institutional%20Co-filing %20Group%202nd%20Feb%202015%20Final.pdf.

Alvarez & Marsal Taxand LLC. 2015. *Oil and Gas Exploration & Production (E & P) Incentive Plan Design Report.* Accessed September 3, 2015. http://www.alvarezandmarsal.com/sites/default/ files/am_tax_oilandgas_e-preport.pdf.

Ansar, A., B. Caldecott, and J. Tilbury. 2013. *Stranded assets and the fossil fuel divestment campaign.* Smith School of Enterprise and the Environment. Accessed April 3, 2015. http://www. smithschool.ox.ac.uk/research-programmes/stranded-assets/SAP-divestment-report-final.pdf.

Asgari, S., A. Afshar, and K. Madani. 2013. "Cooperative Game Theoretic Framework for Joint Resource Management in Construction." *Journal of Construction Engineering and Management* 140 (3): 04013066-1–13.

Aumann, R. J., and M. Maschler. 1964. "The Bargaining Set for Cooperative Games." In *Advances in GameTheory*, Annals of Mathematics Studies No. 52, edited by M. Dresher, L. S. Shapley, and A. W. Trucker, 443–476. Princeton: Princeton University Press.

Axelrod, R. 1980. "Effective Choice in the Prisoner's Dilemma." *The Journal of Conflict Resolution* 24 (1): 3–25.

Axelrod, R. 1984. *The Evolution of Co-operation.* New York: Basic Books, Inc.

Bernoulli, D. 1954. "Exposition of a New Theory on the Measurement of Risk." *Econometrica* 22 (1): 23–36.

Bogle, J. C. 2010. "Restoring Faith in Financial Markets." *The Wallstreet Journal.* Accessed September 3, 2015. http://www.wsj.com/articles/SB10001424052748703436504574640523013840290.

BP plc. 2014. *Annual Report.* Accessed September 3, 2015. http://www.bp.com/en/global/corporate/ investors/annual-reporting.html.

Caldecott, B., G. Dericks, and J. Mitchell. 2015. *Stranded Assets and Subcritical Coal: The Risk to Companies and Investors.* Accessed January 24, 2016. http://www.smithschool.ox.ac.uk/ research-programmes/stranded-assets/publications.php.

Caldecott, B., N. Horwath, and P. McSharry. 2013. *Stranded Assets in Agriculture: Protecting Value from Environment-related Risks.* Accessed January 24, 2016. http://www.smithschool.ox.ac.uk/ research-programmes/stranded-assets/publications.php.

Carbon Tracker Initiative. 2013. *Unburnable Carbon 2013: Wasted Capital and Stranded Assets.* Accessed April 3, 2015. http://www.carbontracker.org/our-work/.

Carbon Tracker Initiative. 2014. *Carbon Supply Cost Curves: Oil Capital Expenditures.* Accessed April 3, 2015. http://www.carbontracker.org/our-work/.

CERES. 2015. CERES - Shareholder Resolutions. Accessed September 3, 2015. http://www.ceres. org/investor-network/resolutions.

Clark, G., A. Feiner, and M. Viehs. 2014. *Stockholder to Stakeholder.* Smith School of Enterprise and the Environment. Accessed April 3, 2015. http://www.smithschool.ox.ac.uk/library/index.php.

Covington, H., and R. Thamotheram. 2015. *The Case for Forceful Stewardship (Part 1).* Accessed September 3, 2015. https://preventablesurprises.com/programmes/climate-change/.

Davis, J. H., F. D. Schoorman, and L. Donaldson. 1997. "Towards a Stewardship Theory of Management." *The Academy of Management Review* 22 (1): 20–47.

Dawes, R. M. 1980. "Social Dilemmas." *Annual Review of Psychology* 31 (1): 169–193.

Dimson, E., O. Karakas, and X. Li. 2012. Active Ownership. Review of Financial Studies, Forthcoming, (December), 1–48. Access November 5, 2015. http://papers.ssrn.com/abstract= 2154724.

Eccles, R. G., I. Ioannou, and G. Serafeim. 2012. "The Impact of Corporate Sustainability on Organizational Processes and Performance." *Management Science Forthcoming.* Accessed November 5, 2015. http://papers.ssrn.com/sol3/papers.cfm?abstract_id=1964011.

The Economist Intelligence Unit. 2015. *The Cost of Inaction: Recognising the Value at Risk from Climate Change.* Accessed September 3, 2015. http://www.economistinsights.com/financial- services/analysis/cost-inaction.

Farrar, J. 2015. "Fossil Fuel Divestment Is Not the Way to Reduce Carbon Emissions." *The Guardian.* Accessed April 3, 2015. http://www.theguardian.com/commentisfree/2015/mar/25/ wellcome-trust-fossil-fuel-divestment-not-way-reduce-carbon-emissions.

Faust, D. 2013. *Fossil Fuel Divestment Statement*. Harvard University. Accessed September 3, 2015 http://www.harvard.edu/president/fossil-fuels.

Fehr, E., and U. Fischbacher. 2003. "The Nature of Human Altruism." *Nature* 425 (6960): 785–791.

Gibbons, R. 1992. *A Primer in Game Theory*. Harlow: Pearson Education.

Goeree, J. K., and Holt, C. A. 1999. "Stochastic Game Theory: For Playing Games, Not Just for Doing Theory." *Proceedings of the National Academy of Sciences of the United States of America* 96 (19): 10564–10567.

gofossilfree.org. 2015. Commitments. gofossilfree.org. Accessed September 22, 2015. http://gofossilfree.org/commitments/.

Goodman, A., and R. R. W. Fields. 2015. "Board-Shareholder Engagement: Current & Future Trends." *Ethicalboardroom.com*. Accessed May 8, 2015. http://ethicalboardroom.com/activism/board-shareholder-engagement-current-future-trends/.

Haldane, A. G., and R. Davies. 2011. The Short Long - Speech. Accessed September 3, 2015. http://www.bankofengland.co.uk/archive/Documents/historicpubs/speeches/2011/speech495.pdf.

Hansson, S. O. 2005. *Decision Theory*. Accessed September 3, 2015 http://web.science.unsw.edu.au/~stevensherwood/120b/Hansson_05.pdf.

Hardin, G. 1968. "The Tragedy of the Commons." *Science* 162 (June): 1243–1248.

Harsanyi, J. C. 1973. "Games with Randomly Disturbed Payoffs: A New Rationale for Mixed-strategy Equilibrium Points." *International Journal of Game Theory* 2 (1): 1–23.

Howard, N. 1971. *Paradoxes of Rationality: Theory of Metagames and Political Behavior*. Cambridge, MA: MIT Press.

Ishibuchi, H., and N. Namikawa. 2005. "Evolution of Iterated Prisoner's Dilemma Game Strategies in Structured Demes under Random Pairing in Game-Playing." *IEEE Transcations on Evolutionary Computation* 9 (6): 552–561.

Janssen, M. A. 2008. "Evolution of Cooperation in a One-shot Prisoner's Dilemma Based on Recognition of Trustworthy and Untrustworthy Agents." *Journal of Economic Behavior and Organization* 65 (3–4): 458–471.

Johnson, S. 2015. "Compulsory Stewardship by Passive Managers Moves Closer." *The Financial Times*. Accessed January 24, 2016. http://www.ft.com/cms/s/0/3917d0d0-e812-11e4-894a-00144feab7de.html#axzz3yFP6jymf.

Kanazawa, S., and L. Fontaine. 2013. "Intelligent People Defect More in a One-shot Prisoner's Dilemma Game." *Journal of Neuroscience, Psychology, and Economics* 6 (3): 201–213.

Kay, J. 2012. "The Kay Review of the UK Equity Market and Long-term Decision Making." Accessed April 3, 2015. https://www.gov.uk/government/publications/kay-review-of-uk-equity-markets-and-long-term-decision-making-implementation-progress-report.

Kim, J., and J. D. Schloetzer. 2013. *Global Trends in Board-shareholder Engagement*. The Conference Board. Accessed September 3, 2015. https://www.conference-board.org/publications/publicationdetail.cfm?publicationid=2618.

Komorita, S. S. 1976. "A Model of the N-Person Dilemma-type Game." *Journal of Experimental Social Psychology* 12 (4): 357–373.

Kreps, D. M., P. Milgrom, J. Roberts, and R. Wilson. 1982. "Rational Cooperation in the Finitely Repeated Prisoners' Dilemma." *Journal of Economic Theory* 27 (2): 245–252.

Kruitwagen, L. 2015. "Conditions for Effective Stewardship of Companies Subject to Climate Change Risk." MSc Thesis, Imperial College London.

Kuhn, S. 2014. "Prisoner's Dilemma." *The Stanford Encyclopedia of Philosophy*. Accessed September 3, 2015. http://plato.stanford.edu/entries/prisoner-dilemma/.

Lewis, M. C., and S. Voisin. 2014. *Stranded Assets, Fossilised Revenues*, Kepler Cheuvreux. Accessed April 3, 2015. https://www.keplercheuvreux.com/pdf/research/EG_EG_253208.pdf.

Local Authority Pension Fund Forum (LAPFF). 2015. "And Statoil Makes Three as Transatlantic Gap Grows." *News*. Accessed January 24, 2016. http://www.lapfforum.org/news/and-statoil-makes-three-as-transatlantic-gap-grows.

Madani, K. 2010. "Game Theory and Water Resources." *Journal of Hydrology* 381 (3–4): 225–238.

Madani, K. 2013. "Modeling International Climate Change Negotiations More Responsibly: Can Highly Simplified Game Theory Models Provide Reliable Policy Insights?" *Ecological Economics* 90 (6): 68–76.

Madani, K., and K. Hipel. 2011. "Non-Cooperative Stability Definitions for Strategic Analysis of Generic Water Resources Conflicts." *Water Resources Management* 25 (8): 1949–1977.

Manhart, K., and C. A. Diekmann. 1989. "Cooperation in 2- and N-Person Prisoner's Dilemma Games: A Simulation Study." *Analyse & Kritik* 11 (2): 134–153.

McCall, A. L., and D. F. Larker. 2014. "Researchers: The Power of Proxy Advisory Firms." *Insights by Stanford Business*. Accessed September 3, 2015. https://www.gsb.stanford.edu/insights/researchers-power-proxy-advisory-firms.

McGlade, C., and P. Ekins. 2015. "The Geographical Distribution of Fossil Fuels Unused When Limiting Global Warming to 2°C." *Nature* 517 (7533): 187–190.

McKibben, B. 2012. "Global Warming's Terrifying New Math." *The Rolling Stone*. Accessed April 3, 2015. http://www.rollingstone.com/politics/news/global-warmings-terrifying-new-math-20120719.

Mesterton-Gibbons, M. 2000. *An Introduction to Game-Theoretic Modelling*. 2nd ed. Providence, USA: American Mathematical Society.

Miller, J. H. 1996. "The Coevolution of Automata in the Repeated Prisoner's Dilemma." *Journal of Economic Behavior and Organization* 29 (1): 87–112.

Nash, J. 1950. "Equilibrium Points in N-Person Games." *Proceedings of the National Academy of Sciences of the United States of America* 39 (1): 48–49.

Neumann, J. Von., and O. Morgenstern. 1944. *Theory of Games and Economic Behavior*, 60th Anniv. Princeton, NJ: Princeton University Press.

Nordhaus, B. W. 2015. "Climate Clubs: Overcoming Free-riding in International Climate Policy." *The American Economic Review* 105 (4): 1339–1370.

Orsagh, M. 2014. *Shareholder Engagement: Bridging the Gap Between Boards and Investors*. CFA Institute. Accessed May 8, 2015. http://blogs.cfainstitute.org/marketintegrity/2014/03/26/shareholder-engagement-bridging-the-divide-between-boards-and-investors/.

Pettit, P., and R. Sugden. 1989. "The Backward Induction Paradox." *The Journal of Philosophy* 86 (4): 169–182.

PIRC. 2015. BP AGM - Who's Next to Aim for A? Accessed September 3, 2015 http://pirc.co.uk/pircnews/bp-agm-who-is-next-to-aim-for-a.

Pothos, E. M., G. Perry, P. J. Corr, M. R. Matthew, and J. R. Busemeyer. 2011. "Understanding Cooperation in the Prisoner's Dilemma Game." *Personality and Individual Differences* 51 (3): 210–215.

PRI. 2015. PRI - Clearinghouse. Accessed September 3, 2015. http://www.unpri.org/areas-of-work/clearinghouse/.

PWC. 2015. *Key Issues: Shareholder Engagement*. Center for Board Governance. Accessed May 8, 2015. http://www.pwc.com/us/en/corporate-governance/shareholder-engagement.jhtml.

Ray, D., and R. Vohra. 1999. "A Theory of Endogenous Coalition Structures." *Games and Economic Behavior* 26: 286–336.

Reinsvold, C. H. 2015. "The Oil and Gas CEO." *Oil&Gas Financial Journal* 11 (9). Accessed September 3, 2015. http://www.ogfj.com/articles/print/volume-11/issue-9/features/the-oil-and-gas-ceo.html.

Rezaei, G., M. Kirley, and J. Pfau. 2009. "Evolving Cooperation in the N-player Prisoner's Dilemma: A Social Network Model." *Lecture Notes in Computer Science* 5865 LNAI: 43–52.

Ross, S. 1973. "The Economic Theory of Agency: The Principal's Problem." *The American Economic Review* 63 (2): 134–139.

Rouhani, O. M., D. Niemeier, C. R. Knittel, and K. Madani. 2013. "Integrated Modeling Framework for Leasing Urban Roads: A Case Study of Fresno, California." *Transportation Research Part B: Methodological* 48 (2): 17–30.

Royal Dutch Shell plc. 2015. *Annual Report 2014*. Accessed September 3, 2015. http://www.shell.com/global/aboutshell/media/reports-publications.html.

Shenoy, P. P. 1979. "On Coalition Formation: A Game-Theoretical Approach." *International Journal of Game Theory* 8 (3): 133–164.

Skancke, M., E. Dimson, M. Hoel, M. Kettis, G. Nystuen, and L. Starks 2014. *Fossil-Fuel Investments in the Norwegian Government Pension Fund Global: Addressing Climate Issues Through Exclusion and Active Ownership.* Expert Group appointed by the Norwegian Ministry of Finance.

Smith, J. M. 1982. *Evolution and the Theory of Games.* Cambridge: Cambridge University Press.

Spedding, Paul, K. Mehta, and N. Robins. 2013. *Oil & carbon revisited-Value at risk from "unburnable" reserves,* HSBC. Accessed April 3, 2015. http://daily.swarthmore.edu/wp-content/uploads/2013/02/HSBCOilJan13.pdf.

Standard & Poor's. 2013. *What A Carbon-Constrained Future Could Mean For Oil Companies ' Creditworthiness.* Standard & Poor's. Accessed April 3, 2015. http://www.standardandpohttps//www.standardandpoors.com/ratings/articles/en/eu/?articleType=PDF&assetID=1245348784590name2=Content-Disposition&blobheadervalue1=application/pdf&blobkey=i.

Standard & Poor's. 2015. *How Environment and Climate Risk Factor into Global Corporate Ratings.* Standard & Poor's. Accessed January 1, 2016. https://www.environmental-finance.com/content/research/how-environmental-and-climate-risks-factor-into-global-corporate-ratings.html.

Szilagyi, M. N. 2003. "An Investigation of N-person Prisoners Dilemmas." *Complex Systems* 14: 155–174.

Total, S. A. 2015. *Total Annual Report.* Accessed September 3, 2015. http://www.total.com/en/media/news/press-releases/2014-annual-reports.

Vyrastekova, J., and Y. Funaki. 2010. *Cooperation in a Sequential N-person Prisoner's Dilemma: The Role of Information and Reciprocity?* (Unpublished work). Accessed September 3, 2015. www.ru.nl/publish/pages/516298/nice_10-103.pdf.

Wong, S. 2010. "Why Stewardship Is Proving Elusive for Institutional Investors." *Butterworths Journal of International Banking and Financial Law* 2010 (Jul/Aug): 406–411.

Yahoo! Finance. 2015a. Chevron Corporation (CVX). Accessed September 3, 2015. http://finance.yahoo.com/q/mh?s=CVX+Major+Holders.

Yahoo! Finance. 2015b. Exxon Mobil Corporation (XOM). Accessed September 3, 2015. http://finance.yahoo.com/q/mh?s=XOM+Major+Holders.

Appendix A: Development of a 1v1 Prisoner's Dilemma

The canonical Prisoner's Dilemma (PD) was initially developed by Dresher & Flood in 1950 to model strategic options during the cold war (Aumann et al. 1964). The PD's characteristic traits make it one of the most written-of social dilemmas, with interest spanning from economics, psychology, and political science (Dawes 1980), natural resource management (Madani 2010), evolutionary biology (Smith 1982), and artificial intelligence and machine learning (Miller 1996). A single-shot prisoner's dilemma is considered with elements described by Table A1. The notation and methodology used herein are typical of any introductory-level game theory study (e.g. Gibbons 1992; Mesterton-Gibbons 2000).

Pure strategy payoffs are given in matrix form as in Figure 2, subject to the constraint of Equation (1).

$$T_i > R_i > P_i > S_i. \tag{1}$$

The Nash Equilibrium of this matrix-form game is (D,D). Even with asymmetric payoffs, as long as the ordinal nature of each player's payoffs holds, the Nash Equilibrium remains (D,D). Relaxing the order of player i's payoffs results in a *common knowledge* PD, where player i, knowing the other's payoffs, will still choose mutual defection, provided $P_i > S_i$ (Kuhn 2014). The one-shot nature of this game lends itself better to study in fields of psychology and sociology, with research on topics such as intelligence (e.g. Kanazawa and Fontaine 2013), trustworthiness (e.g. Janssen 2008), or personality (e.g. Pothos et al. 2011).

Appendix B: Development of a 1v1 Iterated PD

The single-shot game developed in Appendix A is capable of modelling many interactions where two agents interact only once. The uncooperative Nash Equilibrium (D,D) is dissatisfying both for its generally negative connotation and its failure to predict the cooperative equilibria regularly observed between real individuals and organizations (Fehr and Fischbacher 2003; Pothos et al. 2011). Repeated interactions between agents have the potential to create conditions of trust and mutual cooperation, resulting in improvements in both private outcomes and the overall system efficiency (Kreps et al. 1982; Axelrod 1984). The repeated PD is called the *iterated prisoner's dilemma* (IPD).

Deterministic IPD

In the IPD, players engage in a PD game which repeats for multiple rounds. Elements of a deterministic IPD are described in Table A2. A deterministic IPD is characterized by the pure strategies and payoffs of the players being common knowledge.

The payoff of the players may be additive, per Equation (2), or averaged over multiple rounds.

$$V_i = \sum_{t=0}^{\tau} v(a_{i,t}, a_{-i,t}). \tag{2}$$

The strategy space for players is now much more sophisticated, with players able to choose from a variety of rules or sequences of cooperation or defection. Some simple strategies are shown in Table A3. Axelrod (1980) first proposed an open-entry strategy competition where submitted algorithms would compete in an iterated Prisoners' Dilemma. Axelrod (1984) explored the characteristics of successful strategies and drew comparisons to real-life examples of sustained mutual cooperation.

For IPDs of any finite length with complete and perfect knowledge, a single Nash Equilibrium exists. Players use reverse (backward) induction to determine that the strategy to *always defect* strictly dominates all other strategies. While theoretically sound, this equilibrium is unsatisfying, especially at large numbers of iteration (Pettit and Sugden 1989). Similarly, for IPDs of infinite or indeterminate length, no single Nash Equilibrium strictly dominates all others. Players must play strategies which are best responses to each other. The following development of the IPD is typical to introductory-level game theory (e.g. Gibbons 1992; Mesterton-Gibbons 2000).

For an IPD of infinite or indeterminate length, Nash Equilibria may be identified with the inclusion of the discounting factor, δ. The discounting factor represents either the relative value of a payoff received in a future period, as in an infinite IPD, or the probability that the present round will be the final round, as in an indeterminate IPD. The sum of an infinite series of discounted values converges to a convenient expression (Equation (3)), allowing the direct comparison deterministic payoffs and the development of Nash

Equilibria.

$$v + v\delta + v\delta^2 + \ldots + v\delta^\tau = \sum_{t=1}^{\tau=\infty} v\delta^t = \frac{v}{1-\delta}. \tag{3}$$

An additional constraint (Equation (4)) is typically introduced in order to disincentivize strategies in which two players alternate T and S payoffs.

$$R > \frac{T+S}{2}. \tag{4}$$

In the simple case of an IPD between two *Grim Trigger* strategies with symmetrical payoffs, the conditions for a subgame-perfect Nash Equilibrium can be explicitly defined. Mutual cooperation must be preferable in each subgame relative to a temptation payoff followed by perpetual mutual defection. This is described by Equation (5).

$$\frac{R}{1-\delta} > T + \frac{\delta P}{1-\delta}. \tag{5}$$

Following Axelrod's successful computer tournament in 1980, an ongoing annual competition pits a wide range of strategies against each other. Strategies now range in complexity from the original simple strategies as in Table A3, to sophisticated strategies using probabilistic models.

Mixed-strategy IPD

Deterministic IPDs involve explicit assumptions about the cooperative rational nature of the players, and only have cooperative Nash Equilibria for infinite or indeterminate length games. To examine the conditions which best enable routine cooperation from self-interested players, a mixed-strategy IPD is more useful. Following Harsanyi (1973), mixed-strategy weighting can be used to represent belief spaces, allowing the development of Bayesian Nash Equilibrium (BNE). These beliefs may be updated as Bayesian inferences developed from sequential behaviour, as in Goeree and Holt (1999). Thus a mixed-strategy IPD adds the elements of Table A4 to the elements of a deterministic IPD and single-shot PD.

The pure strategy chosen by a player at time t is determined randomly by the mixed-strategy expected payoffs of each pure strategy, per Equation (6).

$$s_i = \text{rand} \begin{cases} C \\ D \end{cases} \text{ with } \begin{array}{l} P_C = P(\pi_C^e, \pi_D^e) \\ P_D = 1 - P_C \end{array} \tag{6}$$

An evolutionary algorithm, as in Goeree and Holt (1999), is used to weight expected payoffs into probabilities, per Equation (7). A relaxing factor, μ, can be adjusted to suit the importance of payoffs in determining the random development of player actions.

$$P_C = \frac{e^{\pi_C^e/\mu}}{e^{\pi_C^e/\mu} + e^{\pi_D^e/\mu}} \text{ with } \mu = (0, \infty). \tag{7}$$

Expected payoffs are the mixed-strategy payoffs developed for a bounded horizon of L periods per Equation (8). Mixed-strategy payoffs are weighted by common knowledge beliefs $\theta_{s,i}$ (of a player i to play a strategy s).

$$\pi^e_{s,i} = \sum_{t=t_0}^{t_0+L} \sum_{i=1,2} \sum_{s=C,D} \theta_{s,i} * \theta_{s,-i} * v_i(s_i, s_{-i}) * \delta^{t-t_0}. \tag{8}$$

Common knowledge beliefs are updated after each round. The beliefs are updated based on the number of times a player adopts strategy per Equation (9). By updating beliefs based on observed actions, cooperative actions increase the probability of mutual cooperation and defection actions increase the probability of mutual defection. The history of observed actions is limited by the memory of the player.

$$\theta_{s,i} = \frac{\text{count } (H(Q_i) = s)}{\text{size } (H(Q_i))}. \tag{9}$$

The sequentially updating beliefs result in a Markov chain of mixed probabilities and payoff states per Equation (10).

$$\pi^e s, i = \delta^0 \sum \left\{ \begin{array}{l} \theta_{C,-i,0} * v_i(S, C) \\ \theta_{D,-i,0} * v_i(S, D) \end{array} \right\} + \delta^1 \sum \left\{ \begin{array}{l} \theta_{C,i,1} * \theta_{C,-i,1} * v_i(C, C) \\ \theta_{D,i,1} * \theta_{C,-i,1} * v_i(D, C) \\ \theta_{C,i,1} * \theta_{D,i,1} * v_i(C, D) \\ \theta_{D,i,1} * \theta_{D,-i,1} * v_i(D, D) \end{array} \right\} + \ldots$$

$$+ \delta^L \sum \left\{ \begin{array}{l} \theta_{C,i,L} * \theta_{C,-i,L} * v_i(C, C) \\ \theta_{D,i,L} * \theta_{C,-i,L} * v_i(D, C) \\ \theta_{C,i,L} * \theta_{D,-i,L} * v_i(C, D) \\ \theta_{D,i,L} * \theta_{D,-i,L} * v_i(D, D) \end{array} \right\} \tag{10}$$

The updating of beliefs for each round, $\theta_{s,i,t}$, requires a result of the previous round. A Monte Carlo method is used to randomly generate a strategy pair for each round according to probabilities established by mixed beliefs at each round, illustrated by Equation (11).

$$s_i, s_{-i} = \text{rand} \left\{ \begin{array}{ll} C, C & P_{C,C} = \theta_{C,i,L} * \theta_{C,-i,L} \\ D, C & P_{D,C} = \theta_{D,i,I} * \theta_{C,-i,L} \\ C, D & P_{C,D} = \theta_{C,i,L} * \theta_{D,-i,L} \\ D, D & P_{D,D} = \theta_{D,i,L} * \theta_{D,-i,L} \end{array} \right. \text{with} \tag{11}$$

The results presented in Section 4.1 represent the average of 10 complete iterations, with 40 Monte-Carlo-generated pairs in each round. The relaxing factor, μ, was unity.

Appendix C: Development of an NvN IPD

The NvN IPD (NIPD) is an abstraction of the 1v1 IPD which has application to a greater set of social coordination and common problems. The NIPD can be used to describe challenges with pollution, public services, energy and water conservation, etc.; all situations where an individual receives a higher payoff for any defective action, but all payoffs are higher with collective cooperation. Due to the larger number of players involved, conditions for cooperation are often more elusive than in the IPD. In the NIPD, harm from defection is dispersed among multiple players, defection is more anonymous, and any reinforcing punishment strategies directed against a defector have negative externalities on all other players (Dawes 1980).

Many authors have studied the NIPD. For large N, an uncooperative equilibrium of self-optimizing agents develops quickly (e.g. Komorita 1976). In order to provide nontrivial results, authors seek mechanisms which induce cooperation in the population. Some studies use compound games (i.e. large games featuring many 1v1 subgames) and spatial considerations to inspire cooperation (Axelrod 1984; Ishibuchi and Namikawa 2005; Rezaei, Kirley, and Pfau. 2009). Other use evolutionary and personality diversities (whether in behaviour or payoffs) to find conditions which induce cooperation (Axelrod 1984; Manhart and Diekmann 1989; Szilagyi 2003).

Calculation of behaviour and equilibria in the NIPD can be an NP-hard optimization problem. Dawes (1980) suggests that elements of knowledge (e.g. communication and public disclosure), morality, and trust have the greatest impact on the development of cooperation in real social dilemmas.

Deterministic NIPD

An NIPD based on Vyrastekova and Funaki (2010) and Manhart and Diekmann (1989) is developed here. Both works use agent personalities in the form of asymmetric payoffs to explore cooperation. Elements of the NIPD are described in Table A5.

As in the IPD, players face the choice to either cooperate or defect. In the NIPD, the reward for cooperation grows with the number of players cooperating. However, for the same number of players cooperating, the defectors receive a greater payoff. Equations (13)–(16) describe the payoff conditions of the NIPD.

$$\text{with } k = \frac{N_C}{N}, \ k' = \frac{N_C + 1}{N}, \tag{12}$$

$$V(D, k') > V(D, k), \tag{13}$$

$$V(C, k') > V(C, k), \tag{14}$$

$$V(C, k') < V(D, k), \tag{15}$$

$$V(C, k = 1) > V(D, k = 0). \tag{16}$$

With payoffs R for cooperation and T for defection, Figure A1 shows how, given Equation (15) above, D dominates C for any k. The Nash Equilibrium of the NIPD is sustained defection by all players. As N becomes large, the threat of future sanctions is insufficient to ensure conditions for cooperation. Any credible threat against a defecting player is diluted with negative externalities to other players, making the conditions for cooperation more difficult.

To develop useful cooperation scenarios from the NIPD, the condition of Equation (15) will be relaxed to Equation (17). To appropriately model the commons and free-riding problems the NIPD simulates, the payoff for additional cooperation will have diminishing returns as in Figure A1.

$$V(C, k) < V(D, k). \tag{17}$$

With symmetric payoffs the Nash Equilibrium occurs at some deterministic $k > 0$. However with asymmetric mixed-strategy payoffs based on each player's individual beliefs, the Bayesian Nash Equilibrium need not occur at a deterministic value of k. This allows for the development of more unique insight and less prescriptive model behaviour.

Mixed strategy NIPD

The NIPD may also be developed in cases where payoffs are asymmetric. Payoffs R and T, for cooperation and defection, respectively, may be weighted by an individual factor U_j. Payoff conditions described as above still hold, with a new K described in Equation (18). Equations (19) and (20) describe asymmetric payoffs R_j and T_j.

$$\text{with } \; K_i = \frac{\sum_{j=1}^{N_C} U_{j \neq i}}{\sum_{j=1}^{N} U_j}, \; K_i' = \frac{\sum_{j=1}^{N_C} U_{j \neq i} + U_i}{\sum_{j=1}^{N} U_j}, \tag{18}$$

$$v_i(C, K_i) = R_i = \alpha K_i'^{\gamma}, \tag{19}$$

$$v_i(D, K_i) = T_i = K_i + \beta. \tag{20}$$

As in the mixed-strategy IPD, players develop an expected payoff based on their beliefs of the other players' actions. Elements of a mixed-strategy NIPD are given in Table A6. Mixed-strategy expected payoffs are given by Equations (21) and (22).

$$\pi_i^e(C, K_i) = \alpha K_i'^{\gamma} = \alpha \left[\frac{U_i}{\sum_{j=1}^{N} U_j} + \frac{1}{\sum_{j=1}^{N} U_j} \sum_{j=1}^{N} U_{j \neq i}(P_C = \theta_{C,j}) \right]^{\gamma}, \tag{21}$$

$$\pi_i^e(D, K_i) = K_i + \beta = \left[\frac{1}{\sum_{j=1}^{N} U_j} \sum_{j=1}^{N} U_{j \neq i}(P_C = \theta_{C,j}) \right] + \beta. \tag{22}$$

The expected payoffs are now dependent on a joint probability distribution of N discrete variables, each with the value U_j or 0 according to a probability $\theta_{C,j}$. To determine

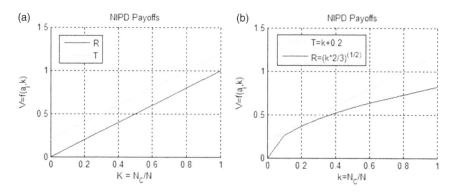

Figure A1. (a) Pure NIPD Payoffs. (b) Relaxed NIPD payoffs, example.

the probability density function deterministically would require the evaluation of 2^N states, a computationally demanding task as N gets large. A Monte-Carlo method is used to sample states of U_j to develop a probability density function with sufficient confidence. Expected payoffs are calculated from the probability density function and players choose their action with the same evolutionary algorithm as in Equation (7).

Table A1. Elements of a single-shot PD.

Game	$g = g_i(A, v)$
Players	$i = \begin{cases} 1 \\ 2 \end{cases}$
Action space	$A_i = [\text{COOPERATE, DEFECT}] = [C, D]$
Pure strategy	$a_i \in A_i$
Pure strategy payoffs	$v_i = f(a_i, a_{-i})$

Table A2. Elements of a deterministic IPD.

Game	$G = G(s, V, \tau)$
Game length	$\tau = [1, \infty]$
Strategy	$s_i = (a_{i,1}, ..a_{i,t}, \ldots a_{1,\tau})$
Discount factor	$\delta_i = [0, 1)$
Payoff	$V_i = V(\delta_i, s_i, s_{-i})$

Table A3. Simple iterated prisoners' dilemma strategies.

Strategy	Description
Grim trigger	Cooperate until opponent defects, then always defect
Tit-For-Tat	Always reciprocate opponent's last move
Pavlov	On a payoff of P or S, change strategies

Table A4. Elements of a mixed-strategy IPD.

Subgame History	$H_{t-1} = \{a_{1,1}, a_{2,1}; a_{1,2}, a_{2,2}; \ldots a_{1,t-1}, a_{2,t-1}\}$
Discount factors	$\delta_i = (0 \ 1)$
Beliefs	$\theta_{s,i} = \begin{cases} \theta(H_{t-1,-i}) \\ 1 - \theta(H_{t-1,-i}) \end{cases}$
Foresight	L_i
Memory	Q_i
Expected payoffs	$\pi_i^e = F(V_i, \delta_i, \theta_i, L_i)$

Table A5. Elements of an NIPD.

Game	$g = g_i(A, v)$
Players	$i = 1, 2, \ldots, N$
Action space	$A_i = [\text{COOPERATE, DEFECT}] = [C, D]$
Pure strategy	$a_i \in A_i$
Pure strategy payoffs	$v_i = f(a_i, k)$

Table A6. Additional elements of a mixed-strategy NIPD.

Subgame history	$H_{t-1} = \{a_{i,1}, a_{j \neq i,1}; a_{i,2}, a_{j \neq i,2}; \ldots a_{i,t-1}, a_{j \neq i,t-1}\}$
Beliefs	$\theta_{s,i} = \begin{cases} \theta(H_{t-1,-i}) \\ 1 - \theta(H_{t-1,-i}) \end{cases}$
Expected payoffs	$\pi_i^e = F(v_i, \theta_i)$

A comparative analysis of the anti-Apartheid and fossil fuel divestment campaigns

Chelsie Hunt, Olaf Weber and Truzaar Dordi

ABSTRACT

Divestment from the fossil fuel industry is campaigned as a means to address carbon-induced anthropogenic climate change, much like the anti-Apartheid divestment movement that was campaigned as a mean to address the country's human rights violations. However, there is a gap in current literature that objectively compares the similarities and differences between the two campaigns. Discrepancies may arise from an evolving understanding of what constitutes a socially responsible investment or the underlying strategy and intended outcomes of the campaigns themselves. Through a comparative content analysis this paper identifies differences and similarities of both campaigns.

1. Background

1.1 The purpose of divestment and social responsible investing

Divestment is most broadly defined as the process of selling assets, such as stocks, for financial or social goals (Merriam-Webster 2015). Divestment can be conducted because of financial reasons, for instance if a certain industry underperforms, or because of ethical reasons, for instance, if firms conduct businesses that are not in-line with the investor's morals. In the context of this research, divestment is seen as a form of socially responsible investing (SRI), in that it applies exclusionary screening to investment decisions. It is a socially motivated action to realign financial capital with an agent's moral or ethical ideologies (Kaempfer, Lehman, and Lowenberg 1987) with the intention to coerce transformative change via political compulsion or other obligation (Ansar, Caldecott, and Tilbury 2013, 2).

Divestment, as a form of social activism against perceived injustices, has been pursued across the late twentieth century; most famously against the racial conflicts and human rights violations of the South African Apartheid government (Arnold and Hammond 1994) and most recently against the impact of carbon-intensive fossil fuel production on anthropogenic climate change (Ansar, Caldecott, and Tilbury 2013, 2). To analyze the fossil fuel campaign, this research compares the fossil fuel divestment movement to the anti-Apartheid divestment movement. For consistency between the different terms used across literature, the movements will be labeled as 'fossil fuel divestment' and 'anti-Apartheid divestment' going forward.

1.2 Divestment as a form of SRI

Divestment can be classified as a form of SRI because it integrates non-financial (ethical, environmental, and social) criteria into investment decisions. An early form of SRI has been the avoidance of 'sin stocks', from sectors such as tobacco or gambling, by investors who integrate personal values and societal concerns within their investment decisions (Schueth 2003; Shank, Manullang, and Hill 2005; Statman 2006). However, SRI can also be seen as a management tool used by prudent investors who utilize social and environmental criteria to assess investment risks (Weber 2010). The underlying purpose of screening and excluding investments (Kinder and Domini 1997) that contradict an investor's position holds across divestment campaigns as well (Demetriades 2011). Although, while excluding investments is the main method used by divestment campaigns historically, in can be combined with other methods, such as positive selections. The divest-invest movement, for example, combines exclusionary approaches with investment strategies in renewable energy industries or other climate solutions (DivestInvest 2015).

This study aims to address the gap in research that compares the divestment campaigns. While there is research on the anti-Apartheid divestment movement (Arnold and Hammond 1994; Grossman and Sharpe 1986; Teoh, Welch, and Wazzan 1999) and some key studies about the newer fossil fuel divestment campaign (Ansar, Caldecott, and Tilbury 2013, 2; Brooks 2013; Grady-Benson 2014), there is an unexamined gap in research comparing both campaigns.

2. Research question and hypothesis

In an effort to compare the anti-Apartheid and the fossil-fuel-free divestment campaigns this research asks two questions:

(1) What are the main themes that arise across the anti-Apartheid divestment literature and are such themes common between both the anti-Apartheid and fossil-fuel-free campaign?
(2) Do the common themes identified share similarities or differ between the divestment campaigns?

By highlighting the differences and similarities amongst the shared themes this paper can offer support to whether the intended outcomes of the divestment campaigns are dependent upon the prevalent characteristics (approaches) to each theme. This is important because advocates of the fossil-fuel-free divestment movement cite the anti-Apartheid divestment campaign as an example of a successful divestment campaign that led to the ultimate end goal of overthrowing the South African government (Ansar, Caldecott, and Tilbury 2013, 2; FossilFree 2015; Tutu 2014). Hence, noting that using divestment as a tactic could be replicable and successful in another instance. The anti-Apartheid campaign was analyzed because it was the largest campaign to date, with the largest amount of academic research support, and is what fossil fuel campaigners commonly use to highlight previous success.

3. Theoretical approach

The study applied a grounded theory (Glaser and Strauss 2009) approach to code and to compare two divestment campaigns. Because a comparison between two divestment campaigns has never been conducted before, our analysis started at the same time as the data collection that was based on a standardized data collection process described below. Throughout the data collection, the different concepts of divestment have been detected and finally led to the category system presented below (Corbin and Strauss 1990) that has been used to compare the divestment initiatives.

4. Method

Initial analysis began with gathering literature on the anti-Apartheid divestment movement. The anti-Apartheid divestment movement is a strong basis to begin the literature review because of the relatively more expansive literature and more importantly, the purpose of this analysis is to assess how the newer fossil fuel divestment movement compares to the historical anti-Apartheid divestment movement. The analysis begins by extracting the abstracts of the most relevant SSCI catalogued journal articles found across Google Scholar, JSTOR, and Scopus, when using the search term 'Divestment AND South Africa'. As of August 2015, 28 articles were extracted dating from 1986 onwards.

The extracted abstracts were subsequently run through a word frequency counter to identify the most commonly used keywords across the aggregated literature. The 20 most relevant keywords were identified through a process of exclusionary screening; keywords that directly related to the anti-Apartheid divestment movement (South, Africa), phrases commonly found in abstracts (study, results), and variations of root words (corporate, corporation) were all excluded. Of the 20 keywords identified, each word was referenced at least 8 23 times across all abstracts.

In the context of the grounded theory approach, the study conducted open coding to group common keywords into exhaustive categories. The process was double-checked by two researchers. At first glance, the keywords relate to politics (sanction, state), finance (fund, return), or reputation (social, pressure). However, a more comprehensive review of the abstracts suggests that there is also an important distinction in the literature, on the relation between doing well financially and doing good for society (Hamilton, Jo, and Statman 1993; Posnikoff 1997; B. J. Richardson and Cragg 2010). Thus, we grouped the identified keywords and their related articles, into five common categories. Over the 28 publications, this approach identified the following five themes according to the keywords highlighted in Table 1: to encourage governmental response (political action), limit financial capital (financial action), raise awareness through reputation (reputational action), risk mitigation by investors (fiduciary approach), and the adoption of new business approaches (business approaches). The characteristics of each of these themes are explained in detail below.

Table 1. Open coding keywords and categories.

Political		Financial		Reputational		Fiduciary		Business	
Sanction	18	Invest	23	Social	16	Return	11	Company	22
Policy	14	Fund	16	Pressure	14	Cost	11	Corporation	16
State	8	Financial	9	Interest	13	Economic	10	Firm	15
Public	8			Benefit	12	Market	9		
				Responsible	8	Institutional	9		

Next, the five identified themes were assessed in the context of the fossil-fuel-free campaign, to examine where the campaign shares similarities or differs from the anti-Apartheid campaign. Notably, while a comprehensive search of reports, papers, and applicable websites on the fossil-fuel-free campaign was conducted, the majority of sources emerge from news reports and websites with limited academic research to support a rigorous and un-biased analysis of the current divestment movement.

The fact that there is more literature on the anti-Apartheid divestment campaign is not surprising. The anti-Apartheid campaign existed for at least 10 years from 1980 to 1990 (Teoh, Welch, and Wazzan 1999) while the fossil fuel divestment campaign only arose in 2012 (Howard 2015). Interestingly, as will be demonstrated below, the themes found in the literature on the anti-Apartheid divestment campaign can be found in the current fossil fuel divestment movement as well. Consequently, under each theme the similarities and differences between the campaigns are described and analyzed.

5. Results

Firstly, to provide context, a brief summary of the purpose, strategy and outcome of Table 2 presents and summarizes each campaign.

The fossil-fuel-free campaign has been reinforced through the publication of an IPCC report in 2014 that suggests only a small portion of the fossil fuels can be burned in order to achieve the two-degree limit in temperature rise (Field et al. 2014). Representatives of the campaign, such as 350.org (an NGO that focuses on keeping the amount of GHGs in the atmosphere below 350 ppm by campaigning) believe that industry leaders are responsible for climate change. Thus, with regard to their strategy, the anti-Apartheid campaign mainly focused on the Apartheid government as the originator of the perceived injustice, whereas the fossil fuel campaign mainly addresses the fossil fuel industry.

Table 2. Timeline, purpose, strategy, and outcome of the divestment campaigns.

	Anti-Apartheid campaign	Fossil fuel campaign
Timeline	Late 1970s to early 1990s	2012 to present
Purpose	Destabilize the South African economy to weaken the government	Limit the fossil fuel sector from financial capital needed to expand and continue their business as usual
Strategy	Target the incumbent government through depriving the economy of financial capital and consequently weakening the economy and triggering the debate in invested institutions.	Target the incumbent industry through depriving the industry of financial capital and triggering the debate in invested institutions
Intended outcome	Collapse or abolish the government	Changing the industry

Consequently, the outcomes of the two campaigns differ. While the anti-Apartheid divestment campaign focused on abolishing the political regime in South Africa, the fossil-fuel-free campaign focuses on decreasing CO_2 emissions caused by fossil fuels such as coal and oil. It strives to force the energy sector to move away from fossil fuels to renewable and carbon neutral energy sources to 'people-centric solutions to the climate crisis' (350.org 2015). While there is no consensus in the literature about exactly how the anti-Apartheid campaign influenced political change in South Africa, the fossil-fuel-free campaign is still active and data about its impact cannot be implied.

The comparative analysis highlighted in Table 3 further summarizes the similarities and differences between the two campaigns concerning the five overarching themes identified. Both campaigns focus on divestment mechanisms to create change. As will be explained, the anti-Apartheid movement had a myriad of ways to stop and remove capital from the South African economy. To win back a positive stakeholder reputation, entities involved in South African business and economy only had to withdraw operations from South Africa mostly without changing their core business. This, however, does not hold for the fossil fuel campaign that wants the fossil fuel industry change their business completely. Divestment advocates also used risk management approaches across both campaigns to have investors agree to an exclusionary approach if ethical reasons are not of interest to them. In both cases, share prices either of South African companies or of companies form the fossil fuel sector decreased. Therefore, after having started from an ethical-moral position, in both campaigns divestment for South Africa and the fossil fuel industry made sense from a purely financial perspective as well.

Table 3. Summary of the differences and similarities of the anti-Apartheid campaign and the fossil fuel campaign.

Themes	Anti-Apartheid campaign	Fossil Fuel campaign
Political action	Divest from companies to coerce political outcome	
	'Means to' remove government	Engage government toward 'intended outcome'
Financial action	Established by institutional and private investors and expanded to target mainstream institutional investors such as pension funds	
	Legislated trade and investment sanctions and corporate divestment	Primarily corporate divestment
Reputational action	Raise public awareness in general and in invested institutions and seek reputational advantages	
	Firms withdraw operations from South Africa	Firms change core business
Fiduciary approach	Common arguments but conflicting evidence to identifying and quantifying risks in the beginning, but change to financial outperformance in later stages	
	Potential financial losses in the beginning of the campaign because of portfolio reduction triggered discussion about fiduciary duty. Later financial outperformance because of declining returns of South African investments.	Potential financial losses in the beginning of the campaign because of portfolio reduction triggered discussion about fiduciary duty. Later financial outperformance because of declining returns of fossil fuel investments
Business approach	Use of exclusionary screening driven by normative arguments	
	No suggested reinvestment.	Sometimes suggested reinvestment strategy through divest–invest movement and renewables as alternative investment strategy in the same industry

Political action

Though both campaigns aim to encourage governments to take political action against their injustices, the campaigns differ in their expected political outcomes. While the anti-Apartheid campaign used divestment to destabilize the government, force its resignation, disestablish the Apartheid, and foster equal rights for all citizens of South Africa (Beaty and Harari 1987; Kaempfer, Lehman, and Lowenberg 1987), the fossil fuel campaign strives to raise political awareness of the climate change problem propagated by the fossil fuel industry, to convince the government to withdraw political support for the industry.

While the South African liberation movement fought for social transformation as early as 1955, strategies of divestment and sanctions were not pursued until the late 1970s to gain international recognition against the suppressed injustice (Arnold and Hammond 1994). Anti-Apartheid legislation was first enacted through the mandatory disclosure of business activities indicating corporate complicity of the Apartheid by American companies (Arnold and Hammond 1994). Later, several additional laws over the course of the Apartheid, such as the United States Comprehensive anti-Apartheid Act, the Rangel Amendment, and a myriad of US state and local level laws that prohibited investments in companies with operations within South Africa supported the campaign (Meznar, Nigh, and Kwok 1994). Hence, divestment was used as a tool for interest groups outside of South Africa to entice policy change in a foreign nation when few direct channels are available (Kaempfer, Lehman, and Lowenberg 1987) and was supported by many South African activists.

The fossil fuel divestment organization (350.org 2015) states that the fossil-fuel-free divestment movement hopes to ' … break the hold that the fossil fuel industry has on our economy and our governments' (350.org 2015, 1). Their political goal is to encourage government action in the form of domestic regulations or policies that limit the productive capacity of the fossil fuel industry. Political incentives to reduce the impact of fossil fuel use on climate change include market-based mechanisms, such as carbon pricing (World Bank 2014) or cutting subsidies (Victor 2009), command and control tools to limit the burning of fossil fuels, extraction or output limits to proliferate stranded assets (Ansar, Caldecott, and Tilbury 2013, 2), and transferring public investments to low carbon infrastructure (Corfee-Morlot et al. 2012). However, it is important to recognize that the fossil fuel industry still holds significant political sway, especially in resource dependent countries. Consequently, Fossil Free MIT states that 'political will, rather than technology, is now the bottleneck in mitigating climate change, and loosening the grip of the fossil fuel industry on our democracy, is a prerequisite to effect political action on climate' (Fossil Free MIT 2014, 1). By changing governments' attitude to the fossil fuel industry, divestment strives to force fossil fuel companies to diverge away from business as usual activities (Brooks 2013) that have negative impacts on climate change.

In comparing the theme of political action between the divestment campaigns, it is important to recognize that the anti-Apartheid campaign was country specific across all sectors, while the fossil fuel campaign is global but confined to one sector. Therefore, when considering political coercion in the case of the fossil fuel campaign one needs to convince governments worldwide to change their outlook on their energy sector.

Financial action

In addition to political coercion, divestment also aims to encourage financiers to withdraw investments from firms or other investees that do not meet their ethical criteria or at least to make them aware to analyze their exposure and response to the problem of apartheid and climate change. By divesting from companies with operations in South Africa, the intention was to pressure these companies to end business activities in and with South Africa, by selling their portion of South African assets and operations (Kaempfer, Lehman, and Lowenberg 1987). The idea of the campaign was that through divestment, foreign financial investment could be restricted, weakening its economy. This however, is only valid if other foreign companies would not open operations in South Africa and South African companies would be unable to continue 'business as usual' operations.

Gosiger (1986) expands the definition of financial involvement beyond the direct involvement of corporations operating in South Africa to include bank loans, direct investment, and shareholdings as well. Therefore, the divestment movement was expanded from divesting US equities with operations in South Africa, to selling of shares on the South African markets and pushing foreign institutions to stop lending and investing in South Africa by both private investors and lenders (Kaempfer, Lehman, and Lowenberg 1987). Also state-legislated investment sanctions that prohibited firms from owning physical capital in the country of South Africa complemented divestment.

Comparably, the fossil fuel divestment campaign aims to weaken the financial security of this industry by augmenting their current cost of capital (Renneboog, Ter Horst, and Zhang 2008) and raising the cost of new capital for firms (Knoll 2002) caused by a decrease in share price and higher capital cost. Compared to other industries, the fossil fuel industry relies on high amounts of financial capital to invest in new projects. In 2014 alone, the industry raised nearly $900 billion from bank loans, bonds, equity, and project financing (Brogan 2014, 1). However, some state that divestment from fossil fuel industries alone would be inadequate in constraining capital. Less scrupulous investors who take the opportunity for lower cost investments just could repurchase the shares of companies with large market capitalization.

Additionally, while there have been some activities by financiers, including the Bank of America, Citigroup, Morgan Stanley, JPMorgan Chase, Wells Fargo, and Credit Suisse, choosing to withdraw from financing the underperforming coal mining sector, 'it's surprising that social activists haven't tried to mount more campaigns against funding sources before' (Sorkin 2014, 1). BankTrack is starting to trace 'the involvement of banks in financing business activities with a negative impact on people and planet' (Bank-Track 2015, 1) but only a few banks and other institutional investors have significantly pulled out of financing the fossil fuel sector as of yet. So far, 21 rather small banks that were not invested in coal anyway have signed the Paris Pledge to quit coal, while other banks continued to invest over $500 billion in the coal industry between 2005 and 2014 (BankTrack 2015). In fact, even with the 2015 UNFCCC climate talks, the World Bank increased fossil fuel financing by 23% in 2014, to $3.4 billion in loans, grants, guarantees, risk management and equity for fossil fuel projects (OCI 2015).

The main similarity between the two campaigns is that at the beginning institutions like churches and universities that were the most responsive to social pressure and have openly communicated their intention to divest, made the first step forward with intent to restrict financial capital. By 1980, Protestant and Roman Catholic churches and universities had pledged to divest $250 million from banks with ties to South Africa, cumulatively (Teoh, Welch, and Wazzan 1999). A project launched by 350.org also calls on educational and religious institutions, governments, and other organizations that serve the public good (FossilFree 2015). Started as a student run campaign, it has urged many universities at a minimum to comment on their stance and direction on the issue.

The main difference between the campaigns with regard to financial action is that, albeit the fossil fuel movement is still in its infancy, financial action directly targets the fossil fuel industry. Comparably, the South African movement utilized direct divestment from the South African market, divestment from foreign holdings, halting of direct investment by foreign banks, and trade sanctions in addition to divestment from firms. As highlighted above, banks and other institutional investors currently have limited involvement with the fossil-fuel-free campaign, though they are involved in the industry as lenders, project financiers, and investors. Unfortunately, the literature does not inform about which restriction to financial capital, if at all, did weaken the South African economy. The same is valid for the fossil fuel divestment movement; it is still not clear whether divestment has a direct financial effect on the business activities of the fossil fuel sector (MacAskill 2015; Ritchie and Dowlatabadi 2014).

Reputational changes

The reputation of a firm's brand is an increasingly important consideration for many businesses today, with over 50–70% of their value attributable to their name and goodwill (Richardson and Cragg 2010). Thus, at the risk of reputational defamation, divestment can be motivation for ethical behavior by high profile firms.

Amongst other aims, divestment from South Africa aimed to raise public awareness against predominant multinational companies complicit with the ongoing apartheid, and to disclose those firms that ignored or even supported the injustice. In 1978, the Investor Responsibility Research Centre (IRRC) documented a comprehensive list of companies with direct investments in South Africa and of some banks with loans to the South African public sector, which has been used as a database for those advocating a complete divestment strategy from South Africa (Grossman and Sharpe 1986).

While the IRRC raised public awareness of firms active in Apartheid South Africa, the Sullivan code, first introduced in 1977, was endorsed as a means to differentiate between perceivably responsible organizations amongst the multinational firms. Curiously, the Sullivan code was introduced as a measure of corporate codes of conduct for multinational firms conducting business in South Africa during the Apartheid (Seidman 2003) and used as a 'moral justification for continuing business operations in South Africa amidst mounting pressure for withdrawal' (Arnold and Hammond 1994, 115). Nevertheless, in order to encourage behavioral change, a means to identify practices supporting the Apartheid is imperative in this case.

Fossil fuel divestment similarly aims to retract the industry's social license that it depends upon to operate (Caldecott, Tilbury, and Carey 2014). The fossil fuel campaign garners public awareness through initiatives hosted by organizations such as 350.org, successfully raising public awareness through organization's inaugurating 'Do the Math' campaign and through events like the New York's 'People's Climate March', which successfully enticed over 50 billion in divested funds the following day (Grady-Benson and Sarathy 2016). While these activities do not directly address the reputation of businesses, 350.org also provides a publicly available list titled The Carbon Underground 200, which identifies the top public oil, gas, and coal companies around the world, ranked by their reported reserves and potential carbon emission of these reserves, to streamline the divestment process for funds (FossilFree 2015). BankTrack adopts a similar approach to the reputation of banks, by tracking bank investments with regard to controversial activities such as coal financing and lists them on its website and in other publications (Chan-Fishel 2007; Collins 2012; Collins 2015; Pimentel 2012).

In comparing actions addressing the reputation of investors and investees, both campaigns are similar in the means by which they raise and encourage public awareness through public activism and the confounding disclosures presented through the IRRC and Carbon Underground 200. Furthermore, NGOs such as BankTrack also start to differentiate between investors being involved in the fossil fuel sector and those that are not. Generally, however, the fossil fuel campaign does not use a tool, like the Sullivan code to differentiate proactive firms amongst violators, mainly because campaign supporters believe that a differentiation between 'good' and 'bad' representatives in the oil and coal industry cannot be made.

Moreover, the campaigns differ in opportunities to act relative to investees with bad reputation. It was relatively easy for consumers and investors to substitute firms and investees involved in Apartheid South Africa. For example, buying comparable products from companies acting more ethically in South Africa (based upon the Sullivan principles) or divesting shares and buying into the strong housing market in the US (Lansing and Kuruvilla 1988). The dependence on the global fossil fuel industry and demand for fossil fuels will continue to exist at least for some time until substitutable products are price competitive and are produced on a mass scale for global consumption and use.

Notably, targeting business operations in the context of the anti-Apartheid campaign and the core business type in the context of the fossil fuel campaign will yield different results. Knoll (2002) suggests that exclusionary screening has a marginal direct effect when it screens the business type rather than their business operation. Simply, it is easier for a firm to end business operations in South Africa than to radically change their whole business especially in cases of continuing demand as for fossil fuels.

Generally, at the beginning of the campaign divestment rather had a negative reputation effect on investors because of the fear to underperform with regard to financial returns. Over time and with growing financial risks of both, South African investments and fossil fuel investments, there has been a change with regard to reputation. From this point on divestment was not a purely morally driven, but financially questionable, but could be justified from a financial point of view as well.

Fiduciary approach

Recognizing that divestment shares common characteristics across politics, financiers, and reputational responsiveness, the last two themes relate to the notion that socially responsible investments must benefit both shareholders (abiding to fiduciary law 'to do well') and the remaining stakeholders (defined by its merits 'to do good') (Friede, Busch, and

Bassen 2015), if it is to legitimize the value of pursuing the campaign (Kotler and Lee 2006). Both considerations seem to be equally important for prospective divestment campaigns.

A survey conducted by Grady-Benson and Sarathy (2016) found that often fossil fuel divestment campaigns were rejected on the basis that (i) it was perceived to present significant transitional or risk induced cost (it could not 'do well') or (ii) the result would be have been negligible on the controversial business and on their carbon emissions (it could not 'do good'). This section first highlights the role of prudent financial decisions, to assess whether divestment could in fact, do well for the investor, and whether it is in-line with or contradictory to their fiduciary duty. First, fiduciary duty is discussed under an exclusively financial perspective, meaning to guarantee best possible financial returns to investors (Dorfleitner, Halbritter, and Nguyen 2016). Later, we will also discuss the broader view of fiduciary duty that also takes non-financial performance into account (Lydenberg 2014; Richardson 2011; Sandberg 2011).

The financial case for divestment during the Apartheid was and still is conflicting across research. Some fiscally conservative trustees viewed divestment as contrary to the exclusive purpose of fiduciary duty by (Ennis and Parkhill 1986). They feared divestment would prompt increased investment risks, increased transaction costs, reduced portfolio diversification, financial losses from high-risk stocks in a South Africa-free portfolio, and loss of endowments from corporate donors and alumni associated with South Africa related companies (Gosiger 1986). Yet other investors argue that adopting a more comprehensive method of screening would illuminate the growing risks of economic instability, internal turmoil, and organizational mismanagement that led to the Apartheid's collapse (Dobris 1986). Thus, from a pure financial return perspective it is unclear whether divestment violated fiduciary duty. It seems that, given the economic decline of South Africa, divestment did not breach fiduciary duty at least in later stages. On the one hand, divestment reduces a portfolio's diversification and therefore increases risks; but on the other hand, this is only valid if the portfolio reduction does not correlate with financial risks. However, given the decreasing economic development of South Africa during Apartheid, divesting from South African positions would have been prudent from an exclusively financial return perspective from 1981 to 1994 as well and consequently would not contradict fiduciary duty, as Figure 1 demonstrates.

Much like the anti-Apartheid campaign, opponents of fossil fuel divestment are quick to refute the campaign, amongst claims that divestment would breach the investor's fiduciary duty to its shareholders; yet these results are equally conflicting. A 2012 study by Sonecon consultancy attests that the financial returns from oil and natural gas stocks over the 2000s far out performed the overall performance of American college and university endowments (Shapiro and Pham 2012). Another report by Fischel (2015) proclaims that the 'costs to investors of fossil fuel divestiture are highly likely and substantial, while the potential benefits – to the extent there are any – are ill-defined and uncertain at best' (Fischel 2015, 3). Building on Fischel's report, another recent study claims that divestment could cost millions in lost returns annually, when university endowments reduce portfolio diversification (Cornell 2015). Notably, however, the three studies all indicate in their footnotes that the petroleum industry, the American Petroleum Institute and the Independent Petroleum Association of America, commissioned their research. Yet, arguments against divestment have motivated universities like Harvard, Yale, MIT,

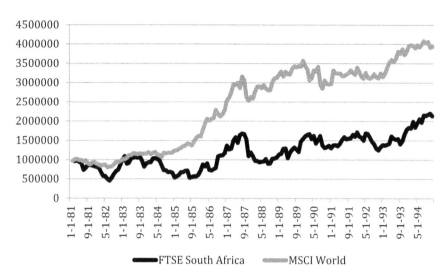

Figure 1. Cumulative return of FTSE South Africa and MSCI World 1981–1994. Source: Thomson Reuters, Datastream.

Columbia, and NYU to reject divestment, under the conjecture that it could hinder their financial performance and breach their fiduciary duty.

In contrast, other parties including Rockefeller Brothers Fund, Stanford University, and Norway Pension Fund, see divestment differently (Arabella Advisors 2015; Cripps 2014). A recent publication on university endowments from 2010 to 2014 suggests that selling fossil fuel holdings can provide a comparable or surplus benefit when reinvested in sectors with higher income potential and less volatility, fixed-income green bonds, and even by mitigating energy and water inefficiencies on campus (Ritchie and Dowlatabadi 2015). This is attested by a number of analyses by organizations such as Mercer (Francis 2015), Northstar Asset Management (Goodridge 2013), Impax Asset Management (Richardson 2013), the Carbon Disclosure Project (CDP 2013), and Corporate Knights (Corporate Knights 2014). Other financial intermediaries, such as the insurance industry have also taken interest in the fossil fuel divestment campaign, recognizing the direct risks carbon- induced climate change poses for their business (Kousky and Cooke 2009). Thus, divestment can be presented as a measure to build resilience against the transitional risks of incumbent assets, associated with the unforeseen or premature write-offs of stranded assets (Ansar, Caldecott, and Tilbury 2013, 2) and therefore is in-line with fiduciary duty particular in time of a downturn of the fossil fuel sector.

Stranded assets are assets that 'suffer from unanticipated or premature write-offs, downward revaluations or are converted to liabilities' (Ansar, Caldecott, and Tilbury 2013, 2). In the case of the fossil fuel industry, the carbon bubble may devalue fossil fuel resources. The carbon bubble asserts that no more than one-third of the current reserves of fossil fuels can be consumed prior to 2050 if climate warming should be limited to 2°C assuming that carbon capture and storage or other technologies will not significantly contribute to decreasing emissions (Rubin 2015). So far, however, the resources have been valued as if they could be sold for the usual market prices. A change in their value would have significant impacts on the share prices of the businesses

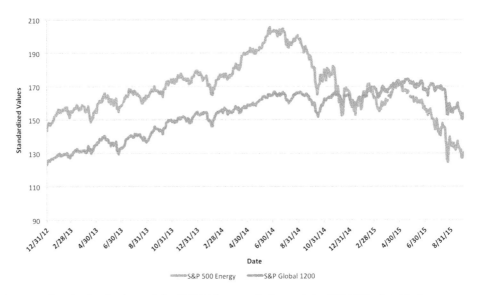

Figure 2. Standardized values of the S&P 500 energy index and the S&P1200 global index.

owning the resources and consequently would lead to a significant devaluation of investments in the fossil fuel industry, as recently stated by the Governor of the Bank of England (Carney 2015).

Recent oil and coal demand and price developments do give some insight into consequences of decreased income in the fossil fuel sector on investments, as Figure 2 demonstrates. Evidently, the share price development of S&P Global 1200 has outperformed the development in the energy sector since September 2014 and has led to an underperformance of investments in the energy sector compared to the global market.

Thus in both the case of South Africa and fossil fuels, divesting form controversial assets has been financially prudent and would not violate fiduciary duties at least in later stages of the campaigns.

In addition to a pure financial approach to fiduciary duty, other authors interpret the concept as fulfilling the will of beneficiaries (Richardson 2011; Sandberg 2011). Consequently, benefits do not have to be exclusively financial, but can be social and environmental benefits as well. Thus, if divestment because of social responsibility is in-line with the will of beneficiaries, it does not violate fiduciary duties. Therefore, it could be argued that both divestment campaigns have been in-line with fiduciary duties.

Business approach

The last theme of divestment aims to build on integrating non-financial, ethical criteria into investment decisions (Cleveland and Reibstein 2015) to address attitudes and concerns of investors. This approach can be summarized as SRI or responsible investment (Weber 2015). SRI offers the opportunity to integrate an ethical perspective into financial decision-making, using non-financial environmental, social, and governance (ESG) indicators in addition to conventional financial indicators and consequently to create a societal impact (Weber 2014). Accounting for ESG criteria is a growing trend; finding growth in all sectors for responsible investments since 2005, the Global Sustainable Investment Review finds that in 2012 over $13.6 trillion USD in investments (representing 21.8% of the total assets managed) have ESG criteria embedded within investment decisions (Global Sustainability Investment Alliance 2013).

The divestment campaigns push this concept forward by alerting stakeholders of the need not only be aware of certain types of criteria but to not invest in stocks that go against their moral and ethical values. This did not only address stakeholders but also triggered investors to re-think their investment strategies and their responsibility for problems such as apartheid and climate change. It is a theme of the divestment movement to offer new investment approaches such as the use of exclusionary criteria for investments to formulate new strategies other than just that of shareholder maximization. Offering this new investment approach undermined the arguments of the South African apartheid regime and the fossil fuel industry that both guarantee prosperity and high financial returns.

The human rights violations of the Apartheid are not disputed; racial segregation against the non-white community led to extreme inequalities, not only in the form of poverty, but across education, health and basic infrastructure as well (Ozler and Hoogeveen 2005). Thus, it was indisputable that the intended outcome of the Apartheid divestment campaign was to eliminate the intolerable treatment of the non-white community (Ngeleza and Nieuwhof 2005). This established a strong normative argument for the case of divestment. However, finding suitable re-investment opportunities to change the current portfolio was a more difficult argument, particularly if reinvestments should have similar risk/return characteristics within the same asset class and sector (Fabozzi, Gupta, and Markowitz 2002).

The normative argument of who is responsible for the carbon-induced climate change is comparably less convincing than that of the Apartheid. While there is no doubt that producing and burning fossil fuels is a major source for climate change, it is not easy to allocate responsibility and consequently actions. Responsibility could be placed on the producer, but also on the consumer who finally buys the product and is responsible for the main part of the emissions (Bergerson, Charpentier, and MacLean 2009). Yet, the fossil fuel divestment movement exclusively focuses on the supply side and ignores the demand side. It only pushes the extractors and producers to diverge from business as usual (Brooks 2013). Moreover, the fossil-free campaigners advocate not just for divestment but also for re-investment into renewables or alternative sources of energy and abatement. The idea of a new business approach for the fossil-fuel-free movement is not just to stop investing in the fossil fuel sector but also to invest in companies that can help us transition to a carbon-free society. Divest-Invest states 'we are foundations divesting from fossil fuels and switching to clean energy investments, joining college, health, pension funds and religious endowments doing the same' (FossilFree 2015).

Although the investment market has expanded significantly since 1980, the MSCI World Index, for instance, has grown over 1100% from January 1980 to January 2015, it is unclear, if this increase in the global market place would make it easier for fossil fuel divestment advocates alternative stocks that still fulfill their risk, return, sector allocation, etc. profile. Additionally, the main difference is that to be an ethical investor in the case of the anti-Apartheid movement, one just needed to divest whereas with the fossil fuel divestment movement it is considered ethical to re-invest into the green, carbon-free society, for instance, in renewable energy. Therefore, this added obligation for the ethical investors can make re-investment decisions much more complicated. More research into the reallocation of capital needs to be conducted.

6. Conclusion

The comparative analysis of literature on divestment suggests that both campaigns are similar in their purpose of raising awareness against controversial practices, across common themes of political, financial, and reputational action and through fiduciary and business approaches. However, the divestment campaigns do have many similar and different characteristics within each theme creating differences amongst their strategy (to target the government and the industry respectively) and their intended outcome (to collapse the government and manage the industry respectively). It is therefore important to recognize that pursuing the fossil fuel divestment movement in the same manner as the anti-Apartheid movement would not be a reasonable strategy, given the differences of the intended overall strategy and outcome, perceived best practices or successes of the anti-Apartheid campaign.

In the context of political action during the Apartheid, foreign (mostly American) laws and regulations prohibited the involvement in companies with operations in South Africa (Meznar, Nigh, and Kwok 1994). Comparably, close ties between the fossil fuel industry and local governments may bottleneck political incentives against the fossil fuel industry (Fossil Free MIT 2014). Moreover, while the anti-Apartheid campaign used divestment as a means to target the government, the fossil fuel campaign focuses directly on the industry and on the awareness inside the very powerful investment industry.

With regard to financial aspects, the South African campaign expanded beyond simply divestment, to boycotts and sanctions against both institutions and banks involved in the Apartheid (Teoh, Welch, and Wazzan 1999). The fossil fuel campaign comparably focuses primarily on divesting away from capital-intensive publicly traded major carbon emitters (Carbon Underground 200).

Both campaigns are similar in their means of raising awareness, by organizations like the IRRC or 350.org. However, while the South African campaign adopted the Sullivan principles to differentiate between proactive and complicit firms (Seidman 2003) the fossil fuel campaign does not have a comparable tool to differentiate proactive firms from violators because there are no investments in the fossil fuels sector that would support strategies moving away from fossil fuel. Moreover, while customers could express disapproval by choosing not to buy a South African complicit product (Smith 1987), fossil fuel products may not be as easily substitutable even in case of bad reputation.

In both campaigns, fiduciary aspects have been and are discussed. Divestment made sense form a pure financial return point of view at least after a certain time because the South African economy of the 1980s and the fossil fuel sector experienced a phase of decreasing financial returns. Thus, from a purely financial perspective divestment did not violate fiduciary duty at least after the decline of the South African economy and the fossil fuel sector. In addition, given that fiduciary duty means that activities address the will of the investors, both campaigns did not violate fiduciary duties in cases their beneficiaries supported the exclusionary approach.

South African divestment campaigns were driven as a means of activism (Teoh, Welch, and Wazzan 1999) while the fossil fuel campaign has proven to also be enticing for larger endowments like that of the Norwegian Pension Fund or the Rockefeller Brothers Fund. Particularly, the engagement of these big institutional investors made many investors evaluating their involvement in these controversial investments. Fossil fuel divestment is perceived as a form of SRI, integrating non-financial considerations in a manner that is attractive for investors to pursue, divesting only when it makes financial sense and holding no guidelines or exclusionary lists as much as the Sullivan principles in the anti-Apartheid movement. However, addressing the suppliers of fossil fuels is only one part of the story; as long as the demand continues there will be carbon emissions related to it. Surely, the problem of demand is bigger in the case of fossil fuel divestment than in the anti-apartheid divestment movement.

Generally, as stated prior, we conclude that there are both similarities and differences between the two campaigns. Yet, even for the anti-Apartheid campaign, the efficacy of the campaign is still unclear about whether it created a change or not. Nor is it certain that the decreasing oil price in 2014–2015 and a falling share prices in the fossil fuel industry are effects of the fossil fuel campaign. This cause–effect relationship has yet to be established for both the anti-Apartheid and fossil fuel divestment campaigns. In order to analyze the question about cause and effect, event studies that show the effect of certain events, such as fossil fuel campaign announcement and share prices might shed light on this issue. However, it is certain that both campaigns increased the awareness of investors and made them thing about the effect of their investments.

Disclosure statement

No potential conflict of interest was reported by the authors.

Notes on contributors

Chelsie Hunt is student in the Sustainability Management Master's Program at the School for Environment, Enterprise and Development, University of Waterloo, Canada.

Olaf Weber is professor at the School for Environment, Enterprise and Development, University of Waterloo, Canada.

Truzaar Dordi is student in the Sustainability Management Master's Program at the School for Environment, Enterprise and Development, University of Waterloo, Canada.

References

350.org. 2015. "Home: We're building a global climate movement." http://350.org/.

Ansar, A., B. Caldecott, and J. Tilbury. 2013. *Stranded Assets and the Fossil Fuel Divestment Campaign: What does Divestment Mean for the Valuation of Fossil Fuel Assets*. Stranded Assets Programme, SSEE, Working Paper. University of Oxford.

Arabella Advisors. 2015. *Measuring the Growth of the Global Fossil Fuel Divestment and Clean Energy Investment Movement*. Washington, DC: Arabella Advisors.

Arnold, P., and T. Hammond. 1994. "The Role of Accounting in Ideological Conflict: Lessons from the South African Divestment Movement." *Accounting, Organizations and Society* 19 (2): 111–126.

BankTrack. 2015. "About BankTrack." Accessed from http://www.banktrack.org/show/pages/about_banktrack.

Beaty, D. T., and O. Harari. 1987. "South-Africa-White Managers, Black Voices." *Harvard Business Review* 65 (4): 98–105.

Bergerson, J., A. Charpentier, and H. MacLean. 2009. "Understanding the Canadian Oil Sands Industry's Greenhouse Gas Emissions." *Environmental Research Letters* 4 (1): 1–8.

Brogan, A. 2014. *Funding Challenges in the Oil and Gas Sector: Innovative Financing Solutions for Oil and Gas Companies.* Moscow: Ernst and Young.

Brooks, M. 2013. "Banking on Divestment." *Alternatives Journal* 39 (6): 48–49.

Caldecott, B., J. Tilbury, and C. Carey. 2014. "Stranded Assets and Scenarios." Smith School of Enterprise and the Environment. University of Oxford. http://www.smithschool.ox.ac.uk/research-programmes/stranded-assets/Stranded%20Assets%20and%20Scenarios%20-%20Discussion%20Paper.pdf.

Carney, M. 2015. "Breaking the Tragedy of the Horizon – Climate Change and Financial Stability." Paper presented at the City Dinner, London. Speech given at Lloyd's of London.

CDP. 2013. *Carbon Reductions Generate Positive ROI.* London: Carbon Disclosure Project.

Chan-Fishel, M. 2007. "Time to go Green Environmental Responsibility in the Chinese Banking Sector." BankTrack.

Cleveland, C. J., and R. Reibstein. 2015. "The Path to Fossil Fuel Divestment for Universities: Climate Responsible Investment." SSRN 2565941.

Collins, B. 2012. "Bankrolling Climate Disruption: The Impacts of the Banking Sector's Financed Emissions." *Bank Track* 1–48.

Collins, B. 2015. "The End of Coal? Coal Finance Report Card 2015." http://www.banktrack.org/manage/ems_files/download/the_end_of_coal_2015_pdf/the_end_of_coal_2015_0.pdf.

Corbin, J. M., and A. Strauss. 1990. "Grounded Theory Research: Procedures, Canons, and Evaluative Criteria." *Qualitative Sociology* 13 (1): 3–21.

Corfee-Morlot, J., V. Marchal, C. Kauffmann, C. Kennedy, F. Stewart, C. Kaminker, and G. Ang 2012. Towards a Green Investment Policy Framework: The Case of Low-Carbon, Climate-Resilient Infrastructure", Environment Directorate Working Papers, No. 48, OECD Publishing, Paris.

Cornell, B. 2015. "The Divestment Penalty: Estimating the Costs of Fossil Fuel Divestment to Select University Endowments." *SSRN 2655603.*

Corporate Knights. 2014. *Carbon Neutral and Carbon Inverse Portfolios.* Toronto, ON: Corporate Knights Capital.

Cripps, P. 2014. *$1.8bn Coalition Divest from Fossil Fuels, Reinvest in Clean-Tech.* London: Environmental Finance.

Demetriades, K. 2011. *A Look at Corporate Social Responsibility and Firm Performance: Evidence from South Africa.* Johannesburg, SA: WiredSpace.

DivestInvest. 2015. Home. http://www.divestinvest.org/.

Dobris, J. C. 1986. "Arguments in Favor of Fiduciary Divestment of South African Securities." *Neb. L. Rev.* 65: 209–234.

Dorfleitner, G., G. Halbritter, and M. Nguyen. 2016. "The Risk of Social Responsibility – Is it Systematic?" *Journal of Sustainable Finance & Investment* 6 (1): 1–14. doi:10.1080/20430795.2015.1123993.

Ennis, R. M., and R. L. Parkhill. 1986. "South African Divestment: Social Responsibility or Fiduciary Folly?" *Financial Analysts Journal* 42 (4): 30–38.

Fabozzi, F. J., F. Gupta, and H. M. Markowitz. 2002. "The Legacy of Modern Portfolio Theory." *The Journal of Investing* 11 (3): 7–22.

Field, C. B., V. R. Barros, K. Mach, and M. Mastrandrea. 2014. *Climate Change 2014: Impacts, Adaptation, and Vulnerability.* Cambridge: Cambridge University Press.

Fischel, D. R. 2015. "Fossil Fuel Divestment: A Costly and Ineffective Investment Strategy." http://divestmentfacts.com.

FossilFree. 2015. "Divestment Commitments." http://gofossilfree.org/commitments/.

Fossil Free MIT. 2014. "Fossil Fuel Divestment: Building a Social Movement for Collective Climate Action." Climate Colab, Proposal for shifting behavior for a changing climate 2014.

Francis, A. 2015. *Climate Change: New Investment Risk Demands Action by Investors, Cautions New Research.* Toronto, ON: Mercer.

Friede, G., T. Busch, and A. Bassen. 2015. "ESG and Financial Performance: Aggregated Evidence from more than 2000 Empirical Studies." *Journal of Sustainable Finance & Investment* 5 (4): 210–233. doi:10.1080/20430795.2015.1118917.

Glaser, B. G., and A. L. Strauss. 2009. *The Discovery of Grounded Theory: Strategies for Qualitative Research*. London: Transaction Publishers.

Global Sustainability Investment Alliance. 2013. "2012 Global Sustainability Investment Review." http://gsiareview2012.gsi-alliance.org/pubData/source/Global%20Sustainable%20Investement%20Alliance.pdf.

Goodridge, J. 2013. *To Paraphrase Mark Twain: The Cost of Fossil Fuel Divestment has been Greatly Exaggerated*. New York, NY: Northstar Asset Management.

Gosiger, M. C. 1986. "Strategies for Divestment from United States Companies and Financial Institutions Doing Business with or in South Africa." *Human Rights Quarterly* 8 (3): 517–539.

Grady-Benson, J. 2014. "Fossil Fuel Divestment: The Power and Promise of a Student Movement for Climate Justice." Pitzer Senior Theses. Paper 55. http://scholarship.claremont.edu/pitzer_theses/55.

Grady-Benson, J., and B. Sarathy. 2016. "Fossil Fuel Divestment in US Higher Education: Student-Led Organising for Climate Justice." *Local Environment* 21 (6): 661–681.

Grossman, B. R., and W. F. Sharpe. 1986. "Financial Implications of South African Divestment." *Financial Analysts Journal* 42 (4): 15–29.

Hamilton, S., H. Jo, and M. Statman. 1993. "Doing Well While Doing Good? The Investment Performance of Socially Responsible Mutual Funds." *Financial Analysts Journal* 49 (6): 62–66.

Howard, E. 2015. "The Rise and Rise of the Fossil Fuel Divestment Movement the Guardian." http://www.theguardian.com/environment/2015/may/19/the-rise-and-rise-of-the-fossil-fuel-divestment-movement.

Kaempfer, W. H., J. A. Lehman, and A. D. Lowenberg. 1987. "Divestment, Investment Sanctions, and Disinvestment: An Evaluation of Anti-Apartheid Policy Instruments." *International Organization* 41 (03): 457–473.

Kinder, P. D., and A. L. Domini. 1997. "Social Screening: Paradigms Old and New." *The Journal of Investing* 6 (4): 12–19.

Knoll, M. S. 2002. "Ethical Screening in Modern Financial Markets: The Conflicting Claims Underlying Socially Responsible Investment." *The Business Lawyer* 57 (2): 681–726.

Kotler, P., and N. Lee. 2006. *Corporate Social Responsibility: Doing the Most Good for Your Company and Your Cause*. New York: Wiley.

Kousky, C., and R. M. Cooke. 2009. "Climate Change and Risk Management: Challenges for Insurance, Adaptation, and Loss Estimation. RFF Discussion Paper No. 09-03-REV. Resources for the Future, Washington, DC."

Lansing, P., and S. Kuruvilla. 1988. "Business Divestment in South Africa: In Who's Best Interest?" *Journal of Business Ethics* 7 (8): 561–574.

Lydenberg, S. 2014. "Reason, Rationality, and Fiduciary Duty." *Journal of Business Ethics* 119 (3): 365–380.

MacAskill, W. 2015. "Does Divestment Work." *New Yorker*, October 20. http://www.newyorker.com/business/currency/does-divestment-work.

Merriam-Webster. 2015. "Divest." http://www.merriam-webster.com/dictionary/divest.

Meznar, M. B., D. Nigh, and C. C. Kwok. 1994. "Effect of Announcements of Withdrawal from South Africa on Stockholder Wealth." *Academy of Management Journal* 37 (6): 1633–1648.

Ngeleza, B., and A. Nieuwhof. 2005. "The Role of International Campaigns for Boycott, Divestment and Sanctions." *Al Majdal*, no. 26: 10–14.

OCI. 2015. *OCI, (2015). Still Funding Fossils: World Bank Group Energy Finance FY2014. Oil Change International*. Washington, DC: Oil Change International. http://priceofoil.org/content/uploads/2015/04/world-bank-april-2015-FINAL.pdf.

Ozler, B., and J. Hoogeveen. 2005. "Not Separate, Not Equal: Poverty and Inequality in Post-Apartheid South Africa." William Davidson Institute Working Paper No. 739. Ann Arbor: University of Michigan.

Pimentel, G. 2012. *An Introduction to the Brazilian Banking Sector and its Sustainability Practices.* Sao Paolo: Banktrack and Amigos da Terra Amazonia Brasilera.

Posnikoff, J. F. 1997. "Disinvestment from South Africa: They Did Well by Doing Good." *Contemporary Economic Policy* 15 (1): 76–86.

Renneboog, L., J. Ter Horst, and C. Zhang. 2008. "Socially Responsible Investments: Institutional Aspects, Performance, and Investor Behavior." *Journal of Banking & Finance* 32 (9): 1723–1742.

Richardson, B. J. 2011. "From Fiduciary Duties to Fiduciary Relationships for Socially Responsible Investing: Responding to the Will of Beneficiaries." *Journal of Sustainable Finance and Investment* 1 (1): 5–19.

Richardson, D. 2013. *Beyond Fossil Fuels: The Investment Case for Fossil Fuel Divestment.* London: Impax Asset Management.

Richardson, B. J., and W. Cragg. 2010. "Being Virtuous and Prosperous: SRI's Conflicting Goals." *Journal of Business Ethics* 92 (1): 21–39.

Ritchie, J., and H. Dowlatabadi. 2014. "Understanding the Shadow Impacts of Investment and Divestment Decisions: Adapting Economic Input–Output Models to Calculate Biophysical Factors of Financial Returns." *Ecological Economics* 106: 132–140.

Ritchie, J., and H. Dowlatabadi. 2015. "What Divesting may Yield: Revisiting "The Grasshopper and the Ant" in the Context of University Endowments." *Journal of Environmental Investing* 6 (1): 51–74.

Rubin, J. 2015. *The Carbon Bubble: What Happens To Us When It Bursts.* Toronto, ON: Random House.

Sandberg, J. 2011. "Socially Responsible Investment and Fiduciary Duty: Putting the Freshfields Report into Perspective." *Journal of Business Ethics* 101 (1): 143–162.

Schueth, S. 2003. "Socially Responsible Investing in the United States." *Journal of Business Ethics* 43 (3): 189–194.

Seidman, G. W. 2003. "Monitoring Multinationals: Lessons from the Anti-Apartheid Era." *Politics & Society* 31 (3): 381–406.

Shank, T. M., D. K. Manullang, and R. P. Hill. 2005. "Is It Better to be Naughty or Nice?" *The Journal of Investing* 14 (3): 82–88.

Shapiro, R. J., and N. D. Pham. 2012. "The Financial Returns from Oil and Natural Gas Company Stocks Held by American College and University Endowments." *SSRN 2542148.*

Smith, N. C. 1987. "Consumer Boycotts and Consumer Sovereignty." *European Journal of Marketing* 21 (5): 7–19.

Sorkin, A. 2014. "A New Tack in the War on Mining Mountains." *The New York Times*, March 9, p. B1.

Statman, M. 2006. "Socially Responsible Indexes." *Journal of Portfolio Management* 32 (3): 100–109.

Teoh, S. H., I. Welch, and C. P. Wazzan. 1999. "The Effect of Socially Activist Investment Policies on the Financial Markets: Evidence from the South African Boycott*." *The Journal of Business* 72 (1): 35–89.

Tutu, D. 2014. "We Need an Apartheid-Style Boycott to Save the Planet." http://www.theguardian.com/commentisfree/2014/apr/10/divest-fossil-fuels-climate-change-keystone-xl.

Victor, D. G. 2009. "The Politics of Fossil-Fuel Subsidies." *SSRN 1520984.*

Weber, O. 2010. "Social Banking: Products and Services." *SSRN 1621822.*

Weber, O. 2014. "The Financial Sector's Impact on Sustainable Development." *Journal of Sustainable Finance & Investment* 4 (1): 1–8. doi:10.1080/20430795.2014.887345.

Weber, O. 2015. "Responsible Investment in Canada." In *The Routledge Handbook of Responsible Investment,* edited by N. Beinisch, J. P. Hawley, T. Hebb, A. G. F. Hoepner, and D. Wood, 70–80. London: Routledge.

World Bank. 2014. *State and Trends of Carbon Pricing 2014.* Washington, DC: World Bank Publications.

Index

For Product Safety Concerns and Information please contact our EU
representative GPSR@taylorandfrancis.com
Taylor & Francis Verlag GmbH, Kaufingerstraße 24, 80331 München, Germany